MW00623834

DRAGONS, JOHN, AND
Every Grain of Sand

EDITED BY

Shane J. Wood

A gift from
Lincoln Christian University
Alumni Association

ESSAYS ON THE BOOK OF REVELATION
IN HONOR OF DR. ROBERT LOWERY

DRAGONS, JOHN, AND
Every Grain of Sand

EDITED BY

Shane J. Wood

Copyright © 2011 College Press Publishing Co.
All Rights Reserved
Printed and bound in the United States of America

Cover design by Shane J. Wood

International Standard Book Number 978-0-89900-935-3

For Dr. Robert Lowery

Professor, Spiritual Father,

Mentor, and Friend

LIST OF CONTRIBUTORS

Craig L. Blomberg, PhD (University of Aberdeen, Scotland)
Distinguished Professor of New Testament
Denver Seminary, Littleton, Colorado

Paul Boatman, DMin (Eden Theological Seminary)
Seminary Dean; Professor of Pastoral Care and Counseling
Lincoln Christian University, Lincoln, Illinois

Otniel Ioan Bunaciu, PhD (Reformed Seminary of Cluj, Romania)
Professor of Historical Theology
TCM International Institute, Europe and Central Asia
Dean, Facultatea de Teologie Baptista
Universitatea din Bucuresti

Craig A. Evans, PhD (Claremont Graduate University)
Payzant Distinguished Professor of New Testament
Acadia Divinity College, Nova Scotia, Canada

Gary Hall, PhD (Union Theological Seminary of Virginia)
Professor of Old Testament
Lincoln Christian University, Lincoln, Illinois

Fred Hansen, PhD Candidate (University of Dublin, Ireland)
Professor of Biblical Languages
Lincoln Christian University, Lincoln, Illinois

J.K. Jones, DMin (Dallas Theological Seminary)
Pastor of Spiritual Formation
Eastview Christian Church, Normal, Illinois
Adjunct Professor
Lincoln Christian University, Lincoln, Illinois

Paul Kissling, PhD (University of Sheffield, UK)
Professor of Old Testament
TCM International Institute, Europe and Central Asia

Brian Lowery, MDiv (Lincoln Christian University)
Managing Editor, PreachingToday.com
Christianity Today International, Carol Stream, Illinois

Yulia Lubenetz, PhD (University of Bucharest, Romania)
Instructor of Church History
Tavriski Christian Institute, Kherson, Ukraine

I. Howard Marshall, PhD (University of Aberdeen, Scotland)
Emeritus Professor of New Testament; Honorary Research Professor
of New Testament
University of Aberdeen, Scotland

Mark E. Moore, PhD (University of Wales, UK)
Professor of New Testament and Hermeneutics
Ozark Christian College, Joplin, Missouri

Matt Proctor, MA (Lincoln Christian University)
President of Ozark Christian College; Professor of New Testament
and Preaching
Ozark Christian College, Joplin, Missouri

Mark Scott, DMin (Denver Seminary)
Academic Dean; Professor of Preaching and Testament
Ozark Christian College, Joplin, Missouri

Jeff Snell, DMin (Southern Baptist Theological Seminary)
Doctor of Ministry Director; Associate Dean; Associate Professor of
Preaching
Lincoln Christian University, Lincoln, Illinios

Carmen Trenton, MDiv (Lincoln Christian University)
Adjunct Professor of Biblical Languages
Lincoln Christian University, Lincoln, Illinois

**Tony Twist, PhD (Indiana University), DMin (Southern Baptist
Theological Seminary)**
President of TCMI Institute; Professor of Leadership and Spiritual
Formation
TCM International Institute, Europe and Central Asia

Neal Windham, DMin (Azusa Pacific University)
Professor of New Testament and Christian Spirituality
Lincoln Christian University, Lincoln, Illinois

Shane J. Wood, PhD Candidate (University of Edinburgh, Scotland)
Professor of New Testament and Spiritual Formation
Ozark Christian College, Joplin, Missouri

ABBREVIATIONS IN THIS VOLUME

Abbreviations of Commonly Used Periodicals, Reference Works, and Series

ANF	*The Ante-Nicene Fathers*
AUSS	*Andrews University Seminary Studies*
Bib	*Biblica*
BR	*Biblical Research*
BSac	*Bibliotheca Sacra*
BT	*The Bible Translator*
CBQ	*Catholic Biblical Quarterly*
CD	Karl Barth, *Church Dogmatics*
CurTM	*Currents in Theology and Mission*
DBI	L. Ryken, J. C. Wilhoit, and T. Longman III (eds.), *Dictionary of Biblical Imagery*
DLNTD	R.P. Martin and P.H. Davids (eds.), *Dictionary of the Later New Testament & Its Developments*
DNTB	C.A. Evans and S E. Porter (eds.), *Dictionary of New Testament Background*
EDNT	H. Balz and G. Schneider (eds.), *Exegetical Dictionary of the New Testament*, 3 vols.
EvQ	*Evangelical Quarterly*
ExpTim	*Expository Times*
HeyJ	*Heythrop Journal*
Int	*Interpretation*
JBL	*Journal of Biblical Literature*
JETS	*Journal of the Evangelical Theological Society*
JSNT	*Journal for the Study of the New Testament*
JSNTSup	Journal for the Study of the New Testament— Supplement Series
JSOT	*Journal for the Study of the Old Testament*
JTS	*Journal of Theological Studies*
NIDNTT	C. Brown (ed.), *The New International Dictionary of New Testament Theology*, 4 vols.
NIDOTTE	W. A. VanGemeren (ed.), *New International Dictionary of Old Testament Theology and Exegesis*, 5 vols.
NovT	*Novum Testamentum*
NPNF	*Nicene and Post-Nicene Fathers*
NTS	*New Testament Studies*
OTP	J. H. Charlesworth (ed.), *The Old Testament Pseudipigrapha*
RevExp	*Review and Expositor*
SNTSMS	Society for New Testament Studies Monograph Series
ST	*Studia theologica*
TDNT	G. Kittel and G. Friedrich (eds.), *Theological Dictionary of the New Testament*, 10 vols.
TDOT	G. Johannes Botterweck and H. Ringgren (eds.), *Theological Dictionary of the Old Testament*, 11 vols.
TS	*Theological Studies*
TToday	*Theology Today*
TynBul	*Tyndale Bulletin*
TZ	*Theologishe Zeitschrift*
WTJ	*Westminster Theological Journal*
WW	*Word and World*
ZAW	*Zeitschrift für die alttestamentliche Wissenschaft*
ZNW	*Zeitschrift für die neutestamentliche Wissenschaft*

Abbreviations for Books of the Bible
with Apocrypha and Early Christian Literature

OT = Old Testament

Gen	Judg	Neh	Song	Hos	Nah
Exod	Ruth	Esth	Isa	Joel	Hab
Lev	1-2Sam	Job	Jer	Amos	Zeph
Num	1-2Kgs	Ps	Lam	Obad	Hag
Deut	1-2Chr	Prov	Ezek	Jonah	Zech
Josh	Ezra	Eccl	Dan	Mic	Mal

NT = New Testament

Mt	Acts	Eph	1-2Tim	Jas	Rev
Mk	Rom	Phil	Titus	1-2Pet	
Lk	1-2Cor	Col	Philem	1-2-3Jn	
Jn	Gal	1-2Thes	Heb	Jude	

Jdt = Judith

Wis = Wisdom of Solomon

Barn = *Epistle of Barnabas*

Abbreviations of Pseudepigrapha
and Early Jewish Literature

2Bar	*2 (Syriac Apocalypse of) Baruch*	*SibOr*	*Sibylline Oracles*
1En	*1 Enoch*	*TLevi*	*Testament of Levi*
PssSol	*Psalms of Solomon*	*TJos*	*Testament of Joseph*

CONTENTS

INTRODUCTION

"Don't have the inclination to look back on any mistake.
Like Cain, I now behold this chain of events that I must break.
In the fury of the moment I can see the Master's hand
in every leaf that trembles, in every grain of sand."
—Bob Dylan, *Every Grain of Sand*—

S ay it simpler," he remarked.

The entire class grew silent. Taken off guard, I gathered myself, looked at my thesis paragraph, and reduced the four hundred words down to one hundred.

Yet again he said, "Say it simpler."

In disbelief, I looked back at my paper and tried to fight away thoughts of frustration and self-preservation so that I would be able to "simplify" my thesis—a battle I felt like I had won when I responded this time with only twenty-five words.

But he looked me in the eyes and said, "Shane . . . say it simpler."

Two to three minutes of silence passed—which from my chair seemed like two or three hours. In bewilderment, I sat paralyzed—with nothing to say and unsure how to respond.

Dismissing this pregnant pause, Dr. Lowery spoke, "Shane, I want you to be able to say your thesis so simply that your three-week-old child you have at home will be able to understand it."

After three years of being Dr. Lowery's Research Assistant, thirty-eight credit hours in one of his classrooms, and dozens of conversations over meals, on car rides, and in his office, this moment from my first "Dr. Lowery exegetical class" is the memory that most consistently resurfaces. It was in this moment that I began to realize the depth of his scholarship— that I began to see his passion for communicating God's word. It was in this moment that I began to understand his desire to challenge his students to engage with transformation that can only occur through great discipline and an immense amount of humility. It was in this moment that Dr. Lowery was not just my professor, but he was my pastor . . . he was my friend— because he cared enough about me not to let me stay the way that I was. This moment reminds me that scholarship is not measured by the amount of esoteric vernacular you can imbue into a single pericope; instead, through diligent study and humble observation, true scholarship, particularly Christian scholarship, takes the difficult and makes it simple so that transformation can take place in the life of the individual and in the life of the church.

Revelation: Burden or Blessing?

"I gaze into the doorway of temptation's angry flame
and every time I pass that way I always hear my name.
Then onward in my journey I come to understand
that every hair is numbered like every grain of sand."
— Bob Dylan, *Every Grain of Sand* —

When it comes to the study of the book of Revelation, the spectrum of adjectives can hardly be exhausted, for some find the book confusing, others find it elucidating. Some fear it, others revere it, and many don't quite know *what* to make of it. Some obsess over the book; others neglect it as if it didn't exist. Some read it daily, others read it yearly, and many only read it on leap years—or so they say. Regardless of where you find yourself right now, the intention of this volume is to bring balance to your study and perspective on the book of Revelation— so that in your life the message of John on Patmos may ring true.

The book of Revelation offers a challenge to its audience. Whether the hearers are the comfortable pew-sitters of Laodicea or the persecuted saints of Smyrna, the book of Revelation confronts each with the same message of transformation—some with the clarion call to repentance and others with the gentle whispers of perseverance. This same challenge is offered still today to John's readers in the twenty-first century, but with all of the baggage that this book has accumulated over the past two-thousand years, oftentimes it is simply too much to bear, and we are tempted to set it aside for another traveler to carry on this sojourn. Yet we must fight this temptation and embrace the challenge of John written in the language of blessing in Rev 1:3, "Blessed is he who reads and those who hear the words of the prophecy, and heed the things which are written in it. . ." (NASB).

Dragons, John, and Every Grain of Sand

"I hear the ancient footsteps like the motion of the sea.
Sometimes I turn, there's someone there, other times it's only me.
I am hanging in the balance of the reality of man,
like every sparrow falling, like every grain of sand."
—Bob Dylan, *Every Grain of Sand*—

This book is separated into three sections, each with seven chapters. The sections each correlate to a word in the title as well as a method of study taught by Dr. Lowery in his classes. The book of Revelation is inundated with themes and images, like: furniture, weather, beasts, harlots, and *dragons*. These pictures run throughout the fabric of the tapestry and give the book its contour, color, and character. As a result, section 1, entitled: *"Dragons: General Studies in the Book of Revelation,"* focuses on the analysis of themes that impact Revelation—whether in small sections of the text (Craig A. Evans), throughout the entire text (Gary Hall, Neal Windham, and Fred Hansen), or even outside of the text itself (Paul J. Kissling, Yulia Lubenets, and Otniel Ioan Bunaciu).

Although these images can provide stimulating pictures, they can also provide enigmatic difficulties. From the two witnesses in Revelation 11 (Jeff Snell) to the woman in Revelation 12 (Mark Scott), section 2 entitled, *"John: Difficult Texts in the Book of Revelation,"* examines the passages and images in the Apocalypse that traditionally prove to be the most troubling.

This includes 666 in Rev 13:18 (Shane J. Wood), the beast and the prostitute in Revelation 17 (Brian Lowery), the millennium in Revelation 20 (by Craig L. Blomberg from the Historic Premillennial perspective and by I. Howard Marshall from an Amillennial perspective), and the release of Satan in Rev 20:7-10 (Shane J. Wood). These chapters invite the reader to engage these problematic texts and thereby be put in a position to hear the voice of *John* more clearly.

The final section, named after Dr. Lowery's favorite Bob Dylan song, is entitled: *Every Grain of Sand: Application and the Book of Revelation.* Beginning with the christological pictures in the Apocalypse (Mark E. Moore), this section looks at topics like suffering (Carmen Trenton) and identity (Paul E. Boatman) as a means of transformation for the Christian through the book of Revelation (Tony Twist). Application of this sort must always be the goal of theological studies. As Bob Dylan's song emphasizes, God's movement in our lives is sometimes unseen, but his movement is revealed in the details of life and in the ancient voices of his word. The message of Revelation, then, must be taught (Matt Proctor) and preached in our churches (J.K. Jones). It is the transforming power of the Apocalypse which causes me to unite with Dr. Lowery in a resounding "Yes!" to the question "Does Studying Revelation Really Matter?" (Shane J. Wood).

Out of honor to my mentor, to dignify a teacher to many, and in tribute to a husband, father, and papa, this book is offered to the church to mine the riches of the message from Patmos — some difficult and some simple — so that you can hear and heed the words of this prophecy and be blessed.

Shane J. Wood

Dragons:

GENERAL STUDIES IN THE
BOOK OF REVELATION

OBSERVATIONS ON THE JUDAIC CHARACTER OF THE POLEMIC IN THE SEVEN LETTERS

Craig A. Evans

The background and polemics of the Johannine Writings, usually understood as comprising the Gospel of John, the three letters of John, and (sometimes) the Revelation of John,[1] have from earliest times been understood as reflecting in one way or another incipient Gnosticism. Following the lead of early Church Fathers, B.F. Westcott argued in the nineteenth century that the fourth evangelist adopted the language of Gnosticism in order to fight Gnosticism.[2] Taking a very different tack in the twentieth century, Rudolph Bultmann argued that the language of the fourth evangelist was in places Gnostic because the evangelist had himself been a Gnostic and disciple of John the Baptist.[3]

In recent years, however, interpreters have sought to understand the background and polemics of the Johannine Writings in other ways. Ongoing study of the Dead Sea Scrolls, marked by spiritual and ethical dualism and a variety of wisdom and interpretive traditions,[4] as well as study of Philo and other "intertestamental" literatures, has tended to situate the Johannine writings in the context of Judaism and the synagogue. J. Louis Martyn's study of the synagogue as context for the polemic and apologetic in the fourth Gospel has influenced a generation of scholars, even if some of his points remain disputed.[5]

In what follows I build on Martyn's general thesis. Although the focus will be on the seven letters in Revelation 2–3, I will call attention to various elements in the Gospel and the Epistles. What we shall find is a coherent polemic and apologetic very much aimed at a skeptical synagogue, a synagogue that rejects the claim of the Johannine Christians that the Messiah has come and that Messiah is Jesus of Nazareth and that his suffering and death in fact fulfill prophetic expectations.

The Polemic in the Seven Letters

The brief study that follows offers a preliminary survey of the Judaic elements present in the letters of the risen Christ to the seven churches in Revelation 2–3, especially with respect to the polemics. We shall observe important lines of continuity with the Judaic elements in the polemics of the fourth Gospel and the letters.

The Revelation of the Risen Christ

The book of Revelation gains its name from its opening words: ἀποκάλυψις Ἰησοῦ Χριστοῦ ἣν ἔδωκεν αὐτῷ ὁ θεὸς — "(This is) a revelation of Jesus Messiah, which God gave to him."[6] Although in the OT the noun ἀποκάλυψις is relatively rare (and never in the sense of divine revelation), the verb appears in the OT and later literature in reference to God revealing his word to his prophet or servant (e.g., 1Sam 3:7,21; 9:15; TLevi 18:2; TJos 6:6; Joseph and Aseneth 16:7; Apocalypse of Moses 1:1).

The Judaic character of the book of Revelation becomes apparent in its opening chapter. The giving of a revelation "to show to his servants" (δεῖξαι τοῖς δούλοις αὐτοῦ) echoes prophetic language, as we see in Amos 3:7, where the prophet declares that God does nothing "unless he reveal his instruction to his servants the prophets" (ἐὰν μὴ ἀποκαλύψη παιδείαν αὐτοῦ πρὸς τοὺς δούλους αὐτοῦ τοὺς προφήτας). John receives and bears testimony to the "word of God" (τὸν λόγον τοῦ θεοῦ), just as the word of God comes to the prophets of old (e.g., Jer 1:2, ἐγενήθη λόγος τοῦ θεοῦ πρὸς αὐτὸν).

The beatitude in v. 3, "Blessed [μακάριος] is he who reads aloud the words of the prophecy, and those who hear [ἀκούοντες], and who keep [τηροῦντες] what is written therein" (v. 3), is reminiscent of a beatitude from Proverbs: "Blessed [μακάριος] is the man who will listen [εἰσακούσεταί] to me . . . keeping secure [τηρῶν] the posts of my entrances" (LXX, Prov 8:34).

In v. 4 ("from the 'One Who Is and Who Was and Who Is to Come'") we have an allusion to Exod 3:14, where God says to Moses, "I am 'The One Who Is'" (ἐγώ εἰμι ὁ ὤν). Students of Greek readily observe the grammatical oddity in Revelation, in that the definite article and noun that follow the preposition ἀπό are in the nominative and not the expected genitive (ἀπὸ ὁ ὢν καὶ ὁ ἦν καὶ ὁ ἐρχόμενος). Of course, the solecism is quite deliberate, making the allusion to Exod 3:14 more obvious and at the same time treating the divine disclosure as though it were an indeclinable name (as many Semitic names are).[7] The mysterious "seven spirits before the throne" of God are to be understood in the light of Jewish literature, especially the Dead Sea Scrolls, as referring to seven principal angels that minister in the presence of God.[8]

In v. 6 (Christ "made us a kingdom, priests [βασιλείαν, ἱερεῖς] to his God and Father"), we have an allusion to Exod 19:6 ("you shall be for me a royal priesthood [βασίλειον ἱεράτευμα] and a holy nation").[9] The allusions to Exod 3:14 and 19:6 underscore the Judaic self-understanding of the seer and his churches. They stand in full continuity with the people of Israel, who long ago were led by the man to whom God revealed himself and who under his leadership came to stand before the mountain, from which God would give his law and make his covenant with his people.

In v. 7 ("Behold, he is coming with the clouds, and every eye will see him, every one who pierced him; and all tribes of the earth will wail on account of him") we have a paraphrase and conflation of Dan 7:13 ("he was coming upon the clouds of heaven") and Zech 12:10 ("they look on him whom they have pierced, they shall mourn for him, as one mourns for an only child").

In v. 8 ("'I am the Alpha and the Omega,' says the Lord God, 'Who Is and Who Was and Who Is to Come, the Almighty'") we again have an allusion to Exod 3:14 ("I am 'The One Who Is'"). The sobriquet the "Almighty" (παντοκράτωρ) occurs some 200 times in the OT and related literature.

In v. 10 John says he was "in the spirit" (ἐν πνεύματι), a phrase that occurs several times in the OT (e.g., Mic 3:8 "in the Spirit of the Lord"; Ezek 11:24 "he took me up in the Spirit of God . . . in a vision, in the Spirit of God"; 37:1 "the Lord brought me out in the Spirit").

In v. 12 (and v. 13; cf. 1:20; 2:1) John says he turned and saw "seven golden lampstands" or menorahs. The golden menorah was first fabricated for the wilderness Tabernacle (Exod 25:31-40) and later became one of the most important appointments in the Temple. The seven-branched candelabrum was a popular symbol in Jewish religious art in the first century, as is amply attested through archaeological finds.[10]

In vv. 13-15 ("one like a son of man . . . his head and his hair were white as white wool, white as snow; his eyes were like a flame of fire, his feet were like burnished bronze, refined as in a furnace, and his voice was like the sound of many waters") we find allusions to Dan 7:13 ("one like a son of man"), 9 ("his raiment was white as snow, and the hair of his head like pure wool; his throne was fiery flames, its wheels were burning fire"); 10:6 ("his face like the appearance of lightning, his eyes like flaming torches, his arms and legs like the gleam of burnished bronze, and the sound of his words like the noise of a multitude"), completing an important part of the allusion in v. 7 above. The description "voice was like the sound of many waters" parallels the last part of Dan 10:6, but stands verbally closer to Ezek 1:24 ("like the sound of many waters"); 43:2 ("his coming was like the sound of many waters").

In v. 16 ("from his mouth issued a sharp two-edged sword") we hear an echo of Isa 49:2 ("He made my mouth like a sharp sword") and perhaps also an echo of Isa 11:4 ("he shall smite the earth with the rod of his mouth, and with the breath of his lips he shall slay the wicked").

In v. 17 ("I am the first and the last") we have an echo of Hebrew Isa 44:6 ("I am the first and I am the last"); 48:12 ("I am the first, I am the last").[11]

In v. 18 the risen Christ says, "I have the keys of Death and Hades." According to Jewish tradition it is God himself who possesses the "key of the sepulchers" and it is he who will "open your graves and lead you from your graves, my people" (*Tg. Neof.* Gen 30:22; cf. *b. Sanh.* 113a God alone possesses the "key of raising the dead"). The Christ, the seed of David, who now holds "the key of Death and Hades," may also allude to Isa 22:22 ("I will place on his shoulder the key of the house of David"). This passage is certainly alluded to in Rev 3:7 (see below).

In v. 19 ("what is and what is to take place [ἃ μέλλει γενέσθαι] hereafter") we hear echoes of the language of Isa 48:6 (ἃ μέλλει γίνεσθαι); Dan 2:28,29,45 ("God has made known to the king what shall be hereafter").

In v. 20 John prepares the reader for the letters to the seven "angels" of the seven churches. Judging by the description of the risen, exalted Christ, with its many allusions to words, phrases, and imagery from the OT and related traditions, we should not be surprised by the thoroughly Judaic character of these letters, including the polemic. To the seven letters we now turn.

First Letter: To the Church of Ephesus (Rev 2:1-7)

Perhaps the wealthiest and most influential city in western Asia Minor[12] was Ephesus. Some of the city's inscriptions boasted: ἡ πρώτη καὶ μεγίστη μητρόπολις τῆς Ασίας ("The first and great metropolis of Asia"), or words to that effect. A city of about one quarter of a million in the first century, Ephesus was famous for its stunning Temple of Artemis, which was acclaimed one of the Seven Wonders of the World. The city was home to many temples, the famous Library of Kelso (or Celsus), gymnasia, baths, fountains, monumental tombs, thriving public squares, and ornate administrative buildings.[13] Even today, though mostly in ruins, the city is a favorite with tourists.

The risen Christ acknowledges the endurance of the church at Ephesus and its vigorous opposition to "evil men," as well as its testing of "those who call themselves apostles, and they are not, and you found them to be false" (v. 2). But the church has lost its first love (v. 4). If it does not repent and once again do the works it did at first, its lampstand will be removed (v. 5).

This church hates "the deeds of the Nicolaitans" (v. 6). Those in this church that hears the word of Christ and conquers will be granted "to eat of the tree of life, which is in the paradise of God" (v. 7).

These exhortations contain several Jewish elements. The false apostles are almost certainly Jewish,[14] and probably to be identified with the Nicolaitans, which in turn are to be identified with the followers of Balaam, as seen in Rev 2:14 (more on Balaam below). The threat of removal of the lampstand is quite significant, recalling that what is in view here is the menorah, the seven-branched candelabrum, perhaps the best known Jewish religious symbol in late antiquity. If the church at Ephesus does not repent, its menorah will be removed, and its removal means a loss of Jewish identity as much as its loss of Christian witness in the city. But those who repent will "eat of the tree of life, which is in the paradise of God." The allusion here is to the famous Garden of Eden, in which was the Tree of Life, whose fruit was denied to fallen Adam and Eve (Gen 2:9; 3:22,24). The hope of regaining Paradise, as well as the Tree of Life, is deeply rooted in Jewish eschatology (cf. *1En* 25:5; *3En* 23:18; *TLevi* 18:11; *Apoc. Mos.* 28:4; 4Q385a frag. 17a-e, col. ii, line 3).

Second Letter: To the Church of Smyrna (Rev 2:8-11)

A city almost as large as Ephesus, ancient Smyrna was praised by Strabo as the "most beautiful of all" the coastal cities of Asia (*Geogr.* 14.1.37). The city overlooked a harbor and boasted several important structures, such as a stadium, large forum, library, a broad, colonnaded main street, and many prominent shrines, including a temple dedicated to emperor Tiberius.[15]

The polemic in the letter to the church of Smyrna is sharp and angry: "I know your tribulation . . . and the blasphemy by those who say they are Jews and are not, but are a synagogue of Satan" (v. 9). Modern readers will be tempted to hear in this outburst Christian anti-Semitism. But this misses the mark widely. It is a reflection of intramural Jewish dispute. The Jewish believers in Messiah Jesus make up the true people of God, not the Jewish congregation that blasphemes by denying that Jesus is the Messiah[16] and claiming that they — those who reject the Messiah — are the true Jews. On the contrary, the risen Christ says, they are a "synagogue of Satan."[17] This is not anti-Semitic slander, but a struggle among the Jewish people themselves, with some proclaiming their faith in Jesus as Israel's Messiah and others rejecting him and persecuting his followers.

Those who are faithful in the face of persecution will be given the "crown of life" (v. 10) and will not be hurt by the "second death" (v. 11). The metaphor "crown of life" and close approximations have their roots in early Judaism (cf. Jas 1:12 "crown of life"; *TLevi* 8:2 "crown of righteousness"; *TBenj.* 4:1 "crown of glory"; *TJob* 4:10 "receiving the crown"; LXX, Jer 13:18 and LXX, Lam 2:15 "crown of glory"). The expression "second death" appears to have developed in the Aramaic-speaking synagogue, as we see in the Aramaic paraphrases of Scripture, or Targums (e.g., *Tg. Onq.* Deut 33:6 "May Reuben . . . not die a second death"; *Tg.* Isa 22:14; *Tg.* Jer 51:39, 57).

Third Letter: To the Church of Pergamum (Rev 2:12-17)

Pergamum was another impressive city in western Asia, graced by many beautiful buildings, including a theatre, an Asklepeion, and several temples, one dedicated to Dionysius, another to Zeus, and others to the Roman emperors of the first and second centuries.[18]

The letter to the church of Pergamum acknowledges the challenges the struggling community faces. It is, after all, the place where "Satan dwells." In contrast to the "synagogue of Satan" in v. 9, the "throne of Satan" (v. 13) in the letter to the church of Pergamum probably refers to Roman not Jewish opposition to the Christian movement.[19] Nevertheless, the author, writing from a Jewish perspective, makes use of this ancient Semitic term, which traditionally referred to the evil, sometimes personified, that opposes the will of God.

The description in v. 12 that the words of Christ are like a "sharp two-edged sword" once again, as in Rev 1:16, echoes Isa 49:2. But the allusion to Isa 11:4 ("he shall smite the earth with the rod of his mouth") this time is assured, because of what is said a few verses later, in v. 16: If the lapsed do not repent: "I will come to you soon and war against them with the sword of my mouth."

The major complaint is that members of the Pergamum church "hold the teaching of Balaam" and the "teaching of the Nicolaitans" (vv. 14-15). In Jewish Scripture (Num 22:5-8 *et passim*) and lore (4Q339 frag. 1, lines 1-2; *b. Ber.* 7a; *Sanh.* 106a), as well as in Jewish Christian teaching (Jude 11; 2Pet 2:15-16), Balaam rises to the level of an all-time villain who sought to destroy the Jewish people. This Balaam, of course, "taught Balak to put a stumbling block before the sons of Israel, that they might eat food sacrificed to idols and practice immorality."[20] Our Jewish author is much stricter in matters of *kasruth* than what we see in Paul (1Cor 8:1,4,7,10; 10:19). Paul, of course, is primarily concerned with the "weak" Christian, whose superstitions regarding pagan gods and idols make it impossible for him with a clear conscious to eat meat sacrificed to idols. Here in Rev 2:14 the idea of eating meat sacrificed to idols is repugnant in any situation and in any frame of mind, much as we see in the case of the Maccabean martyrs, who refused to eat pork and take part in Seleucid sacrifices (2 Maccabees 6-7).

The one who conquers these temptations will receive "some of the hidden manna" (v. 17). Manna, of course (from the Hebrew, literally meaning "What is it?"), is the famous food provided the Israelites during their wilderness sojourn (Exod 16:4-36). In Jewish interpretation this food took on all sorts of interesting properties and associations. In some tradition it is the heavenly bread that will be provided in the age to come (2 Bar. 29:8; Gen. Rab. 82.8 [on Gen 35:17]), for it will convey eternal life (*Joseph and Aseneth* 16:14 "everyone who eats of it will not die for ever").

The faithful will also be given a "white stone." Although the precise meaning here is uncertain, in light of the context, it is probable that it was understood as a token of innocence and guarantee of membership in the congregation of the faithful.[21] Not only is a stone received, it has one's name written on it, a "new name," for confidentiality. This makes the best sense in light of the synagogue's efforts to "blot out" the names of the Christians from the membership book (see Rev 3:5 below).

Fourth Letter: To the Church of Thyatira (Rev 2:18-29)

Only recently excavated, Thyatira was known for trade and its high quality purple dye.[22] It will be recalled that Paul's convert Lydia, a "seller of purple goods," was from Thyatira (Acts 16:14).

In the letter, the congregation is admonished for tolerating "the woman Jezebel, who calls herself a prophetess, and she teaches and leads astray. . ." (v. 20). Jezebel, of course, was the infamous Phoenician princess who married Israel's King Ahab (1Kgs 16:29-31), promoted the worship of Baal (1Kgs 16:31), murdered many of Israel's prophets who had remained faithful to Yahweh (1Kgs 18:4,13), and goaded her husband into murdering Naboth so that he might take possession of the man's property (1Kgs 21:5-16). In fulfillment of the word of a prophet the evil woman was murdered and dogs ate her corpse (2Kgs 9:30-37). It is no surprise that Jezebel was vilified in later Jewish traditions (e.g., in *2Bar* 62:3 we hear of the "curse of Jezebel" in reference to Israel's tragic legacy of idolatry).[23]

As in the letter to the church at Pergamum, here the risen Christ inveighs against the "Jezebel" of Thyatira, who encourages believers to "eat food sacrificed to idols" and to "commit adultery" (v. 20). Whereas the charge of engaging in πορνεύω is probably metaphorical (as in Judg 2:17; 8:27), the reference to eating the meat sacrificed to idols should be taken literally (see comment on v. 14 above).

The warning that the Lord "will strike her children dead" (v. 23) is the harshest in the seven letters. These children should be understood as Jezebel's followers, not her literal children. There is no hiding from the Lord, for he "searches the mind and heart," as he always has done (1Chr 28:9).

He who overcomes the temptations and false teaching of the false prophetess Jezebel will be given "power over the nations" (v. 26), and "he shall rule them with a rod of iron, as when earthen pots are broken in pieces" (v. 27). These words unmistakably allude to Ps 2:8-9, the Psalm that celebrates the victory the Lord's Messiah has over the nations, which he will "break

with a rod of iron, and dash them in pieces like a potter's ves-
sel." The risen Christ will also give to him "the morning star"
(v. 27). Here we may have an allusion to the morning star of Isa
14:12, which in Judeo-Christian interpretation was understood
as Satan (or Lucifer). If so, perhaps the believer is assured that
he will have power over Satan. But the morning star of Rev 2:27
may refer to the messianic star (Num 24:17; *TLevi* 18:3; Mt 2:2).
If so, this may mean that Christ will share his messianic power
and glory with his believers.[24]

Fifth Letter: To the Church of Sardis (Rev 3:1-6)

Sardis is located some 100 kilometers due east of Smyrna. It
is estimated that the city's first-century population was 120,000,
including many Jews and at least one synagogue. Like the other
major cities of Asia Minor, Sardis was favored with beautiful
buildings, including the Temple of Artemis. Much of the city
was rebuilt following the earthquake of AD 17.[25]

The risen Christ assures the faithful person of Sardis that he
will be clad in "white garments" (v. 5a). Given the eschatological context of the book of Revelation, it is likely "white" is best
understood in the light of Daniel, who says the righteous will
"purify themselves, and make themselves white" (Dan 12:10;
cf. 11:35), perhaps even as the Ancient of Days is himself clad
"white as snow" (Dan 7:9; cf. Eccl 9:8; 1QM 7:10). The faithful
person may be assured that his name will not be blotted out of
the "book of life" (v. 5b). The tradition of a book from which
one hopes not to have one's name blotted out originates in
Exod 32:32 (where Moses is willing to be blotted out of God's
book, if in exchange God will forgive Israel's sin). In time this
"book" was referred to in various ways, among them "book of
life" (*Joseph and Aseneth* 15:3 "your name is written in the book
of life"; *Ordinance of Levi* 59 "carried in the book of remembered
life"; *TBenj.* 11:4 "he will be inscribed in the holy books").

For Jewish Christians ejected from the synagogue (as in Jn
9:22; 12:42; 16:2), which would result in loss of membership and
their names struck from the roll,[26] Christ's promise that their
names will not be blotted out of the book of life would have
been very reassuring.

Sixth Letter: To the Church of Philadelphia (Rev 3:7-13)

The risen Christ levels no complaints against the church of Philadelphia. There is again reference to opponents as "those of the synagogue of Satan who say they are Jews and are not, but lie" (v. 9). Christ describes himself as the one who "has the key of David, who opens and no one shall shut, who shuts and no one opens" (v. 7). We have here a clear allusion to Isa 22:22 ("I will place on his shoulder the key of the house of David; he shall open, and none shall shut; and he shall shut, and none shall open").

The interesting references to the "temple of my God," "city of my God," and the "new Jerusalem" — imagery that recalls Ezekiel's vision of the new Jerusalem — have been thrown into a new light thanks to the discovery of the New Jerusalem texts at Qumran (1Q32, 2Q24, 4Q554, 5Q15, 11Q18). At the very least it shows how important this theme was to Jews who longed for Israel's redemption.

Seventh Letter: To the Church of Laodicea (Rev 3:14-22)

Laodicea, famous for its hot and cold springs, streams of water, and aqueducts, as well as its great wealth, has only been partially excavated. An impressive gate, two theatres, a bathhouse, and a stadium are among the ruins of once great edifices.[27]

The risen Christ describes himself as "the Amen, the faithful and true witness, the beginning of God's creation" (v. 14). The word amen (אָמֵן/ἀμήν) occurs more than two dozen times in the OT. It is even more frequent in the Targums. The words "faithful and true" (πιστὸς καὶ ἀληθινός) are part of the meaning of amen. One sees this in Isa 1:21, when the prophet laments over Jerusalem's sinful condition: "How the faithful [נֶאֱמָנָה/πιστή] city has become a harlot." The description "beginning of creation" immediately recalls Gen 1:1. Of course, as the eternal Son of God, who existed in the very bosom of the Father (Jn 1:18), Christ may be compared to Wisdom, who was in God's presence before the "beginning of the earth" (Prov 8:22-23).

Recalling the words of Prov 3:12, Jesus tells the church of Laodicea: "Those whom I love, I reprove and chasten" (v. 19).

Although they are lukewarm, he urges them to be zealous and to repent, assuring them: "Behold, I stand at the door and knock; if anyone hears my voice and opens the door, I will come in to him and eat with him, and he with me" (v. 20). These words may allude to the beckoning call of the lover in the Song of Songs: "Hark! my beloved is knocking: 'Open to me [κρού-ει ἐπὶ τὴν θύραν· ἄνοιξόν μοι]'" (Song 5:2).

Those who respond, those who conquer, will sit with Jesus on his throne, just as he conquered and sat on the throne of his father (v. 21). This remarkable promise takes us back to the words of Jesus, who promised his disciples that someday they would sit on twelve thrones, judging the twelve tribes of Israel (Mt 19:28; Lk 22:28-30; cf. Dan 7:9; Ps 122:1-5), and who threatened his priestly accusers: "You will see the Son of man seated at the right hand of Power, and coming with the clouds of heaven" (Mk 14:62; cf. Dan 7:13; Ps 110:1). These dominical utterances, spoken before Easter and spoken in a new way decades after Easter, are firmly rooted in the Scriptures of Israel.

Concluding Remarks

Given the Judaic orientation of much of the polemic in the letters to the seven churches and its coherence at points with the fourth Gospel's apologetic that is clearly oriented toward the synagogue, I am convinced that we need to take a fresh look at the references to the opponents and false teaching in the Johannine Epistles. These opponents are not Gnostics or Hellenizers; they are Jewish skeptics and members of synagogues, who reject the claims that Christian Jews make about Jesus.

The affirmation in the Gospel of John, that the "Word became flesh and dwelt among us" (Jn 1:14), is not a counterthrust against docetic Gnosticism. It is an affirmation that the eternal Logos of God, God's wisdom, has, in a manner not unlike the very glory of God descending and occupying the leather tent of Exodus 40, entered into the human realm as a human being.

The opponents of the Johannine community, as reflected in the Johannine Epistles, are not docetic Gnostics, who reject the

30

corporeal reality of Jesus; they are Jews who deny that the Messiah has come at all. They deny Jesus. They assert that the Messiah has in fact not come in the flesh. In short, he has not arrived! This is the meaning of 2 John 7, "Many deceivers have gone out into the world, who do not confess Jesus as the Messiah having come in the flesh." This is the meaning of 1 John 2:22, "Who is the liar, other than the one who denies, (by saying,) 'Jesus is not the Messiah.'" These liars and deceivers are those who deny the messianic identity of Jesus. They simply reject the affirmation of John 20:31, "These things are written that you believe that the Messiah, Son of God, is Jesus." This confession is affirmed in 1 John 4:2, "By this we know the Spirit of God: Every spirit that confesses Jesus as the Messiah having come in the flesh is of God."

The struggle seen in the Gospel of John, in which those who confess Jesus are threatened with expulsion from the synagogue, continues in the Epistles of John and in the Revelation of John, particularly as seen in the letters to the seven churches. To be sure, the book of Revelation is very concerned about state persecution, but the most troubling difficulty facing these struggling churches is the opposition of synagogues that simply do not believe that Israel's Messiah has come and that the Messiah is none other than the crucified and resurrected Jesus of Nazareth.

THE PLAGUES OF THE EXODUS IN THE BOOK OF REVELATION

Gary Hall

Introduction

The event of the exodus had a great impact on the rest of the OT. Numerous words and motifs were picked up from this first major act of God's redemptive plan and used to develop a trajectory throughout Israel's history. The adaptation of themes begins in Joshua 4 (crossing the Jordan River) and continues through the history books and prophets.[1] It should be no surprise that the book of Revelation, which is so dependent on the OT, would continue the adaptation of the great themes and motifs from the book of Exodus. In fact Dr. Lowery uses the allusions to Exodus in Revelation as a good example of John's typological use of the OT.[2]

The many themes and images from Exodus require some selectivity in a short essay. I have chosen to concentrate on the usage of the plague images in Revelation. The plagues in the book of Exodus form a major theme in the event and provide a basis for some fruitful reflection. The plagues are closely tied to the theological reasons for the Exodus and may shed light on John's allusions. We are also aided by the fact that the plague imagery has a trajectory through the OT before we arrive at the New.

The Purpose of the Plagues in Exodus

Scholars offer a variety of nuanced interpretations of the purpose of the plagues. This is perhaps because the texts themselves offer several reasons why God will afflict the Egyptians:

[1] The Exodus will be God's great act of redemption for Israel which will convince Israel that he alone can redeem them (6:6-8);[3] [2] it will require that he multiply his wonders in Egypt (7:3); [3] it will result in Pharaoh and Egypt learning that he is God (5:2 [Pharaoh asks, "Who is Yahweh that . . . I should let Israel go?"], 7:5,17; 8:10,22; 9:14; 14:4,18);[4] [4] it will demonstrate his power over Pharaoh (15:6,12,15; Deut 9:29);[5] [5] it will show Yahweh more powerful than the gods of the Egyptians as each plague attacks one of the Egyptian deities (12:12; 18:10-11; Num 33:4);[6] [6] the cosmic struggle reflects the struggle in the moral order since Pharaoh's genocidal actions against Israel violated God's created moral order which impacted the cosmic order (and therefore the plagues are acts of judgment, 6:6; 7:4; 12:12).[7] Following Fretheim in this last concept, Peter Enns carries it further and speaks of a creation—uncreation—recreation scheme. In Exodus 1 Pharaoh sought to overturn Genesis 1 by denying Israel fruitfulness. So God unleashed the forces of creation against him. The plagues were reversals of creation—animals harm humans, light ceases, water brings death, and humans die. But each plague ceases and God restores creation.[8]

The various views are not contradictory, but is there a theme that has prime significance? The concentration of statements with the verb "to know" (ידע) in chapters 5 through 14 (16 times) suggests a central theme of the plague account. Before the first plague Pharaoh says, "I do not know Yahweh and I will not let Israel go" (5:2). At the crossing of the Red Sea at the end, God announced, "I will gain glory for myself over Pharaoh and all of his army: and the Egyptians will know that I am Yahweh" (14:4,18). In between are nine affirmations that the events will cause several audiences (Israel, Egypt, the nations) to know that God is Yahweh—especially 9:14, "For this time I will send all my plagues upon you yourselves, and upon your officials, and upon your people, so that you may know that there is no one like me in all the earth" (NRSV). This knowledge would come as the result of several crucial events, primarily the signs and wonders that God will perform through the plagues. In the process he also demonstrated his power over creation and therefore his power over all Egyptian gods and over the

Pharaoh as their representative in Egypt. Therefore, the route to knowledge of Yahweh involved a cosmic battle. The plagues take the form of natural events which echo in some places the creation of the world. They seem to exhibit a reversal of God's creative acts of Genesis 1. Therefore, there is some truth to the various purposes that scholars have suggested for the plagues, but the major purpose is knowledge of God.[9]

How does a culture that had developed its own concept of deity, grown arrogant in its worldly power, and thought nothing of enslaving foreigners learn who the true God of the universe is? It learns only with great reluctance, determined resistance, refusal to give in, and ultimately great suffering and death. The path to knowledge of Yahweh then was a tortured one for Egypt and had universal implications.[10]

Out of such profound struggle came an abundance of language and images to fuel further thought about cosmic events. Before tracing these thoughts through the OT into Revelation we need to take a brief look at the plagues themselves.

A Closer Look at the Plagues of the Exodus

The literary structure of the development of the plagues in the text has been well established.[11] The pattern is a 3 + 3 + 3 + 1 structure (reminiscent of the 3 + 3 + 1 pattern in the creation account of Genesis 1). For example, the first three plagues conclude with the Egyptian magicians saying that this is the finger of God (8:19). The second three end with the magicians unable to stand before Moses (9:11). The third three end with the statement that the Pharaoh will not see Moses again (10:28-29). Each plague includes common elements such as a warning of its coming (or lack of one), instructions for, timing of, response to, and the agent. Each triad of plagues has a pattern in these areas that parallel the other two. The first two plagues of each triad include a warning (numbers 1, 2, 4, 5, 7, 8) but the third ones do not (numbers 3, 6, 9). Plagues 1, 3, and 7 occur in the morning. No time is given for the others. This literary pattern indicates the instructional and theological nature of the plagues.[12]

The actual plagues have been interpreted in a variety of ways. Some see a "natural" development or connection between them and interconnected natural phenomena in Egypt.[13] This rationalistic interpretation falters on several counts.[14] Fundamentally, the plagues are presented as direct interventions of God and are designed to advance his purposes.

Though commonly referred to as the ten plagues, this language is absent from Exodus 4–11 and the rest of the OT. The most common terms used are "signs" (אֹת) and "wonders" (מוֹפֵת).[15]

The LXX continues this reticence, using πληγη only two times in these chapters, Exod 11:1 and 12:13. Interestingly the LXX translates the normal Hebrew word for plague, דֶּבֶר, as "death" (θανατος) in Exod 5:3; 9:3,15.

We have suggested that the plagues were intended to create knowledge of God, but it was knowledge gained the hard way, for the plagues were devastating divine acts against Egypt, her Pharaoh, and her gods. This is supported by the various verbs used with the plagues. Many are from the domain of divinely initiated destruction. So the plagues would "fall on" Egypt (5:3, פגע). The frogs "struck" the land (נכה – 8:2[H-7:27]); 12:12. Death will strike the Egyptians (נגף – 12:23, 27). The insects are "sent" on the land (שלח – 8:21; see 9:14). The hail "falls" on the land (המטר – 9:18) and "strikes" it down (9:23). The locusts "devour" the land (אכל – 10:5). Ultimately, the Egyptian first born are "killed" (הרג – 13:15). Further, Yahweh "fought" against the Egyptian army (לחם – 14:14,25).[16] This defeat was engineered by God's "strong hand" and "outstretched arm" (Exod 15:6,12,16; Deut 9:29). This language represents retributive justice, that is, divine destruction for violence committed. Egypt experienced the hardship, suffering, and death that she had afflicted on Israel (Exodus 1).

The Influence of the Plagues on the Old Testament

The plagues deeply impressed the authors of the rest of the OT, especially the prophets. The language of these signs and wonders became an integral part of the expressions the prophets used for God's judgment on the nations, and even upon Israel herself.

The language is first taken up in the covenant curses of

Deuteronomy 28. In a long section, Moses warns that covenant disobedience will trigger covenant curses (Deut 28:15-68).[17] These will take the form of natural disaster and enemy attacks. Therefore, Yahweh will cause disease (דֶּבֶר) to cling to them (דבק) until he has destroyed (כלה) them (28:21). He will strike them (נכה) with all sorts of maladies and calamities until they perish (אבד – 28:22). They will be afflicted with the boils of Egypt (v. 27, cf. v. 35). Furthermore, locust will devour their crops (v. 38) just as the locusts did in Egypt. The curses will result in a devastated land and people that will mirror the consequences of God's "signs and wonders" against Egypt (v. 46). God will treat his covenant people the way he treated Egypt with all their diseases (vv. 58-61), an awful specter indeed. Even more incredible, Israel's great salvation will be reversed and the Lord will send her back to Egypt (v. 68)!

The prophets picked up this language because in their role of covenant mediators they found many of the words and ideas fitting expressions of God's coming judgment on Israel's sin and on the nations. Their purpose was to convict the people of their sin so that they would repent and return to their covenant God.[18] Two common nouns from the plague narrative that the prophets use are blood (דָּם) and pestilence (דֶּבֶר). Though often used alone sometimes they appear in a list of other plague-related words. Isaiah 34:1-7 refers to God's judgment on nations that will result in the hills running with blood and God's sword being covered with blood. God's rescue of Israel from her captivity will mean destruction of her oppressors whom God will make drunk on their own blood (Isa 49:26). The result will be that all living things "will know that I, the LORD, am your savior," a repeat of the Exodus plague's theme! Also, Ezekiel often speaks of God's judgments on Israel in plague terms. God will bring famine, wild beasts, blood, sword, and plague on them (5:17). Ezekiel also speaks of blood and plague (5:17) and blood, pestilence, and sword (28:23; cf. 38:22). Especially interesting are Ezekiel's words against Egypt and the Pharaoh in 30:13-19 and 32:2-8. They will experience a host of calamities including sword, darkness over the land, captivity, wild animals, and copious shedding of blood. The result will be that "they will know that I am the LORD" (30:19).

Among the prophets, Jeremiah uses pestilence (דֶּבֶר) the most (17 times). But he almost always includes it in the triad of sword, famine, and pestilence (14:12; 21:7,9; 24:10; 27:8,13; 29:17,18, etc).[19] In fact, pestilence almost always appears in multipart lists in the prophets. In addition to the triad with sword and famine, it is listed with wild beasts, hail, fire, brimstone, drought, fall of cities, damage to crops, war and disaster. These lists in Jeremiah and Ezekiel seem to have come from the real life experiences of the Judeans as they lived through the destruction of their nation.[20] They also parallel the curses found in boundary stones and vassal treaties from the ancient Near East.

Fire (אֵשׁ) occurs often in the prophets describing God's judgment. There is precedent for this in the OT outside of the seventh plague. The idea is grounded in the fact that in the OT fire is associated with God in various ways. Fire is associated with God in theophany (Gen 15:17; Exod 3:2; 13:21,22; 14:24; 19:18; Deut 4:12; 5:4, etc.) and with the idea that God is a jealous God and thus a consuming fire (Deut 4:24; 9:3). Also early in Israel's history God used fire to punish the disobedient (Num 16:35).[21] It seemed natural to associate fire with God's judgment on the wicked (Ps 11:6; 97:3; Isa 30:30; Jer 21:14; Amos 7:4). Fire was particularly destructive, totally consuming its target. Eschatological texts also list fire as one of the means God will use to punish the wicked (Ezek 39:6; Joel 2:30[H 3:3]).

Other plague themes used in judgment texts include hail, darkness, and locusts. Hail would flatten crops and destroy everything (Isa 28:2,17; 30:30; Hag 2:17). Darkness would cover the earth and disrupt the light sources—the sun, moon, and stars (Isa 13:10; 60:2; Jer 13:16; Ezek 32:8; Mic 3:6). The prophet Joel is well-known for his picture of a devastating locust plague as divine judgment (Joel 1–2). An invading army like a locust plague will destroy everything (1:4). The invasion will be accompanied by darkness and fire (2:2-3,10). Stuart affirms that the description of the plague in 1:4 is borrowed almost exactly from Exodus 10:5 and 15.[22] But the locusts are a symbol for an invading army and not literal as in Exodus. This plague curse causes such devastation that it logically results in other covenant curses such as desolation of fields, vines, trees, land,

and drought.[23] Nahum uses the symbolism of the locust plague as judgment on Assyria (Nah 3:15-17). Isaiah employs the imagery for judgment on Assyria (Isa 33:4). Jeremiah uses it to express judgment on Egypt (Jer 46:23) and Babylon (Jer 51:14,27).

Further, Psalms 78 and 105 give an overview of Israel's rebellious history and devote a section to the deliverance from Egypt. Each Psalm lists seven plagues rather than the ten (Ps 78:42-51; 105:26-36).[24] Both Psalms are didactic and intend to teach by negative example (Ps 78:1-4).[25] The ancestors failed at every turn despite the mighty work of God and his patience. Yet he blessed them with the land, the temple, and David (Psalm 78) and kept his promise to Abraham (Psalm 105).[26]

The Influence of the Plagues in Revelation

As John searched for language in the OT to convey his theology of God's judgment, it seems logical he would follow the example of the OT prophets and utilize plague language. At the minimum, one could argue on the basis of shared circumstances and intention—that John's selection was conscious and expected. He did not have to invent ideas or symbols but found already at hand a rich conceptual repertoire from which to draw. This connection is most evident in the description of the seven trumpets in Revelation 8–11 and the seven bowls in Revelation 16, although allusions occur elsewhere in Revelation as well, especially in the seven seals in Rev 6:1-17; 8:1-5.

Seals, Trumpets, and Bowls

The literary pattern of the seven seals, trumpets, and bowls is striking. They follow the 6 + 1 pattern from Genesis 1 and replicated in the plagues pattern (9 + 1) as noted above. There are six seals (Rev 6:1-17), an interlude (Rev 7:1-17), and then the seventh seal (Rev 8:1-5). There are six trumpets (Rev 8:6–9:21), an interlude (Rev 10:1–11:14), and then the seventh trumpet (Rev 11:15-19). This is an archetypical pattern that occurs throughout the OT and John is consciously copying it in Revelation.[27]

The parallels between the seven trumpets (Revelation 8–11) and the seven bowls (Revelation 16) are especially interesting. Each septet presents the plagues striking spheres of creation in the same order culminating in a final judgment scene that involves the same elements of lightning, thunder, earthquake and hail.[28] All but the sixth trumpet alludes in some way to an Exodus plague.

Examination of the linguistic data also suggests conscious borrowing. John utilized several words from the Greek translation of the Exodus plague narrative to refer to the plagues of his trumpets and bowls. The first plague, blood (Greek, αιμα) is reflected in the second and third bowls (Rev 16:3 and 4-7). In the second bowl the sea turns to blood. In the third bowl the rivers and springs become blood (directly alluding to Exod 7:17 and 20). Blood is also a part of the first and second trumpets (Rev 8:7-9) but the dependence is not as clear. The second trumpet includes one-third of the sea turning to blood. Perhaps this is a more general borrowing from the OT prophetic tradition.

The second plague, frogs (βατροχος), is reflected in the sixth trumpet which describes three evil spirits that are like frogs (Rev 16:12-16). The sixth plague, boils (ελκος) is reflected in the first and fifth bowls (Rev 16:2,11). In both instances the pouring out of the bowl causes ugly, painful sores on the worshipers of the beast. The seventh plague, hail (χαλεζαν), is alluded to in three different events in the trumpet and bowl cycles. Hail plus fire and blood are a part of the first trumpet (Rev 8:7). Hail is a part of the divine theophany when the seventh trumpet opened the heavenly realm (Rev 11:19). Also the seventh bowl unleashed the final destruction of the nations and included huge hailstones falling on the people (Rev 16:21). The seventh plague also included fire with the hail, and fire is an important part of the trumpets and bowls. The horses in the sixth trumpet breathed out fire and sulfur that killed (9:17,18).[29] The seventh bowl included fire of lightning (16:18).

The eighth plague, the locusts (ακρις) is reflected in the fifth trumpet (Rev 9:3,7), where powerful locusts come out of the Abyss to torment the people who do not have God's seal on their foreheads. They were fierce looking creatures (Rev 9:7-11).

The ninth plague, darkness (σκοτοω, σκοτιζω) over the earth, is reflected in the fourth and fifth trumpets and the fifth bowl. In the fourth trumpet one-third of the sun, moon, and stars are darkened (8:12). In the fifth trumpet the smoke from the Abyss darkens the sky (9:2). In the fifth bowl the kingdom of the beast is plunged into darkness and sores break out on the people (16:10-11).

Allusions to the fifth plague, pestilence or disease on the Egyptain livestock (Exod 9:1-7), are subtle. The LXX translated the Hebrew דֶּבֶר (pestilence or plague) with the word "death" (θανατος). Death is a prominent theme in Revelation so every reference would hardly be an allusion to Exodus. But in the light of the prominence of allusions to the plagues in the Trumpet and Bowl cycles, perhaps the occurrence of θανατος twice in the fifth trumpet account (Rev 9:6) is a veiled allusion to the fifth plague.[30]

There do not appear to be any direct allusions to the plagues in the seven seals (Rev 6:1-17; 8:1-5). But some borrow heavily from the OT prophetic language of judgment that was heavily influenced by the plagues. For example, the triad sword, famine, death (NIV, plague), results from the fourth seal (Rev 6:7-8). The sixth seal results in the sun turning black and the moon blood red (Rev 6:12).

Other Parallels in Revelation

Plague language in Revelation is not confined to the seven seals, trumpets, and bowls. For example, blood is mentioned in Rev 14:20 as coming from the winepress of God's judging wrath. The image is a clear allusion to Joel 3:13 and especially Isa 63:1-3. The blood is perhaps real here, not metaphorical, but the quantity is hyperbole. Still judgment brings death (shedding of blood) which conveys the same concept of judgment in the three septets.

The two witnesses (Rev 11:4-6) as a part of their defensive equipment have the ability to turn water into blood, a clear reference to Exod 7:17-25.[31] They also have the ability to pour out fire on their foes (v. 5). Fire is another plague word that reinforces the judgment theme. Fire as a judgment idea is used more often than blood outside of the three septets. Probably this is because of its extensive use in the OT prophets as noted earlier. The worshipers of the beast and its images will drink the cup of God's wrath and be tormented with fire (Rev 14:10), a certain punishment drawing also from Isa 51:17, Jer 25:15-18, and Ps 75:8. The great whore will be burned in judgment (Rev 17:16). Also Babylon will suffer the plagues and be burned with fire (Rev 18:8).

Although the book of Exodus does not often refer to the nine events in Exodus 7–11 as plagues, as pointed out above, John uses the word (πληγη) quite often. Most prominent are the references to "the seven angels with the seven plagues" that introduce the seven bowls (Rev 15:1,6,8). Of course the number seven is used because of its symbolic importance, but perhaps John also was influenced by enumeration of seven plagues in Psalms 78 and 105. The phrase also appears in Rev 21:9 to identify the angel who shows John the New Jerusalem.

A general reference to plague is also used to describe the scene of destruction of Babylon in 18:4,8. Later these plagues are promised to those who would dare take away any words of the prophecy of "this book" (Rev 22:18).

Purpose of the Plagues in Revelation

It remains now to determine for what purpose John appropriated the Exodus plague traditions in his septet cycles. We have suggested above that the plagues were cosmic events as acts of judgment intended to convince Pharaoh, the Egyptians, and Israel that Yahweh was God.

John seems to go in a different direction with his septets. First of all, the plagues are not signs and wonders. In Revelation, the beast or his minions perform signs![32] Nor does John use the plagues to foster belief. He never sees knowledge of God as an outcome, the major focus of the plagues in Exodus. Rather, John seems to follow the lead of the OT prophets by using the plagues as symbols of judgment. Especially the trumpets and bowls bring judgment on the enemies of God, the beast, the wicked city, and the followers of the beast.[33]

Also, following the prophets John seems to see the possibility that the plagues might foster repentance. This is especially true of the trumpets, though his comment after the sixth trumpet is that the survivors of the plagues did not repent (Rev 9:20-21).[34] After the fourth and fifth bowls he also remarks that those with the mark of the beast still did not repent (Rev 16:9,11). Therefore, the possibility of repentance as the purpose seems at best indirect. If repentance was possible, it was short lived as the seven bowls are usually viewed as final judgments, not partial like the seven trumpets.[35] "The followers of the Antichrist, however, are like Pharaoh and his people in the time of Moses. Their hearts remain obdurate through all the divine chastisements. So the wrath comes on the last generation to the uttermost, as it did on Pharaoh and his generation."[36]

Beale tempers the repentance theme by pointing out that the theology of the exodus plagues has been formative for the trumpets and that ultimately the trumpets must be understood as punishments on the people. The trumpets are primarily intended to demonstrate God's uniqueness and incomparable omnipotence. They also demonstrate the human hardness of heart.[37] This is so because the trumpets are an answer to the saints' plea in Rev 6:9-11 for the punishment of their persecutors. This connection "explains why the trumpets are not mainly warnings but punishments for unrepentant persecutors and idolaters."[38]

On the other hand, spaced in the interludes between the septets, is the theme of God's glory. Just before the seventh trumpet, an earthquake kills thousands and the terrified survivors glorify God (Rev 11:13). Before the seven last plagues, the seven bowls, the heavenly inhabitants break into a new song of Moses to glorify God for his judgments (Rev 15:3-4). Those who did not repent after the fourth bowl also did not give God glory (Rev 16:9). This theme could very well parallel the Exodus theme of driving Pharaoh to acknowledge God (and thereby bring him glory).

Conclusion

John mined the OT plague tradition for symbols to utilize in his trumpet and bowl septets. The impact of the plagues he described was even more severe than in Exodus because of their world ending, cosmic impact. They are the ultimate uncreation, preparing the way for the new heavens and the new earth. They manifest the justice of God who brings punishment on those who are in open rebellion against him and oppress his people. The plagues might lead some to repentance but the possibility is small; for God's opponents, like ancient Pharaoh and Egypt, are hardened in their hearts, totally recalcitrant, and ripe for God's final justice, total destruction.

"WITNESS" IN THE BOOK OF REVELATION

Neal Windham

In John's Apocalypse, "witness" serves both as a cultural manifestation of Christian fidelity and a necessary act of resistance against evil. As such, it is both prophetic and revolutionary. Yet, more than anything, it is an expression of worship. John uses faithful Christian witness like a crowbar, prying apart truth from lies, saints from sinners, the Living Lord from beastly gods, and authentic worship from pagan blather. As such, its centrality to the purpose of Revelation is secure, for John's vision of enduring hope for the redeemed promises a future bright with God and the Lamb because Christian witnesses have both told the truth about Jesus Christ and, at the same time, faithfully continued to worship their God.

In this essay, we will first survey the state of contemporary scholarship of "witness" in Revelation, followed by an analysis of prominent words in the relevant semantic field. Next, we will identify and trace key phrases often paired with witness throughout the book, culminating in the identification of a major discourse peak in Revelation 19, where all the key elements of witness converge in a scene of triumph for the Faithful Witness, Jesus, and his followers. Finally, we will look at the Roman imperial cult as possibly the principal source of witness-evoking conflict that triggered John's attention to the theme in the first place, concluding with a few words of application for the church in the contemporary world.

Recent Interpreters

Allison Trites's *The New Testament Concept of Witness* sets the stage for the contemporary discussion.[1] In it, he argues that NT appropriation of the language of witness derives from Israel's law courts, with special attention to the controversy in Isaiah 40–55.[2] Here, Israel's opponents are challenged to make the case for their gods, offering arguments which authorize suitable worship. But since these gods are unable to produce any compelling evidence, the case is lost to Yahweh. A subsequent lawsuit between Yahweh and his own people, set in these same chapters, depicts Israel lamenting her "right" before Yahweh as one unnoticed by him. But Yahweh counters as the "eternal, the indefatigable Creator . . . the never-failing source of strength available to his followers."[3]

Trites argues that it is against this background of witness as leveled against Israel's opponents and in favor of her "right" that the NT writers marshal the language of testimony in face of strong ecclesial opposition. Specifically, "both these books [Revelation and the Fourth Gospel] use the words ["witness" and "testimony"] in their primary, forensic sense."[4] His arguments are particularly palatable as related to Revelation 12, but perhaps more important for our purposes is Trites's attention to the "legal contest" between the "martyrs and their earthly accuser, Babylon" in Revelation 18–19,[5] a section I will later argue constitutes part of a critical discourse peak in the Apocalypse, one which appropriates the language of witness in a highly effective, even climactic, rhetorical web of related concerns.

Recently, Olutola K. Peters has built upon the proposals of Trites in *The Mandate of the Church in the Apocalypse of John* by arguing that witness is the major unifying theme of Revelation.[6] Peters builds his case by examining worship, witness, and repentance (which is evoked by worship), along with a number of accompanying subsidiary themes (reading, hearing, waiting, etc.). For Peters, worship and witness are nearly equally fronted throughout Revelation, but in the end witness prevails due to its ubiquitous presence and frequent prominence.[7] The central value of Peters's work is its rich exploration of the many related themes which constitute the ethical mandate of Revelation for the church.[8]

In summary, Trites has demonstrated that witness has legal dimensions in Revelation, while Peters has shown its important connection to worship. While other interpretations of the witness motif exist,[9] Trites's and Peters's studies are most relevant to the arguments of this chapter.

Marturia and *Martus*: The Language of Witness

While the semantic field of witness extends beyond *marturia* ("testimony") and its cognates *martus* ("one who testifies"), *marturion* ("testimony" or "proof"), and *martureo* (to "bear witness") to include words like *propheteia* ("prophecy")[10] and *logos* ("word"),[11] we will limit the focus in this section to the *marturia* group due to its frequency in the Apocalypse.

Much has been made of the phrase "testimony (*marturia*) of Jesus," which appears often in Revelation (1:2,9; 12:17; 19:10; 20:4). The debate surrounds the genitive *Iesou* ("of Jesus"). Is it subjective (placing the accent upon Jesus' own testimony about himself, as disclosed to his witnesses),[12] objective (placing the accent on others' testimony *about* him as they had formulated it on the basis of experiences with the Lord and his people),[13] or some combination of these?[14]

While many commentators now side with the subjective genitive interpretation (for which a very strong case can be made),[15] the objective reading is also attractive since John is in fact "testifying" (a form of *martureo,* the verb) to "whatever things *he* saw" (*hosa eiden*) in 1:2, and is exiled on Patmos due to his testimony (1:9). Admittedly, the phrase "word of God" (1:2,9) begs the subjective reading, as is frequently argued, but even here it is at least possible to suggest that the focus is upon the fact that John offered a word (or testimony) about God and a witness about Jesus based upon his own reporting of encounters with the Lord and/or his people. This is particularly true if, and this is conjectural, John's forced testimony about Jesus before officials of the Roman imperial cult led to his exile.[16] In either case (subjective or objective genitive), the testimony is, in the final analysis, both derived from the risen Lord and delivered by Revelation's faithful witnesses. Perhaps Beale is correct in labeling this genitive "general" (i.e., both subjective and objective).[17] In the final analysis, the meaning of *ten marturia Iesou* ("the testimony of Jesus") awaits further investigation. Its meaning is, I will later argue, closely tied to the larger discourse structure.

The martyr (from Greek *martus*) motif has also generated significant interest in witness studies. Eusebius informs us that second-century Christians suffering great persecution in Gaul refused to allow themselves to be called *martures* ("witnesses"), reserving that title for Christ alone, "the faithful and true witness."[18] Also, at about the same time the Christians in Gaul were being persecuted, Polycarp, bishop of Smyrna, became a martyr. Trites observes that the words *martus, marturion,* and *marturein* are all employed to refer to his martyrdom in *The Martyrdom of Polycarp,* a very clear indication that the Greek root had, by that time, begun to refer to death due to faithful testimony.[19]

But had *martus* come to mean "martyr" in the pages of Revelation? Trites doesn't think so.[20] He argues that *martus* merely meant "witness," as in a court of law. Next, it came to refer to a person who testified to his faith in a court and *subsequently* suffered death as a penalty for his testimony. Both these meanings appear in Revelation. In yet a further development, Trites contends that *martus* began to refer to death "as a part of the witness," and eventually (in the second century) it came to mean "martyr."[21] The closest the NT comes to "martyr" is in Rev 2:3 and 3:14, according to Trites. In his view, the root continues to retain its primary association with witness, not death, throughout Revelation.

On the other hand, Mitchell Reddish, who agrees with Trites' diachronic analysis of the *mart-* root, has, nevertheless, argued that martyrdom is "the primary motif of John's writings."[22] He suggests that "Lamb" is Revelation's "most prominent Christological title," appearing some twenty-eight times.[23] Moreover, it is a Paschal (or suffering) Lamb that John has in mind, one who conquers through martyrdom. Reddish concludes, "In a work addressed to potential martyrs it would be important to remind them that their leader, their Savior, was likewise a martyr victim."[24]

In summary, the language of witness in Revelation often evokes a picture of deep suffering as a result of faithful testimony offered in a legal setting. The testimony itself centers upon God and Christ, and is rooted in the experience of having lived either with Jesus (the apostles) or for him (believers in John's seven churches). While the word "martyr" does not appear in Revelation, it will become fairly common in Christian literature of suffering toward the end of the second century. Still, the *concept* of martyrdom is clearly beginning to emerge in John's day. Suffice it to say that those witnesses whom John commends as faithful speak the truth about God and Jesus when called upon to do so and sometimes die for it (Rev 2:13).

Revelation's Trajectory of Witness

Outlines of Revelation abound, no two of them quite alike. Generally speaking, they follow one of two paths. Either they are chiastic in structure,[25] or they are marked by a roughly linear movement. Grant Osborn's outline illustrates the second approach, the one taken here.[26] According to Osborn, the book's progress gathers around a generally linear movement: prologue (1:1-8), churches addressed (1:9-3:22), God in majesty and judgment (4:1-16:21), final judgment (17:1-20:15), new heaven and new earth (21:1-22:5), and epilogue (22:6-21). Significant for our purposes is that, in Osborn's approach, Revelation 17-20 is the climax of the judgment sequence of the book. This is to say, although instances of judgment appear regularly in earlier chapters (e.g., 6, 8, 11, 12, 15, and 16), there is something final and eternal about the judgments of Revelation 17-20.

At the heart of this section lies Rev 19:10b, which reads, "The testimony of Jesus is the Spirit of prophecy."[27] I submit that these words, as they appear in *this* part of the book, constitute part of a significant discourse peak, useful in providing needed understanding as to the meaning of "testimony of Jesus" throughout the pages of Revelation. In discourse, "It is normal to find a peak towards which the narrative advances, and from which there is a rather rapid descent. The peak is the point of the story: a question is posed . . . and then answered, a paradox is presented . . . and then resolved, a competition is described . . . and then a winner produced."[28] Revelation "delays" its peaking several times since the seventh sign is so often deferred, as with the seventh seal and the seventh trumpet.[29] But there appears to be no delay in Revelation 19. Babylon has fallen, the heavenly multitude collectively shouts "Hallelujah," and the rider on the white horse makes his triumphant appearance. In short, a question ("How long, O Lord?") is here answered, a paradox (God's apparent ambivalence toward evil) resolved, and a winner (the rider on the white horse) produced. This triumphant appearance thus constitutes the key component of Revelation's discourse peak. But why, just after the heavenly chorus and just before the rider appears, do we hear the enigmatic words, "The testimony of Jesus is the Spirit of prophecy"?

In order to answer this question it will be necessary to trace a "trajectory" of witness throughout the book. I do not use the word "trajectory" to suggest a neatly and tightly wound "rise" in John's handling of witness, but a generally forward-moving, momentum-gathering focus upon witness, culminating in the statement, "The testimony of Jesus is the Spirit of prophecy." The trajectory has several focal points in the book, specifically in Revelation 1–2 (John, Jesus, and Antipas), 6:9 (slain witnesses crying out to God), 11–12 (the two witnesses and the woman's witness), 19–20 (triumphant witnesses), and 22 (denouement: the final witness of John and Jesus). It employs six key contextual associations that regularly appear alongside "witness" or "testimony": the *word of God*, the testimony *of Jesus, faithful* witness(es), *suffering, worship*, and *prophecy*.

Word of God

This phrase appears five times in Revelation (1:2,9; 6:9; 19:13; 20:4), often coupled with "testimony" (1:2,9; 6:9). It has been suggested of 1:2 and 1:9 that "Word of God" is a reference to the OT prophetic witness, while the "testimony of Jesus" refers to apostolic testimony.[30] Such a reading would conveniently explain why John joins the phrases, especially in light of his ubiquitous use of the OT,[31] though this reading is not without problems.[32] In any case, witness is coupled with "word of God" in Revelation fairly often; we should pay careful heed to the possible significance of this pairing, particularly in 19:9 ("These are the true words of God") alongside 19:10 ("The testimony of Jesus is the spirit of prophecy").

Testimony of Jesus

As noted earlier in this essay, this phrase appears five times in Revelation (1:2,9; 12:17; 19:10; 20:4). Significant for our purposes is where it occurs, in Revelation 1, 12, 19, and 20, all focal points in the trajectory.

Faithful Witness

Three times John uses this phrase — twice of Jesus (1:5; 3:14) and once of his servant Antipas (2:13). Jesus is the witness *par excellence*, the most faithful of all those summoned to testify to the truth of his divine vocation. That Antipas follows in his footsteps, enduring death at Pergamum, is a sign of persecution. It is also significant for our purposes that the "faithful" witness language appears in 1:5, sandwiched as it is between 1:2 and 1:9, both of which mention the "testimony of Jesus." Notice as well the proximity of "testimony of Jesus" (19:10) and the phrase "Faithful and True" (19:11), which echoes 1:5 ("the faithful witness").

Suffering

Suffering is everywhere present in Revelation, and never more apparent than in texts dealing with witness. Several come to mind. They are: 1:9, "I, John, your . . . companion in suffering . . . on the island of Patmos because of . . . the testimony of Jesus"; 2:13, "in the days of Antipas, my faithful witness, who was put to death . . ."; 6:9, "I saw . . . the souls of those who had been slain because of . . . the testimony of Jesus"; 11:7, "when the (two witnesses) have finished their testimony, the beast . . . will kill them"; 12:11, "they overcame . . . by the blood of the Lamb and by . . . their testimony"; 12:17, "then the dragon . . . went off to make war against . . . those who . . . hold to the testimony of Jesus"; and 17:6, "I saw that the woman was drunk with the blood of . . . those who bore testimony of Jesus." While the suffering of Jesus and the saints is largely past in Revelation

19, it is, however, explicitly mentioned in 19:2 and 19:13. That it is largely past *here* makes perfect sense. The suffering has come to an end; its mention is retrospective.

Worship

In better than half the chapters of Revelation, worship is mentioned explicitly. It is central to the book's message. So we should not be surprised to find it connected to witness. Specifically, this pairing is strong in Revelation 11 and 19. In Revelation 11, where we read about the "two witnesses," John is told to measure the temple of God and count its worshipers (11:1). And in Revelation 20, shouts of "Hallelujah!" precede a declaration that John will not worship an angel who self-describes as a "fellow servant with you and with your brothers who hold to the testimony of Jesus" (19:10). John is then told to "Worship God!"

Prophecy/Prophesy

John frequently mentions prophecy (1:3; 19:10; 22:7,10,18,19) and prophesying (10:11; 11:3,6). Once again, he does so in close proximity to the language of witness, particularly in 1:3, 11:3 and 6, and, most significantly, 19:10, where the "testimony of Jesus" *is* "the spirit of prophecy."

Implications of "Witness" Themes

Having now demonstrated the regular contextual proximity of these six major themes to *marturia* ("witness"), we are finally ready to weigh an interpretation of Rev 19:10b which takes into account our "trajectory." First, a little context. Babylon is, by the beginning of chapter 17, spent. She has reaped the fruit of her blood-soaked adulteries, and her formerly robust commerce has come to a crashing halt (chapter 18). While Satan himself will enjoy one last brief burst of evil (20:7-9), the remainder of Revelation, beginning in 19:1, depicts the Church and her Lord entirely triumphant.

Revelation 19 commences with celestial praise from a "great multitude . . . the twenty-four elders and the four living creatures" (19:1,4). To the roar of racing waters and the crack of

loud thunder, yet more praise erupts (19:6ff.). "The angel" pro-
nounces a blessing on the Lamb's invited wedding guests and
adds, "These are the true *words of God*" (19:9). At this, John,
overwhelmed and obviously confused, attempts to *worship* the
angel. He is sternly warned and then instructed by the angel, "I
am a fellow servant with you and with your brothers who hold
to *the testimony of Jesus. Worship God!* For the *testimony of Jesus is
the Spirit of prophecy*" (19:10). Next, John sees a rider, "*Faithful*
and True" (19:11), whose robe is dipped in *blood*" and "whose
name is *the Word of God*" (19:13). Thus, we observe the convergence of all six witness-related contextual associations mentioned throughout the book in this one climactic text (and all in
the space of two verses) — surely, a point important to establish-
ing this text as part of Revelation's discourse peak in the book's
"trajectory of witness" and overall narrative flow.

Is it not possible that one of John's greatest questions, a question which had perhaps puzzled his readers since 1:2 (and commentators ancient and modern ever since), is here finally being
answered? Just what *is* "the testimony of Jesus"? The discourse
begs an answer, and John, now aware that it is quite possible
even for a faithful witness such as he to mistake God for a lesser
being, is ready to provide one. But in fact it is not John's answer
at all; it is the angel's. "The testimony of Jesus," the angel
announces, indirectly,[33] is to "Worship God!"[34] (not the dragon,
nor the beasts, nor the false prophet; not the angel speaking this
word, and definitely not the emperor or any other pagan deity
[see below], but God). The angel's words are, thus, consistent
with that message, of which negligence caused Israel a painful
sojourn in the wilderness (Exodus 32), continuing struggles in
the period of the judges (Judg 2:10-15), Assyrian deportation
(2Kgs 17:7-23), and Babylonian captivity (2Kgs 24:89–25:21).

Moreover, the angel's command — Worship God! —
addressed a grave theological problem prominent in Asia
Minor — idol worship (Acts 19:23ff.).[35] It was surely an answer
John's auditors needed to hear. Furthermore, to "worship God"
is an explicit and recurrent theme throughout Revelation, and
particularly in texts belonging to the "trajectory of witness"
(Rev 11:16; 19:4,10; 22:9).[36]

Additionally, John discovers this is a testimony inspired by *the* Spirit (not "a spirit") through prophetic agency. The genitive, "Spirit *of prophecy*," is therefore objective, meaning it is the Spirit who inspires this prophecy that the faithful are to worship God. Neither John nor his fellow servants nor the angel is called upon to figure this out on his own. The Holy Spirit will show them. Directing the people of God to worship God, as opposed to some lesser deity, is, in other words, clearly the work of Spirit (Rev 4:2).

Moreover, the text is strongly Trinitarian: "Worship *God!* For the testimony of *Jesus* is the *Spirit* of prophecy," says the angel. In other words, the angel is both indirectly answering the question, "What is the testimony of Jesus?" (to "worship God"), *and* providing a reason to do so (because "the Spirit says so"). This Trinitarian focus accords well with John's emphasis upon worshiping both the One who sits on the throne (4:8,11) and the Lamb (5:12-14). The two are, equally "Lord" in the Apocalypse.[37] Notice as well that "testimony of Jesus" alongside "Spirit of prophecy" forms a slight chiasm, yet one more way of fronting the centrality of God (and the worship of God alone) in this text.[38]

As a final argument for the centrality of this crucial clarification—Worship God!—in the midst of Revelation's discourse peak, in Rev 22:8-9, as John closes his book with critical information about the implied author, we are told, "I, John, am the one who heard and saw these things. And when I had heard and seen them,[39] I fell down to worship at the feet of the angel who had been showing them to me. But he said, '. . . I am a fellow servant with you and with your brothers the prophets and of all who keep the words of this book. Worship God!'" (Rev 22:8-9). This is, of course, an echo of Rev 19:10.[40] As if he could not recover from the nearly disastrous error of earlier falling down before the angel, John concludes that Israel's major blunder with God, worshiping someone other than Yahweh, has now become the church's greatest challenge. And here is why.

The Roman Imperial Cult

"I am a fellow servant with you and with your brothers the prophets and of all who keep the words of this book. Worship

God," the angel tells John (Rev 22:9). Why so great a stress upon angelic and human faith-camaraderie, keeping (*tereo*) the words of this book, and, above all, worshiping *God* near the close of the Apocalypse? Consider the Roman imperial cult. Robert Lowery has written, "Revelation suggests that at the end of the first century, Roman toleration of Christians was fading and was being replaced by growing suspicion and vindictiveness. . . .The Christians in Asia Minor found themselves in a period of transition where the response of the Roman government and populace toward them was changing for the worse."[41] Further, "The overwhelming majority of scholars agree that the Roman cult in which the Emperor was worshiped as a god is the background behind such passages as Revelation 13:1-18; 14:9-11; and 19:19-20."[42] It is to this important possibility which, in closing, I wish to turn our attention.

While scholars have debated the geographic extent and level of required devotion to the imperial cult, there is growing consensus that the cult was prominent during the close of the first century in the Greek East, and particularly so in selected locales in Asia Minor (i.e., Revelation 2–3). S.R.F. Price has argued that its existence there served largely to consolidate imperial concerns like politics, economics, and social standing.[43] The Romans were maintaining order through the cult.

But at what cost to Christians? Elizabeth Schüssler Fiorenza argues that the cost was high.[44] Citing the presence of the cult in Ephesus, Pergamum, Smyrna, Thyatira, Sardis, and Laodicea, she sees parallels with Revelation 13: "Not only threat to life, imprisonment, and execution but also economic deprivation and destitution are to be suffered by those who refuse to take the mark of the beast, that is, to be identified with its followers."[45]

Others have taken a different view, notably Adela Yarbro Collins and Leonard Thompson.[46] Thompson believes that the conflicts were provincial, not empire-wide, that John's problem was with local, traditional religious practices, not the imperial cult.[47] But, one wonders, why the apparent references to Rome in Revelation 17–18 (particularly "Babylon" in 17:5 and the "seven hills" in 17:9), which we have now identified as leading into the major discourse peak for the entire book? It seems that John's determined emphasis upon worshiping God, coupled with clear references to Rome, would support at least a strong possibility that he is at odds with the imperial cult, not merely the local shrines.

Conclusion

Witness (*marturia*) is used by John of Christians who were compelled by officials of the imperial cult (and perhaps local religions as well) to cooperate with their programs in the interest of maintaining a well-ordered, but radically pagan, society. However, because authentic Christian testimony acknowledges only one Lord, believers like John (exiled because of his testimony), proved threatening both to local religious institutions and, ultimately, Caesar. John's encouragement for Christians to remain faithful witnesses in the midst of first-century religious pluralism is a clear call to worship the Christian God, and the Christian God alone. Even John was at one point tempted to worship someone other than this God. Revelation 19:10b marks a turning point in the book as John indirectly identifies the "testimony of Jesus" as a Holy Spirit-inspired mandate to worship God and God alone.

This message resonates loudly with contemporary believers who dwell in the midst of radical pluralism. Testimony has lost its footing to preference and individualism (and thus, to many "little gods"). C.A.J. Coady has put the problem well:

> In the post-Renaissance Western world the dominance of an individualist ideology has had a lot to do with the feeling that testimony has little or no epistemic importance. It is a commonplace that the political, social, and economic thought and practice of the West have been profoundly influenced in recent centuries by certain ideas and ideals stressing the powers, rights, dignities, and autonomy of the individual person.[48]

Coady concludes that if we "cannot dispense with observational and experimental data in natural science, so we cannot do without testimonial data in history. . . . 'It is a fact of observation' we say confidently, even where we are reporting no observations of our own. If we extend this courtesy to our contemporaries why not to our ancestors?"[49]

John's testimony — Worship God! — is clear. May we extend him the "courtesy," having been so much closer to Jesus in particular space and time, of offering the church an authentic witness for all space and time. The message of Revelation is also clear, echoing the first commandment in the Decalogue ("Have no other gods before me") and the Greatest Commandment ("Love the Lord your God — heart, soul, mind, and strength"). John's witness — Worship God! — is none other than the quest of the entire Judeo-Christian tradition.

THE HYMNS OF REVELATION: THEOLOGICAL REFRAINS IN THE APOCALYPSE

Fred Hansen

Introduction

The title of Dr. Lowery's first book, *Revelation's Rhapsody: Listening to the Lyrics of the Lamb*,[1] reflects the musical nature of Revelation. The book is also an encouragement for the people of God to study Revelation itself rather than rely upon the mostly inaccurate and popular pontifications of radio preachers and televangelists. This chapter seeks to combine the musical nature of Revelation with Dr. Lowery's passion for equipping students by undertaking a brief study of the topic of the hymns of Revelation.[2] It will attempt to define hymns, offer insight into how one might study the poetic nature of hymns, and conclude by addressing the function and theology of these hymns as they relate to John's literary purpose and then to contemporary culture.

Identifying Hymns in Revelation

An unfortunate circumstance for the novice to Revelation's hymns is the lack of an accessible, yet comprehensive, treatise on the definition, process, and necessity of identifying hymns — though a number of smaller, helpful chapters and articles regarding hymns do exist.[3] Revelation's commentators often magnify this problem by ubiquitously asserting that certain of John's passages, such as 4:8 and 4:11, are hymns, but they assume the reader's foreknowledge of hymnic criteria.[4] While space prohibits a thorough recounting of such criteria, which is presumably why so few extensive works on the hymns of the apocalypse exist, the nature of this chapter warrants some preliminary discussion.

It is helpful to begin studying the hymns of Revelation with a definition: hymns are liturgical poems, either embedded in narration and paraenesis, or explicitly delineated in direct discourse, that is, recorded speech.[5] Such poems possibly predate the author or the text, and the author interposes them into a literary context. They may be original compilations by the author in a liturgical context, or the church later adopted them as liturgy, whether the author intended it or not.

One will notice that the above definition underscores the poetic aspect of hymns without regard to any discussion of singing. This is because hymns, at least in their original contexts, are not necessarily songs. Unfortunately, many lexicons add to the confusion surrounding hymns by defining the Greek ὕμνος, hymn, as, "a song of praise,"[6] and, "a festive song in praise of gods or heroes".[7] To be sure, when the NT confirms the use of hymns in a half-dozen segments as a form of early Christian worship, without recording the content of the hymns, it is unfailingly in the context of singing.[8] Yet many poems acknowledged as hymns, including several in the Apocalypse, do not incorporate any nouns or verbs referring to songs or singing, including the word hymn, its cognates, or synonyms.[9] With this in mind, through careful examination of the structure and context of many poems, it is within reason to assert they are likely songs, but their original composition does not necessitate this.

Because many poetic treatises do not use terminology associated with singing or music, scholars must often infer NT hymns using a conglomeration of factors. Such factors include analyzing the grammar, syntax, and discourse markers within a Greek text as well as positing literary dependence upon canonical and noncanonical sources, such as the Psalms or the liturgy from Hebraic and Hellenistic synagogues, not to mention early Christian liturgy. These features do not absolutely reveal a text as hymn. In general, the most that grammatical and syntactical analysis reveals about the original text is that it is poetic. Based on studies of early Christian liturgy, one may speculate, even with a high degree of certainty, that these poems are hymns, but uncertainties remain.

An alternative to labeling these poetic compositions as hymns is to name them as homologies.[10] W. Hulitt Gloer, in his short article on hymns and homologies, defines a homology as a confession used by the early church.[11] Similar to hymns, homologies are poetic in structure, but they are uttered confessions, rather than songs. The difference is often one of function within liturgy rather than structure or composition. Knowing this, it may be helpful to study a passage first as poetry and later delineate if it is a hymn or a homology.[12]

Indeed, all study of poetic genres must begin by analyzing issues related to grammar and syntax—whether reading Revelation in Greek or English, because many English translations attempt to maintain the poetic structures of the Greek text. An initial analysis of Revelation's poems will at least consider the following elements.[13]

Introductory Formula[14]

An advantageous aspect of studying Revelation's poetry, as opposed to a Pauline composition, such as Phil 2:6-11, is that John demarcates his poems with a verb of direct discourse.[15] For instance, Revelation 4:8 reads, ". . . the four living creatures . . . have no rest day or night, saying . . ." The participle λέγοντες, "saying," indicates that what is to follow is direct discourse. The same participle precedes apparent poems in at least twenty-six other references, though many are not hymns.[16] Such a clue alerts the reader to search for poetic elements. One can then distinguish the hymns from other poetic compilations by noting the literary co-text and the liturgical context in which they appear; the speculative hymns of the Apocalypse, as opposed to John's numerous other poetic expositions, tend to be longer, in a worship setting, and spoken by a group, rather than an individual.

Rhythm

Two significant categories that contribute to the rhythm of the poem are syllabification and isocolon.

Syllabification. The number of syllables in a poem, and indeed, in each stanza, contributes to the rhythm and flow of the poem. Syllabification is readily understandable even in English translations. Students should begin by counting the syllables of each word in a suspected poem, looking for rhythmic patterns, such as (line one) nine syllables, (line two) eleven syllables, and (line three) eleven syllables, as appears in Rev 4:11.[17] Similarly, in 7:10, one finds a pattern of ten syllables, ten syllables, and five syllables, respectively, in another three-stanza poem. When counting these syllables, it is vital to observe John's use of dactylic syllabification, where a word contains one long and two short syllables or one stressed (accented) and two unstressed syllables.[18] Of course, syllables in English are likely to differ from those in Greek.

Isocolon. Isocolon is defined as, "A sequence of two or more coordinate clauses that consist of similar constructions and a similar number of words and syllables."[19] In Rev 4:11, one will find rhythm through isocolon in a repeated pattern of threes in the clauses, "Holy, Holy, Holy," as it corresponds to "Lord, God, Almighty," and "the one who was, the one who is, and the one who is to come." While this demonstrates a balance of clauses, one may also use isocolon to refer to the syllabification noted above. Many of these clauses also possess rhyming words or alliterative sounds, both of which aid in memory, a key aspect of early liturgy. Several English translations, even if they do not replicate the exact number of syllables or the same rhyming sounds as the Greek, attempt to maintain words that exhibit memorable syllabification, rhythm, and rhyme, thus preserving isocolon and the original lyrical nature.

Rhyme

Although much is lost in English translation, the Greek words of Revelation's hymns display rhyme. Using similar sounding words or homoioteleuta, words with similar endings, John creates lyrical strophes that embed in the memory of the hearer.[20] In 5:9, the words, αὐτοῦ, σου, λαοῦ, ἔθνους, provide a rhyming ending to the first three lines.[21] This same poem ends with ἱερεῖς, γῆς,[22] in its final two lines.

Grammatical and Syntactical Style

Beyond rhythm and rhyme, one should also note if an author expresses patterns by ending stanzas with nouns, verbs, or pronouns, or if the author employs grammatical and syntactical patterns in general. For instance, the opening stanzas of Paul's potential hymn in Col 1:15 end with the pattern of adjective, noun, adjective, noun. Similar grammatical formulas are in the stanzas of Rev 15:3-4 and 19:1-2, where John utilizes pronouns. In 15:3-4, John employs the use of the second person singular pronoun, σου ("of you" or "your"), placing prominence on a series of nouns referring to or representing God. The NIV captures it well, "Great and marvelous are *your* deeds . . . , just and true are *your* ways . . . , bring glory to *your* name . . . , and worship before *you*."[23] In 19:1-2, John alternates the use of various pronouns and the NIV again depicts John's accentuation, "Salvation, glory, and power belong to *our* God, . . . true and just are *his* judgments, . . . who corrupted the earth by *her* adulteries, he avenged on *her* the blood of *his* servants."

Participles and Infinitives

In the Greek of 4:11, John uses a finite verb describing God, "the one who was," but then transitions to two infinite participles, "the one who is and the one who is to come." The emphasis placed on the participles indicating the concurrent nature of God's existence through all time is central to John's vision of an enthroned God.[24] Such analysis often only comes through the study of the Greek manuscript, but students of English, alerted to a potential hymn by commentators, may find similar forms.[25]

Once an initial study of the grammar and syntax is complete, one then has a framework in which to consult commentaries or other books that demonstrate the existence or use of these poems as hymns in a liturgical setting in early Christianity.

Cotextualizing and Contextualizing Hymns in Revelation

After considering the poetic nature of potential hymns in Revelation, one must ask why the above analysis is necessary. The simple answer is that John wishes to make memorable his incredible message. In studying the lyrical aspects of hymns, it is tempting to lose sight of John's purpose in using poetic genres. His goal is to communicate a theological or christological message using unforgettable means. The reader can ascertain these messages within the immediate co-text and context of the hymn.[26] The co-text of each hymn is the proximate narrative.

John Collins, among others, has adequately demonstrated that apocalyptic literature distills its proposals in a narrative framework, leading to the conclusion that hymns are a form of discourse, or direct speech, within narration.[27] This discourse, or dialogue, "is integral to the pace of the plot as it decelerates action and calls attention to detail pinpointing activity, characterization, or motive as displayed in individual scenes."[28] Robert Alter goes so far as to state, "Narration is often relegated to the role of confirming assertions made in dialogue. . . ."[29] Therefore, by slowing the pace of the plot through discourse, John doubly emphasizes his theological message within the co-text of the hymn. Hymns not only pinpoint narrative assertions as discourse, they isolate these assertions with remarkable poetry. Consequently, students of biblical narrative, particularly John's Apocalypse, would do well to examine the relationship between discourse, hymnic or otherwise, and the action sequences in each micronarrative.[30] Such an examination reveals that hymns are theological refrains within each narrative. That is, they repeat and confirm reoccurring messages in each story and in the macronarrative.[31] Therefore, one can assert that hymns are an interpretive and summative key to John's visions and theology.

For instance, in Rev 15:3-4, those singing the song of Moses are recalling, in hymnic worship, the mighty and righteous deeds of God expressed in the surrounding chapters.[32] John's recording of God as the παντοκράτωρ, the Almighty, and the King of the nations,[33] establishes God as judge and God's judgments as true and just. Although John records God's acts of judgment in the adjacent chapters, the focus of the hymn in 15:3-4 is not necessarily upon the specific acts, but rather on those acts as righteous because of the nature and position of God.[34] God as the Almighty and the King is a common theme in Revelation, particularly chapters 4–5. Therefore, one can rightly distinguish this hymn in 15:3-4 as a refrain of the surrounding events and a refrain of John's overarching portrait of a just, all-powerful, and kingly God.

While this view of Revelation 15:3-4 provides a co-textual analysis and example of John's theological themes as found in hymns, one must consider these same hymns in their historical, social, and cultural contexts as well.[35] The NT period is one of competing religions, worldviews, and ideas where the character and work of God are set apart and set above those of others gods. Greeks, Romans, Jews, and Christians live side by side in this world.

An instance of these disparate worldviews is in Pausanias's *Description of Greece*, where he avows that Zeus is the one who was, who is, and who is to come.[36] John's hymn in Revelation 4:11 demonstrates the church's belief that God alone exists and is worthy of such acclaim. He carefully records those adjectives, participles, and other grammatical forms that express the reality, work, and supremacy of God. Thus, John's co-textual interpolations result from his contextual considerations. By expressing these realities concerning God in memorable and poetic fashion, he seeks to ensure the beauty and perpetuity of his lyrical professions in later contexts as well.

Employing the Hymns in Revelation

Considering the amount of time and energy invested in the exegetical process, one might ask why it is necessary to identify the genre and poetic nature of hymnic material beyond John's literary and theological purposes. Ralph Martin suggests at least three reasons why one needs to isolate a hymn: it provides an introduction to the worshiping life of the apostolic church and reminds modern readers that the church was a worshiping community; poetic language suggests a deep spiritual reality which goes beyond the rational and coherent; their easily memorized and highly theological and christological teachings are a polemic against heresy.[37]

All of these assertions are indispensable for the contemporary church. When reflecting on worship, the contemporary church must consider the practices and content of early

Christian liturgy, especially that of the canon, such as the Apocalypse. Their concern for the propagation and defense of the gospel is no less significant than that of the church today, especially in the case of scripture. Those who devise liturgy for the worshiping community without giving attention to the prior centuries of worship assume a posture of historical arrogance. Early liturgy can and does provide a prototypical model,[38] and Christian liturgists today should include John's hymns and homologies in worship.

Moreover, churches of protestant heritage place substantially more emphasis on the rational exposition of God's word to the detriment of the poetic declaration or recitation of God's word. While such exposition is not unwarranted, it lacks symmetry. Revelation's hymns superbly and succinctly capture the essence of God's nature and work and beautifully preserve such pronouncements for generations. Poetry and music, coupled with rational exposition, elicits a fuller response from the community of God to the work of God in history.

Finally, the hymns of the Apocalypse still provide a theological moor for the contemporary church. A potential example exists in current efforts regarding ecological hermeneutics and the Bible. In a seminal work on the subject, a group known as the Earth Bible Team seems to propose that God does injustice to his creation by inflicting judgment on it through ecological means.[39] The hymn of Rev 15:3-4 indicates that John and his readers comprehend all of God's acts as just and righteous. It is not possible for a just and righteous God to do injustice upon his creation. Those who sing this hymn regard the judgments of God in the correlating visions as virtuous. Thus, Revelation's hymns provide a helpful starting place for this and other issues facing present-day Christians. As refrains of John's theology, they are insightful and timeless summations and declarations for a myriad of contexts today.

The study of Revelation's hymns demonstrates that John uses memorable and meaningful poetic forms to refrain his theological and christological assertions. These beautiful hymns and poems reflect the worship and belief of John's audience and they should reflect the same for the church today.

THE EXTRABIBLICAL LITERATURE IN THE BOOK OF REVELATION

Paul J. Kissling

Introduction

The topic which I was asked to address in this essay is as complex as the book of Revelation — so first, some definitions. I mean by "literature" specifically Jewish literature. "Extrabiblical" means literature not in the Protestant canon, although it may be in the Roman Catholic or Orthodox Church canons. Due to the constraints of the chapter, I have decided to use two representative pieces of literature, one from the Apocrypha (4 Ezra) and one from the so-called Pseudepigrapha[1] (2 Baruch), and show how their commonalities with the book of Revelation in terms of genre, general ethos, and vocabulary and theological themes help to illuminate the book of Revelation. While both of these books were written at about the same time as the book of Revelation,[2] I do not know if the author of Revelation had read or had heard read either of these documents. He certainly does not quote them as such. Nevertheless, both of them are of Jewish origin[3] and were read and valued by at least one of the traditional churches.[4]

Genre: Definitions and Analysis

The book of Revelation is a combination of three genres of literature: epistle, prophecy and apocalyptic.[5] The first two of these genres are quite familiar to Bible readers because of their frequency in the rest of the Bible. Apocalyptic, however, is found in the Bible only in the book of Revelation, in parts of

Daniel,[6] and, at most, in a few other scattered passages in the OT. But there are numerous books and portions of books which have come down to us from 200 B.C. until the middle ages which share the apocalyptic genre of the book of Revelation.

In popular usage, the terms apocalyptic and Apocalypse are sometimes defined rather imprecisely and this leads to a significant amount of confusion among ordinary Bible readers and even, at times, among scholars. The most widely cited scholarly definition of the genre is by J.J. Collins: "Apocalypse is a genre of revelatory literature with a narrative framework, in which a revelation is mediated by an otherworldly being to a human recipient, disclosing a transcendent reality which is both temporal, insofar as it envisages eschatological salvation, and spatial, insofar as it involves another, supernatural world."[7] Both of our representative pieces of literature as well as the book of Revelation fit this definition.

This definition can be "unpacked" as follows. The recipient of the revelation is guided by an angel or similar figure. Often this involves an otherworldly journey. This is recounted in the apocalypse as a story of the experience. Since this otherworldly reality is not limited by the world of time and space, the point of the revelation is to see that other world and the future salvation which is involved in bringing it into being.

How does this definition fit the book of Revelation?

While the book of Revelation is a mixture of genres and begins as a circular epistle to the seven churches of Asia Minor (1:4; 2:1–3:22), the narrative of John's[8] heavenly journey begins in 4:1 where he is invited to come up to heaven through an open door and see a vision of the future. The figure who invites him up to heaven and will guide him on his journey is the heavenly Christ (4:1 and 1:10-18). John records for his readers his experience of this visit to heaven. He begins by describing his vision of God (ch. 4) and continues by describing his feeling when initially no one was found worthy to open the scroll with its seven seals (5:1-5). As each seal is opened John describes what he saw. The seventh seal leads to the narrative of the blowing of the seven trumpets the seventh of which leads to the seven bowls. With each level, the reader is taken closer and closer to the end. Ultimately, John sees the new heavens and the new earth (21:1) and the descent of the heavenly Jerusalem onto that earth (21:2; 9-22:6).

How does this definition fit 4 Ezra and 2 Baruch?

Both 4 Ezra and 2 Baruch are (non-Messianic) Jewish apocalypses written in response to the destruction of Jerusalem by the Romans in 70 A.D. Both were written sometime between that date and 100 A.D. or so.[9] As such they form alternative Jewish responses to those events with 4 Ezra and 2 Baruch offering non-Messianic Jewish approaches and the book of Revelation a messianic Jewish approach.[10] In both 4 Ezra and 2 Baruch a divine figure[11] talks during a heavenly journey with a scribal figure purportedly in grief over the destruction of Jerusalem in 587 B.C. In reality, it is the destruction of the second temple in 70 A.D. that is in view. Both scribal figures dispute with the divine figure about the justice of God toward his people in allowing them to be overrun by a powerful pagan empire. In both the divine figure appeals to an eschatological solution which is revealed in symbolic dreams which are interpreted for the scribe by the divine figure. In both, the scribal figure becomes a sort of second Moses who provides hope for the people and commends the attention of the Jewish people to the written scriptures.[12]

General ethos: Apocalyptic Settings

Apocalyptic literature is usually written by and to people from minority (often Jewish) communities who feel threatened by the outside world with its seemingly all-powerful empires. It is literature designed to give comfort and encouragement to its readership so that they may face their current challenges with the assurance that the present and the future is in God's hands and that the future will make their current difficulties worth it all. In a sense, Apocalyptic is literature which uses a different style or genre to perform the same social/religious function which Psalms of lament did and do in another way. Psalms of lament cry out to God about the problems of the individual or community and thus leave the matter in God's hands.

Apocalyptic leaves the matter in God's hands by reassuring its audience that God is in control, even in the midst of pressure and persecution, and that ultimately history will end with God's people being vindicated and the wicked being judged.

In such situations there is clarity about good and evil and who belongs on which side. The books of Revelation, 4 Ezra, and 2 Baruch all give reassurance to people of Jewish background, whether Messianic or not, concerning the pressure which the Roman empire is putting on God's people. In the case of 4 Ezra and 2 Baruch, the Romans have destroyed the temple in Jerusalem and forced the Jewish people to divert the annual half shekel tax which had gone to the temple to go towards the construction of a temple to Jupiter in Rome.[13] The book of Revelation gives comfort to the Christians of Asia Minor who are being actively persecuted by the Roman emperor, probably Domitian.[14]

Vocabulary and Theological Themes: Parallel Imagery

While there is no concrete evidence of direct borrowing by the book of Revelation from 4 Ezra or 2 Baruch or vice versa, the three works do share many features of vocabulary and theological themes in common. In the case of the latter two works this may well be because of some direct or indirect dependence between them. While the presence of common vocabulary and key theological themes could be illustrated with dozens of examples,[15] I have chosen six illustrations.

(1) Silence in Heaven

In Rev 8:1 we read "When the Lamb opened the seventh seal, there was silence in heaven for about half an hour." Beale sees a parallel with 4Ezra 7:30,31 and 2Bar 3:7 where the silence "refers to the divine judgment preceding the new creation."[16] Citing the same parallel passages, he later notes, "There will be a 'primeval silence' at the end of history when all earth's inhabitants die, immediately before the final judgment (4Ezra 7:30 cf. 4Ezra 6:39; 2Bar 3:7)."[17]

This silence immediately prior to the new creation makes a correspondence with the first creation according to both of these passages where an original silence preceded the original creation. In 2Bar 3:7 we read, "Or will the universe return to its nature and the world go back to its original silence?" Fourth Ezra 6:39 states of the first creation, "then the spirit was blowing, and darkness and silence embraced everything; the sound of human voices was not there." Even more interesting is 4Ezra 7:30-31, "After those years my son the Messiah shall die, and all who draw human breath. Then the world shall be turned back to primeval silence for seven days, as it was at the first beginnings, so that no one shall be left. After seven days the world that is not yet awake shall be roused, and that which is corruptible shall perish." Loren Stuckenbruck comments on the wider context in 4Ezra 7:26-44, "The hiatus between the old age and judgment is underscored by a space of time, seven days of primeval silence, which signals the correspondence between Urzeit and Endzeit shared by many apocalyptic writers."[18]

In the ancient world of the book of Revelation and 4 Ezra and 2 Baruch the silence at creation and new creation is not merely the physical fact of the lack of noise as contemporary readers might assume. It is a sort of "pregnant pause" before God's action in creation or new creation begins in earnest and marks the turn of an epoch.

(2) Heads of Beasts Representing Kings of the Empire

In Rev 12:3 a great red dragon with seven heads and ten horns appears. In 13:1 the beast from the sea has ten horns and seven heads. In 17:3 a woman sits on a scarlet beast with seven heads and ten horns. Most serious scholarly commentators assume that these beasts signify the Roman empire in some form. More controversial is the attempt to link the numbers seven and ten to specific Roman emperors. One piece of evidence that this approach is a problem is the fact that commentators seem unable to come to a consensus on precisely what kings are being counted.[19] But whether John has specific kings in mind or not, the book of Revelation is not the only piece of Jewish literature from the end of the first century A.D. which depicts the Roman empire as an unnatural beast with unnatural numbers of appendages.

71

Fourth Ezra 11–12 speaks of an eagle with 12 wings and 3 heads which by common consent represents the Roman empire. Many also agree with Collins that it is "probable that the three heads represent the Flavians—Vespasian, Titus, and Domitian."[20] Both of these passages as well as 2 Baruch 35–39 are modeled on the four kingdom schema in Daniel 7. All three refer to the Roman empire as an enemy beyond even the empires of Babylon, Persia, and Greece.

(3) Rome as Babylon

By common consent among commentators the Babylon referred to in Rev 14:8; 16:19; 17:5; 18:2,10, and 21 is the Roman empire which destroyed the temple in Jerusalem in 70 A.D. and was persecuting both non-Messianic and Messianic Jews ("Christians") in the later decades of the first century. Beasley-Murray helpfully notes:

> The most probable reason for giving the name Babylon to Rome was that as Nebuchadnezzar, king of Babylon, had destroyed Jerusalem in 586 B.C. so Rome had done in recent times. The dirge over Babylon in Revelation 18 views the current tyrant city as another Babylon. The apocalypses 4 Ezra and 2 Baruch were written at the end of the first century of the Christian era and also gave the name of Babylon to Rome for the same reason.[21]

According to Beale, Rome is only referred to as Babylon after 70 A.D. in 4Ezra 3:1-2; 28–31 and 2Bar 10:1-3; 11:1; 67:7 and in the book of Revelation. This is one of his arguments for dating the book of Revelation at the end of the first century rather than prior to 70 A.D.[22]

(4) Seven-Section Structure and Recapitulation

As Nicklesburg[23] notes concerning 4 Ezra, "[T]he book divides cleanly into seven sections, each centering on a revelation." Metzger notes that the first six of the seven sections conclude with a description of the end.[24] The first vision (3:1–5:20) ends with a description of the final woes of judgment (5:1-13); the second vision (5:21–6:34) ends with signs of the end (6:11-28); the third vision (6:35–9:25) recapitulates the signs of the end (8:63–9:25); the fourth vision (9:26–10:59) ends with the woman being transformed into the heavenly Zion (10:25-59); the fifth vision (11:1–12:39) ends with the Messiah judging the fourth kingdom and redeeming his people (12:10-34); the sixth vision (13:1-58) is interpreted as the Son of God judging the nations and regathering the nation (13:25-50). The seventh vision (14:1-48) relates how Ezra dictates the 94 books, 24 of them the published books of the Hebrew Scriptures and 70 secret books to be kept for the wise alone.

This seven section structure also occurs in 2 Baruch, although there is no unanimity about the exact beginning and ending of some sections and whether 2 Baruch 78–87 are original or secondary.[25] In the book of Revelation, Robert Lowery helpfully discusses how each of the seven main sections of the book of Revelation point to the end where the wicked will be punished and God's people will be vindicated — a technique he describes as repetition and recapitulation.[26] In all three documents, the reader is repeatedly brought back to the end when God will judge the wicked oppressors and vindicate the faithful among his people. This parallel warns the reader of Revelation against the temptation to attempt to read it chronologically.

(5) The Righteous Dead and the Record of their Deeds

Beale notes, "The idea that deceased saints 'take with them the record of their deeds' into the afterlife in heaven finds analogy in Jewish and Christian writings."[27] He is referring to Rev 14:13, "And I heard the voice from heaven saying, 'Write, Blessed are the dead who die in the Lord from henceforth: yea, saith the Spirit, that they may rest from their labors; for their works follow with them.'" Second Baruch twice uses the word "treasuries" to refer to the place where the good deeds or righteousness of the faithful are stored until the end (14:12; 24:1). Fourth Ezra 8:33 refers to the "many works laid up with" God for which they "shall receive their reward in consequence of their own deeds."

(6) New Jerusalem Comes Down to Earth

In 2 Baruch 3, Baruch complains about the pending destruction of the temple in Jerusalem which he terms his mother. He is concerned that if the temple is destroyed Israel will be forgotten by the world. The Lord's response shows that the real temple is not being destroyed, only the copy that sits in Jerusalem. The real temple will one day be revealed again. In 4:2-7 Adam was shown the New Jerusalem before the fall and then both Paradise and the New Jerusalem were taken away from him.

> Or do you think that this city of which I said: "On the palms of my hands I have carved you?" It is not this building that is in your midst now; it is that which will be revealed, with me, that was already prepared from the moment that I decided to create Paradise. And I showed it to Adam before he sinned. But when he transgressed the commandment, it was taken away from him—as also Paradise. After these things I showed it to my servant Abraham in the night between the portions of the victims. And again I showed it also to Moses on Mount Sinai when I showed him the likeness of the tabernacle and all its vessels. Behold, now it is preserved with me—as also Paradise. Now go away and do as I command you.

Baruch takes a spiritual journey to see unseen things (6:3), in this case the hiding of the temple vessels in the earth by angels before the Babylonians can get them (6:7) with the promise of a future restoration of the temple. The angel says,

> Earth, earth, earth, hear the word of the mighty God, and receive the things which I commit to you, and guard them until the last times, so that you may restore them when you are ordered, so that strangers may not get possession of them,. For the time has arrived when Jerusalem will also be delivered up for a time, until the moment that it will be said that it will be restored forever. (6:8-9)

Beginning in 4Ezra 9:38 Ezra encounters a woman weeping and in mourning who has been barren for thirty years and then saw the child she was given die on his wedding night. Ezra rebukes her for mourning over the loss of a single child when

Zion has been destroyed (10:6-8). While Ezra is talking with the woman she is suddenly transformed into the glorious Zion come to earth:

> While I was talking to her, behold, her face suddenly shone exceedingly, and her countenance flashed like lightning, so that I was too frightened to approach her, and my heart was terrified. While I was wondering what this meant, behold, she suddenly uttered a loud and fearful cry, so that the earth shook at the sound. And I looked, and behold, the woman was no longer visible to me, there was an established city, and a place of huge foundations showed itself. (10:25-27)

Both 4 Ezra and 2 Baruch encourage their audiences by reassuring them that the tragic destruction of the temple by the Romans in 70 A.D. is not the end of the story. What matters is the heavenly Jerusalem which will one day be established on earth. Whatever the relationship between these two documents they share this common feature.[28]

With these may be compared John's record of seeing the heavenly Jerusalem descend to earth:

> And I saw the holy city, new Jerusalem, coming down out of heaven from God, prepared as a bride adorned for her husband. And I heard a loud voice from the throne saying, "Behold, the dwelling place of God is with man. He will dwell with them and they will be his people, and God himself will be with them as their God." (Rev 21:2-3 ESV)

In all three cases we see the vision of the heavenly Jerusalem come down to earth as a means of reassurance to the audience. But the relationship between the audience and the destruction of the temple in Jerusalem is very different in the book of Revelation and in 4 Ezra and 2 Baruch. For the latter two works the events of 70 A.D. called into question Israel's continuing relationship with her God. The answer is to turn to the scriptures and to look for a future restoration of the heavenly temple. For the audience of the book of Revelation, the destruction of the literal temple was something that Jesus the Messiah had anticipated and was a tragic demonstration of the futility of using violence to attempt to bring in the kingdom. Instead, the temple is the eschatological new creation.[29]

Implications for Reading the Book of Revelation

We have seen that in terms of genre, general ethos, and especially vocabulary and theological themes, the book of Revelation shares many features in common with two contemporary non-Messianic Jewish works: 4 Ezra and 2 Baruch. If we had had the space, the instructive examples of Jewish extrabiblical parallel literature could have been multiplied many times over. It is safe to assume that the original audiences of these works understood what type of literature they were reading. Contemporary readers, however, only understand that type of literature through careful historical study. The contents, genre, and themes of the book of Revelation would have been quite familiar to a late first-century audience steeped in Israel's scriptures and conversant with the extrabiblical literature. For us in the twenty-first century, it is like entering a new world. We must be careful not to make the mistake of thinking that John was writing directly to us.

Two lessons might be drawn from our investigation. First of all, books like 4 Ezra, 2 Baruch and the book of Revelation should be interpreted whenever possible in light of the specific historical circumstances in which they were written. Knowing that 4 Ezra and 2 Baruch are documents written to encourage the Jewish people after the disaster of 70 A.D. and to point to a different future is the only way to make sense of them. The same is true of the book of Revelation. Second, we must be careful not to overliteralize books like these by misreading the genre. Apocalyptic is not intended to be read chronologically. Nor should we look for contemporary literal fulfillments among our political enemies or the circumstances of our specific history. The scorpions which shoot out of their tails are not ancient anticipations of helicopter gunships.

What deSilva has written specifically of 4 Ezra applies also to 2 Baruch and in a less direct fashion to the numerous pre-Christian apocalyptic works extant among the Jewish people prior to the writing of the book of Revelation:

The author writes in response to the destruction of Jerusalem in A.D. 70, and even more directly in response to God's slowness in punishing Rome, the instrument of destruction. In its negation of hope for this age, its hope for reward in the age to come, its visions of the many-headed eagle and the man from the sea, this text *provides an important window into Jewish apocalypticism that offers instructive parallels for NT apocalyptic material.*[30]

THE INTERPRETATION OF REVELATION IN THE CHURCH FATHERS OF THE II–VI CENTURIES[1]

Yulia Lubenets

I n his work *The Apocalypse of St. John* Swete notes that this book has challenged the intelligence of Christian students from the first and invited them to "unravel the meaning" if they can (Rev 13:18; 17:9). The desire to answer the challenge gave start to various schools of interpretation of Revelation from the time of its writing onward.[2] The purpose of this work is to present the ways the Church Fathers of the II–VI centuries understood this book so one can see the roots of different methods which exist until this day. The article starts with a short exposition of the spread and acceptance of the Apocalypse by the early Christians as this information helps comprehend the history of the interpretation of the book. It continues to present the development of the views of the Church Fathers on Revelation within the indicated period.

The Acceptance of the Apocalypse

In his work on Revelation, Mounce asserts that "perhaps more than any other NT book, the Apocalypse enjoyed wide distribution and early recognition."[3] He goes on to explain that since its message deals with the time of persecution which the universal church was about to experience, it probably quickly spread throughout the whole Roman Empire soon after it had been written.

However, it was in the West rather than in the East that the book was accepted and used widely. Weinrich notes that "Revelation was early and steadfastly recognized and used by Western Christian writers."[4] According to him, Tertullian (c.

220), Hippolytus (c. 230), and Cyprian (d. 258) made significant use of it.[5] Weinrich also points out that in Rome the *Shepherd of Hermas* employed Revelation but the point appears to remain debatable. Mounce suggests that both books could have drawn from a common apocalyptic tradition.[6] In any case, it appears that of the Western Church Fathers only Jerome expressed certain doubts about Revelation.[7] The Third Council of Carthage (397) regarded it as a canonical book.[8]

The acceptance of Revelation in the East was not uniform and met with sustained opposition.[9] Dionysius of Alexandria, although considering it inspired, doubted that its author was the Apostle John. Cyril of Jerusalem (315–386), John Chrysostom (347–407), and Theodoret (386–457) questioned the Apocalypse as well. It was not found among the canonical books at the Council of Laodicea (ca. 360), and it was excluded from the official Bible of the Syriac-speaking Christians in the fifth-century.[10] Mounce explains this by the rise of Montanism which looked to Revelation for the support of its apocalyptic extremism. Ian Boxall points out that the Syriac and Armenian Christians were ignorant of the existence of the book for a long time and that may account for its omission in the Syriac New Testament for several centuries.[11]

Over time the East seemed to change its attitude towards Revelation. In the fourth century, Athanasius of Alexandria included it in the list of the canonical books (367). When the decrees of Laodicea and Carthage were confirmed by the Third Council of Constantinople (680), the Apocalypse was accepted as a canonical book.[12] Whatever the reason for the late acceptance of Revelation in the East, it accounts for the fact that the first commentaries and interpretation of the book in that part of the Christian world appeared much later than in the West.

The Interpretation of the Apocalypse in the West

The earliest attempts to interpret Revelation go back to the second century. Both Irenaeus and Justin the Martyr interpreted the Apocalypse, although it is unclear whether they merely commented on certain passages or wrote whole works on the book.[13] Jerome states that Melito, bishop of Sardis (d. 190), wrote *On the Apocalypse of John*,[14] which could have been a commentary on Revelation. Unfortunately the work has been lost. Jerome also notes that Hippolytus wrote commentaries on various books of Scripture, one of them called *On the Apocalypse*.[15]

Although it is unclear whether a full-scale commentary on Revelation was written in the second century, Swete states that the early Church Fathers seem to have been very interested in the themes found in the book, especially in those connected with the coming of Antichrist and the expectation of the Millennium.[16] The latter was perceived as a literal thousand-year kingdom on earth before the Last Judgment.[17] Court states that these early interpreters of Revelation can be seen as adherents to "Millenarian" views because they put a great emphasis on the literal concept of the Millennium. He further notes that this literalism which characterizes the interpretation by the early Church Fathers of Rev 20:1-6 (the textual basis for the Millenarian interpreters) is "the dominant attitude in the reading of the book as a whole."[18]

The interest in the Millennium and the way it was understood can be explained by the fact that the early Church Fathers lived during the age of persecution and experienced its ferociousness.[19] Justin (c. 100–c. 165) died as a martyr and Hippolytus (c. 170–c. 230) was sent to work in the mines. Although Irenaeus (c. 130–c. 200) was not killed, his mentor, Polycarp, was burned at the stake and his predecessor as a bishop of Lyons, Photinus, died as a result of persecution.[20]

Therefore, living during turbulent times of persecution can account for the above-mentioned scholars holding the Millenarian views also shared by Tertullian (160–c. 225). These authors believed that after the second coming of Christ His deceased followers would rise from the dead and live in the renewed earth together with the Christians who were alive. They would enjoy the material blessings during the thousand years under the reign of the Lord. Thus both Irenaeus and Lactantius gave graphic descriptions of the life in the earthly paradise in terms of OT prophets.[21] Undoubtedly this expectation of life in the Millennial kingdom seemed especially attractive during a period of uncertainty and persecution. During the harsh times Revelation "brought them a promise of deliverance and of ultimate security."[22]

Wainwright notes that living during the age of persecution is reflected in the way the Millenarian interpreters of Revelation viewed evil. They tended to see the Roman Empire as the embodiment of the dark powers described in the book.[23] Thus Irenaeus entertained the idea that the number of the beast, 666, can be read as *Lateinos*, indicating the rule of Latins, that is, Romans.[24] Tertullian saw the harlot (Rev 17) as "a figure of the city of Rome."[25] According to Wainwright, Hippolytus identified Rome with the beast from the sea and claimed that Antichrist, symbolized by the beast from the land, would revive the Roman Empire.[26]

Although Millenarian interpretation of Revelation was the most popular one until the fourth century, it was not the only one which existed at the time.[27] Unlike the early Millenarian interpreters, the representatives of the Alexandrian school which believed in the threefold sense of Scripture (literal, figurative, and spiritual) and put a special emphasis on the spiritual meaning tended to interpret Revelation allegorically. Thus Clement of Alexandria (c. 150–215) understood the gates of New Jerusalem which are "made like precious stones" as "the transcendent grace of the apostolic voice" and their brightness as "the inimitable brilliancy of the spirit, the immortality and sanctity of being."[28]

There is some evidence suggesting that another famous Alexandrian, Origen (c.185–254), planned to write a commentary on Revelation, although it remains unknown whether he realized his intent.[29] However, his interpretation of some passages from the book can be found in his works, for example, in the *Commentary on John*. Although it is impossible to obtain detailed information about the views of this Church Father on Revelation as a whole, it can be assumed that Origen adhered to the spiritual interpretation as was the case in his other commentaries and as the tradition of his school would suggest. Thus he interpreted the sealed scroll (Rev 5) as Scripture to which only Christ has the "key of David." According to him, the writing in front of the scroll stands for the "obvious" sense while the one on the back the "remoter and spiritual sense."[30] It is known that Origen criticized those who understood the Scriptures "in a sort of Jewish sense," that is, literally, "drawing from them nothing worthy of the divine promises."[31]

Methodius (d. 311) followed in the footsteps of the representatives of the Alexandrian school favoring the spiritual interpretation of Revelation. Thus interpreting the Woman (Rev 12), he saw the sun in which she is enclosed as "the brightness of the Word" and the moon on which she stands as "the faith of those who are cleansed from corruption in the laver of regeneration."[32] The child the Woman bears represents "baptized believers."[33]

Although the interpretation of individual passages of Revelation can be found in the works of various Church Fathers, the first extensive Western commentary on the book which has survived is by Victorinus (d. c. 304), bishop of Pettau (modern Ptuj in Slovenia). Unfortunately there is not much known about him. Jerome describes Victorinus as "deficient in learning" but not lacking in "the wish to use what learning he has."[34] The statements of Jerome also suggest that the bishop died as a martyr.[35] The approximate date of his death (304) leads one to believe that it happened during the Diocletianic persecution (303–311).

According to Jerome, Victorinus wrote many commentaries.[36] However, only the one on Revelation exists today. According to Weinrich, Victorinus relied on Irenaeus and Hippolytus and interpreted the book "in broadly millennialist terms."[37] Thus he offered a literal interpretation of the first resurrection when the righteous would rise from the dead and rule with Christ for a thousand years, after which the second resurrection would take place and all would be judged.[38]

However, the images of his Millenarian vision are not as vivid as those of his predecessors, although like them he used OT passages (e.g., Isa 60, 61) to demonstrate the fulfillment of apocalyptic promises.[39] Moreover, Daley states that Victorinus interpreted "the Apocalypse's vision in a modestly allegorical way that betrays the influence of Origen."[40] His explanation of some details of the New Jerusalem can serve as an example.

The precious stones represent "the holy men who cannot waver in persecution," the streets of the city — the holy men's "hearts purified of all uncleanness, transparent with glowing light," and the gates made of pearls — "the four virtues."[41] Daley seems right to summarize Victorinus's interpretation of Revelation as one that "reveals above all the mutually tempering influence of Asiatic concreteness and Alexandrian spiritual exegesis."[42]

An important contribution of Victorinus in the interpretation of Revelation is the use of the recapitulation theory which suggests that "visions of the book do not depict a sequential series of future occurrences but rather depict the same realities that repeatedly occur throughout salvation history and are rendered through differing images and symbols."[43] Although Victorinus did not actually formulate the principle of recapitulation, he implied it in his work.[44] When writing about the events following the sound of the trumpets (Rev 8), he stated, that "although the same thing recurs in the phials, still it is not said as if it occurred twice, but because what is decreed by the Lord to happen shall be once and for all; for this cause it is said twice."[45] According to Wainwright, "This idea was to dominate interpretation for many centuries and was prominent in the work of Tyconius and Augustine."[46]

Tyconius (c. 330–390) lived during the reign of Theodosius and his sons when Christianity became the State Religion. Gennadius states that he was of African origin, "sufficiently learned in sacred literature, not wholly unacquainted with secular literature and zealous in ecclesiastical affairs."[47] The same source informs that Tyconius wrote a commentary on Revelation. Unfortunately, the work has been lost, but scholars consider it possible to recreate at least some of his interpretation of the book.

Tyconius lived at the time when the Millenarianism was losing its appeal. Wainwright points out that during the reign of Constantine (324–337) the Roman Empire was nominally converted to Christianity and many Christians became less inclined to associate Rome with the powers of evil. Also the adherents of the Millenarian views believed that Christ would return after the end of the period of persecution, and their expectation did not harmonize with the course of events.[48] According to Wainwright, "the time was . . . ripe for new interpretations of the Apocalypse."[49] One of them was suggested by Tyconius.

According to Gennadius, Tyconius commented on Revelation "regarding nothing in it in a carnal sense, but all in a spiritual sense."[50] For example, when he interpreted the passage about the angel casting down to earth the censer filled with the fire from the altar (Rev 8:5), he wrote: "The Lord received His body, that is, the church, and filled her with fire from the altar to accomplish the Father's will. That is to say that he filled [the church] with the power of loosing and binding, which consists in sacrifices and the propitiation of God. . . . And he cast it upon the earth, for through the preaching of the church knowledge of the future judgment comes to the world." Tyconius proceeds to explain the following thunder as the proclamation of faith, the lightning as the virtues of the believers, and the earthquakes as persecutions.[51]

Unlike the scholars before him, Tyconius rejected the Millennium as a future reality viewing it as a period of time between the first and second coming of Christ.[52] Gennadius also states that Tyconius rejected the idea of two physical resurrections of the dead but believed that there will be a simultaneous one for everybody in the end. However, he did make the distinction between the two resurrections, suggesting that the first one took place at baptism, and the other one in the end of time.[53]

Although Tyconius' commentary on Revelation has been lost, his other work remains. It testifies that he developed "eight Rules for investigating and ascertaining the meaning of the Scriptures"[54] which, some scholars believe, he used in his interpretation of the book. One of them was the principle of recapitulation which had been previously employed by Victorinus. According to another one, Tyconius "would pass insensibly from a name which suggested a particular object to the universal fact which it symbolized; e.g. from Jerusalem to the Church, or from Babylon to the hostile world."[55] Thus instead of elucidating on the subject of Rome and persecuting emperors, Tyconius draws the attention to the ongoing battle between the powers of good and evil.[56]

Wainwright states that, according to the modern reconstruction of Tyconius's interpretation of Revelation, the latter accentuated this contrast between the city of God and the city of the devil, both of which existed at the same time, that is, the faithful in the church and the worldly power, found both outside and inside the church but always hostile to God: "There are two parts in the world, that which belongs to God and that of the devil. That which belongs to the devil is further divided into three parts, which are both within and outside [the church]. These are Gentiles, false brothers and those separated by open error of schism."[57] Bainton notes that Tyconius regarded the whole history "as a poised conflict between the *civitas diabolic* and the *civitas Dei*."[58] Wainwright asserts that if Tyconius really wrote about it, his teaching on the two cities preceded that of Augustine. However, this also remains an assumption.[59]

Gennadius points out that Tyconius was "recognized to have been a Donatist" on the basis of his other works in which he cited the ancient councils.[60] Donatists rejected the authority of the church leaders who showed spiritual weakness during the persecution under the emperor Diocletian. Because their unwillingness to compromise led to conflict and schism in the Church, the Donatists were at times persecuted by the authorities.[61] The fact that Tyconius was recognized to be a Donatist may account for the fact that, while later scholars were obviously influenced by his ideas, they rarely ventured to express their support of them. Thus, although he introduced a new theory about Revelation, "it was Augustine's revision of his theory that had the more lasting effect."[62]

Although Augustine (354–430) refuted the beliefs of Donatists,[63] he seems to have been impacted by Tyconius's view on the Apocalypse. According to Koester, Augustine found that his interpretation "provided a way to read Revelation that could be applied to the interior life of Christians in all times and places."[64] Tyconius's influence on the famous theologian can be seen in the comments of the latter on Rev 20:1-6 found in the *City of God*.[65] This book presents a contrast between the two cities, one of God and the other of the devil.[66] According to Augustine, the human race was divided in two parts, "the one consisting of those who live according to man, the other of those who live according to God. And these we also mystically call the two cities. . . of which the one is predestined to reign eternally with God, and the other to suffer eternal punishment with the devil."[67]

Augustine believed that the Millennium did not mean a literal thousand years but stood for either the remaining part of the sixth Millennium of the world's history or the rest of this age, the fullness of time.[68] Charles notes that this view on the Millennium as an era in the Church's history was widely accepted for the next several centuries.[69] The general transition in the West from Millenarian beliefs to the ones popularized by Tyconius and Augustine may be seen, at least in some way, as the impact of the transition from the age of persecution to the age of recognition and elevation of the Universal Church in the nominally converted Roman Empire. Now that the Church was not a persecuted minority but a respected community, the expectations of the thousand years of material bliss which characterized the views of the Church Fathers in the 2nd and 3rd centuries apparently lost their appeal.

Scholars agree that overall Augustine's interpretation of Revelation can be called spiritualized, allegorical, or mystical, which also can be seen as the influence of Tyconius.[70] Thus the North African theologian sees the abyss into which the devil is confined as the hearts of the sinful people who defy God.[71] According to Augustine, the beast (Rev 20:9) represents the unfaithful people, and his image is the evil (hypocrisy) in those who call themselves Christians yet fail to live according to the teaching of the Son of God.[72] According to Koester, the spiritualized interpretation became the main viewpoint for the next several centuries.[73]

However, Wainwright, while defining Augustine's interpretation as spiritual, points out that the latter's "understanding of prophecy is partly literal," since he obviously believed in a literal second coming of Christ, a physical resurrection at the end of time, and a literal final judgment.[74] He also notes that

Augustine seems to have avoided the claim that the second coming of Christ was at hand. It is especially significant considering that the theologian lived at the time when the Roman Empire was falling apart and "the course of events invited the conclusion that the last days have arrived."[75] Wainwright suggests that Augustine's cautious attitude about setting a date for the Second coming impacted later interpreters of Revelation.[76]

Another Church Father influenced by the ideas of Tyconius was Jerome (d. 420) who revised the commentary of Victorinus, correcting his Millenarian views and adding his own comments which reflected his interest in monastic ideals and his fight with heretics.[77] Overall it appears that Jerome adhered to the spiritual interpretation of Revelation. For example, he sees the golden band worn by Christ walking in the middle of the seven lampstands (Rev 1:13) as "the gospel and the fortitude of the monks" which binds "mind and heart" and contrasts it with the leather girdle of John the Baptist, that is, the law.[78] Wainwright points out that Jerome rejected the Millenarianism in several of his writings. Like Augustine, he believed that the period of time was already there.[79]

However, R.H. Charles, while acknowledging that Jerome adhered to the "spiritualizing method of interpretation" of Revelation, states that the latter "stands at the point of transition between the Realistic and Spiritualizing Methods."[80] For example, although Jerome interprets one thousand years allegorically, he takes the passage about 144,000 virgins of the Israel's tribes literally (Rev 14:4).[81]

Through the works of Augustine and Jerome, the traditions of Tyconius's and Victorinus's way of thinking influenced later Western interpreters of Revelation. Among them are Caesarius of Arles (d. 543), Primasius (d. after 553), and Apringius.[82] According to Swete, these and "most of the writers on the Apocalypse who followed them in the earlier centuries of the Middle Ages, were content with a mystical exegesis which varied in its details according to the fancy of the individual expositor or the needs or ideas of his time."[83]

Revelation in the Eastern Church

Since the canonical status of Revelation was questioned in the East for a long time, the known Eastern full commentaries on the Apocalypse were written later than the Western ones. Daley points out that the apocalyptic literature was "largely neglected in the Greek Christian world since the mid-third century and was revived only several hundreds years later due to the new wave of expectation of the oncoming end of the world."[84]

The first full Greek commentary on the book was composed by Oecumenius in the sixth century. He was probably a layman of high rank who had received a good education. Various manuscripts refer to Oecumenius as "philosophus" and "rhetor."[85] Weinrich notes that his commentaries are characterized by "broad reading, knowledge of contemporary events, and the mild allegory of the Alexandrian exegetical tradition."[86]

These commentaries also show a certain degree of originality since Oecumenius demonstrates no familiarity with any earlier works on Revelation, although his writings contain references to the earlier Greek Fathers.[87] Wainwright suggests that this can be explained by parochialism, an unwillingness to acknowledge indebtedness to the West, or dependence on some other unknown source.[88] Whatever the reason, unlike Western interpreters of Revelation Oecumenius understands the thousand years as Jesus Christ's life on earth. During that time the devil was bound since "it was necessary that the sojourn of our Lord on the earth have a somewhat greater support and protection, to prohibit the unclean demons from attacking it in the same way as they did against humankind before the time of the incarnation."[89]

Yet it was the work of another Greek scholar, Andreas of Caesarea, which became the standard commentary on Revelation for the Eastern Church, both Greek and Russian.[90] Andreas lived in the sixth century and for some time was a bishop of Caesarea.[91] Since he mentions the attacks of Huns, it is believed that he wrote his commentary on the Apocalypse about 515.[92] Andreas was evidently familiar with the writings of the earlier Church Fathers since he quoted many of them in his work, including Papias, Irenaeus, Cyril of Alexandria, and others. Weinrich notes that it is also obvious Andreas knew the commentary by Oecumenius. He often summarizes the views of the latter but offers a different interpretation.[93]

Andreas agrees with the Alexandrians that one should look for the threefold sense of the Scriptures, and that the spiritual one is the most important of the three. Thus it is not surprising that interpreting Revelation he "finds the main worth of the book in its spiritual meaning."[94] However, the scholars note that while adhering to allegorical exegesis, Andreas does not depart completely from the school of Irenaeus and Hippolytus.[95] Therefore, according to Swete, "the greatest of the Greek commentaries on the Apocalypse is a syncretism, blending the methods of Irenaeus, Origen, and Tyconius, while at the same time the writer feels his way towards the later system of interpretation which discovers in St. John's prophecy anticipation of the course of history."[96]

Conclusion

Therefore, when one looks at the interpretation of Revelation by the Church Fathers, it becomes clear that in the 2nd –3rd centuries the expositors of the book including Irenaeus and Hippolytus, were mostly adherents to Millenarian views which can at least partly be explained by the turbulent time of persecution in which they lived.

This approach was the most popular but not the only one within the period. The spiritual or allegorical interpretation was developed by the Alexandrian school, and Origen in the third century played an important role in popularizing it. The influence of Tyconius and Augustine, who lived after the "conversion" of the Roman Empire and the end of the era of persecution, made the spiritual method of interpretation of the Apocalypse the main one in the West. The Millenarian approach with its promises of material bliss on earth, which seemed a comfort during the harsh times, lost its appeal. However, it did not completely disappear and survived until the present day. Yet it was the spiritual interpretation of Revelation which dominated in the commentaries of scholars in the next several centuries after Augustine.

In the East the commentaries on the book appeared some-what later, most likely due to a later acceptance of the book as canonical in that part of the Christian world. The interpretations of Revelation were diverse but the commentary of Andreas of Caesarea became the standard one for the Eastern Church.

Today, Revelation still challenges and comforts the students of the Bible. Scholars and teachers like Dr. Lowery continue the tradition of the Church Fathers of studying it. They believe that "it is as relevant as any other work found in Scripture" and teach others "to find God's timeless words of encouragement and exhortation" in it.[97] May the tradition be carried on until "the old order of things has passed away" (Rev 21:4).

FROM THE PROPHET TO THE PEOPLE:
A REFLECTION ON KARL BARTH'S UNDERSTANDING OF SCRIPTURE

Otniel Ioan Bunaciu

> "There are over 20 million Bibles distributed every year, and the Bible can be read aloud in 70 hours — though you might want to take a nap between the Old and New Testaments. Nine out of every ten Americans own at least one Bible — what's up with the other guy?"[1]

Although I am not an Old or New Testament specialist, I decided to offer a reflection on how to perceive the Scriptures through the understanding of Karl Barth, one of the greatest theologians of the twentieth century. Understanding Scripture is not an easy task and trying to look at it through the "eyes" of Karl Barth may appear to further complicate things, but I am persuaded that the writings of the Swiss theologian can inform and help us gain a fresh perspective on a much debated issue. NT Wright points out the difficulty of this debate that often leads to an impasse.

Debates about the authority of scripture have tended to get off on the wrong foot and to turn into an unproductive shouting-match. This is partly because here, as in matters of political theology, in the words of Jim Wallis "the Right gets it wrong and the Left doesn't get it." And sometimes the other way round as well. We have allowed our debates to be polarized within the false either/or of post-enlightenment categories, so that we either see the Bible as a holy book, almost a magic book, in which we can simply look up detached answers to troubling questions, or see it within its historical context and therefore claim the right to relativize anything and everything we don't immediately like about it. These categories are themselves mistaken; the Bible itself helps us to challenge them; and when we probe deeper into the question, "what does it mean to say that the Bible is authoritative," we discover a new and richer framework which simultaneously enables us to be deeply faithful to scripture and energizes and shapes us, corporately and individually, for our urgent mission into tomorrow's world.[2]

Educated in the spirit of liberal theology, Karl Barth was certainly a child of his age. Disappointed by the fact that his professors supported the World War, Barth began to question whether their position was not in some way tributary to their theology. His disappointment with the results of such theology lead him to abandon liberal theology and its approach to the Scriptures. Barth developed instead a new way to look at the Scriptures. In an autobiographical note he remembers the power and deep meaning of Abel Bruckhardt's hymns which he learned as a child. He writes about the "telling again" of the Gospel stories in those hymns:

> Yes, it was very naïve, but perhaps in the very naivety there lay the deepest wisdom and greatest power, so that once grasped it was calculated to carry one relatively unscathed — although not, of course, untempted or unassailed — through all the serried ranks of historicism and anti-historicism, mysticism and rationalism, orthodoxy, liberalism and existentialism, and to bring one back some day to the matter itself.[3]

His new position became evident during his time as a minister in the village of Safenwill. In 1916 Barth held a conference with the name *Die neue Welt der Bibel*.[4] Here he suggested that the world of biblical events forms God's revelation and this can be interpreted only through itself. He continued to develop these ideas in the *Exegesis of The Epistle to the Romans* where he identifies a hermeneutical circle in the Scriptures defined by the two central elements of the Gospel, the crucifixion and the resurrection. In his first edition of the commentary he emphasized the resurrection while in the second edition he emphasized the paradoxical relationship between the two events which led to his "dialectical theology."[5] Resurrection is understood as a total negation of everything human—so radical that not even time is able to contain the "Yes" of resurrection. The two events encapsulate for Barth the meaning of reality in which, as W. Lindemann suggests,[6] God addresses the problem through crucifixion and answers through resurrection. Crucifixion is proposed to have an epistemological role destroying any possibility to know God outside the paradox between it and the resurrection. This is the severance, in Barth's view, of any connection between Gospel and religion or between Gospel and natural theology.

Revelation as the Word of God

In the period following the second edition of the *Commentary to the Epistle of Romans*, Barth developed his thinking in two directions. First, he moved towards a doctrine of the Word of God that would enable the reflection of the believer on the narratives of the Bible (*Nachdenken*). In order to do this, he did not accentuate the Kierkegaardian "infinite qualitative difference" between man and God in favor of a relationship between them through the Word of God. In his *Prolegomena zür Christlichen Dogmatik*, published in 1927, he introduces a positive doctrine of God as Trinity where the Word is God himself communicated in an historical event (*geschichtliches Ereignis*).[7] This communication can be understood as revelation only through the narration of the Bible, *die offenbarung steht, nein sie geschiet in der Schrift, nicht hinter ihr* (the revelation is, no, it happens in very Scripture, not behind it).[8]

A second direction in his thinking was a development in his polemic against natural theology and religion. The reason for which he left his dialectical theologian colleagues (Bultmann, Gogarten, and Brunner) was because he understood their positions as being in the same category as that of natural theology which he excluded now with more and more rigor. His next step was to try to find an autonomous base for theology; he did this following his study of Anselm.[9] D.F. Ford is of the opinion that Barth interpreted Anslem as offering an *a posteriori* argument about the existence of God, because Anselm's understanding presupposes the existence of faith according to Barth. This position becomes the foundation for Barth's exegesis who negates now any perspective of knowing God outside the hermeneutical circle where, as Ford notes, God gave the proof of his existence in the historical expression of himself which is presented in the Bible and therefore only the biblical stories reproduce this identity with authority.[10]

The result is that Barth develops what was called "objectivity" or "realism" in the interpretation of the biblical message. With regards to God, "objectify" means that his being cannot be taken separate from his action, and this means that God encounters man and acts upon him. This is how he wishes to avoid the weakness of subjectivity, which characterized pietism and liberalism and that led in the end to a dualism between history and interiorization.

It also represents his attempt to return to the understanding of the Word of God held by the Reformers by identifying the Word of God with Jesus Christ and thus grounding it in the eternal being of God. As a result, in his Word, the being of God communicates itself in a personal manner. This is why Barth feels compelled to question the validity of any way of knowing God other than through his Word. Incarnation plays a crucial role because in this act God became, in a unique way, man in Jesus Christ. The implications of this action lead to the understanding that God cannot exist without being "bound" to Jesus Christ, and therefore, he cannot be known in any other way than through Jesus Christ. If God can be known in his own living reality, which is Jesus Christ, then an independent way to know God outside his revelation cannot be maintained — because God known through this other way would be different to God known in the nature of his incarnation.

The Word of God Written

Barth discusses Scripture in chapter 4 of his volume I/1 of *Church Dogmatics* in the context of presenting the three forms of the Word of God. In his understanding, the Bible is the medium through which the Church remembers God's past revelation. Therefore, the link between the book of Revelation and the Church is based on the attestation of the book of Revelation. The writers of the Scriptures are not speaking for themselves, but they are witnesses who point beyond them about something that does not belong to them but was given to them by God (Rev 1:1,11,19). The proclamation of the church, therefore, is based on the remembrance of the past and waiting for a future revelation.

Barth also distinguishes it from the rediscovery by man of his essential relationship with eternity in the way in which Augustine understood God as being the end of what all men search for as they seek to find *vita beata*. Augustine[11] makes a link between *memoria* and the platonic doctrine of *anamnesis*. For him, recollection is the turning of man towards himself to find God in himself — God who is already there. Although, God, in his freedom, could have left the Church to ground herself in herself so that through turning to herself it would find God, Barth points out that God did not choose this way. In Jesus Christ, the Head of the Church, she finds the transcendental part of its being which confronts the earthly side. It is because of this transcendental dimension that the remembrance of God's revelation, which the Church has, is different from the reflection on what is essentially and eternally hers.

By accepting the canon of Scripture, the Church acknowledges that its proclamation as event comes from outside — from a specific canon, which, although it is a categorical imperative, it is historical. Recognizing this canon as the New and Old Testament, the Church accepts that the connection to it has a specific form determined by its content. She cannot renounce these "marching orders" in written form without renouncing her own proclamation.

Barth draws attention to the phenomenological similarity between the proclamation of the Church and the canon of Scripture. Even in the Bible, Barth believes, we deal with Scripture in a secondary sense because it is "the deposit" of the proclamation made in the past. Therefore, Scripture does not claim to be primarily a historical document but a document of the Church. From this perspective, it may be that Jeremiah and Paul are at the beginning of the proclamation of the Church and the preacher today is the end of the same line.

Barth's opinion lies in the same phenomenological similarity — the dissimilarity between Scripture and church proclamation. The former differs fundamentally from the second because it is the foundation of the proclamation — the written word of the prophets and apostles being above any other words being spoken in the Church. This is why the Church is not alone in her proclamation, because when she remembers God's past revelation she is in a direct confrontation. This task of intercession that the Church has must have the character of succession if the message of the proclamation is grounded in God and not in the church. Barth reaffirms the Reformers' conviction that the true apostolic succession is not physical but one of teaching and of spirit.

> The apostolic succession of the Church must mean that it is guided by the Canon, that is, by the prophetic and apostolic word as the necessary rule of every word that is valid in the Church. It must mean that the Church enters into the succession of the prophets and apostles in their office of proclamation, and does so in such a way that their proclamation freely and independently precedes, while that of the Church is related to it, is ventured in obedience on the basis of it, is measured by it, and replaces it only as and to the extent that it conforms to it.[12]

Because the distance between antecessor and successor is so big, he suggests that only the written form of the Scripture can guarantee the succession — although God could have left the canon in oral form if he wanted to. The problem of such a canon is that being so close to the Church she cannot confront it. To distinguish the life of the Church in this tradition is like trying to distinguish in our blood the blood of our parents. That is why through the unwritten tradition the church is not addressed but engaged in a dialogue with itself.[13]

The canon of the Bible is in an ongoing process to be incorporated in the life of the Church — a process in which the Bible is understood and interpreted again and again. The process of exegesis through which the Bible receives authority carries with it the danger that the message of the Bible is confiscated and distorted by the Church. Therefore, Barth thinks that the exegesis of the Bible should be left "open" not for the sake of the "free thinkers" but for the sake of a free Bible. The defense of the text against potential abuse should be left to the text itself. This is so because the canon of the Bible was achieved through the Bible imposing itself through the word of the prophetic and apostolic witnesses of Jesus Christ. The promise made to the Church through the person of Christ is the promise of God's grace and mercy and this is: "*Emmanuel, God is with us!*"

The entire proclamation of the church, led and empowered by the Scripture, must be understood as an event. In this event, the Bible is the Word of God because the human word of the prophets and apostles represents the Word of God; in the same way, in the event of the preaching, the Word of God gives itself to man as the human word of the preacher.

> The fact that God's own address becomes an event in the human word of the Bible is, however, God's affair and not ours. This is what we mean when we call the Bible God's Word. We confess and acknowledge therewith that the recollection of God's past revelation, without which the enterprise of Church proclamation would be impossible, is just as much God's grace and gift as is the actualisation our own proclamation needs. It is not in our own power to make this recollection, not even in the form of our grasping at the Bible. Only when and as the Bible grasps at us, when we are thus reminded, is this recollection achieved.[14]

That is why Barth can say that the Bible is the Word of God in the measure in which God allows her to be his Word and in the measure in which God speaks through it. The initiative belongs again to God, and for man, it is an affirmation of faith. So, the Bible is the Word of God in our faith by the virtue of God's act that confronts our lack of faith.[15]

The content of the Bible preoccupied the biblical authors in the sense that they were "caught" by the biblical object. Barth recounts how he thought that Paul sees and hears something which is above any other thing and beyond his range of observation.[16] In a similar way, Luke, Abraham and Moses point to a movement in the Bible which is like that of the stars rotating around the sun. Barth likes to illustrate with Grünewald's painting of the crucifixion from the altar in the church in Colmar where John the Baptist points with his extended hand

and finger trying to show us something. It is this hand, Barth thinks, that the Bible shows us. If this hand is religion, worship, or experience, we cannot offer an explanation, but in the biblical experiences another element appears to which nothing corresponds because the historical religion of the Bible has the distinction of being not religion and not history but reality and truth.

He distinguishes in this manner between "religion" and what we find in the Bible. The danger that religion keeps facing is that it fools itself when it thinks that it is indispensable. By claiming this, religion enters in competition with the other powers of the world, and the biblical images become too familiar and are treated too lightly. In other words, man tries to take the divine in his possession. Therefore, Barth considers that the decisive characteristic of the Bible is to oppose the history of religion, because the Bible presents an amazing continuity of faithfulness, hope, endurance, and objective attention towards the incomprehensible, un-historical, and nonpsychological truth about God.[17]

The prophets and the apostles did not wish to be what they were, but they had no choice—they had to be what they were. In the center of biblical religiosity is the personal relationship of men with God and not a myth or mysticism, because this personal relationship does not come out of the human subconsciousness. Even sacrifice, so important for the history of religion, is treated with reservation in the Bible as the OT points beyond sacrifice to a final act that will make sacrifice unnecessary. The NT continues this understanding when it claims that through the sacrifice of one all the sacrifices were abandoned.

Usually the Bible debates with the religious world and not with the godless world as it calls to the pagans who worship their Baals. When the pagans declare faith, faith that sometimes cannot be found in Israel, this shows us that man in the Bible is always the first one in his relationship with God—without father or mother to inherit the relationship from. The biblical history in the Old and New Testament is not a history as such but a series of divine acts seen from above and seen from below as a number of unfulfilled trials to achieve something impossible. The Church that we find in the Bible is the tent, and in the heavenly Jerusalem of the book of Revelation the Church is missing. The Bible has only one theological preoccupation and that is with God himself.[18] God is shown as Wholly Other and not another thing among things; this gives the "other worldly" feel to the Bible.

When we try to find God in the Bible we are directed towards Jesus Christ crucified as in Grünewald's painting. Barth points out that the only source for real and immediate revelation of God is death, because Christ opened its gates and brought life from death. ". . . Human correlation with divine life is not virtue, nor inspiration, nor love but fear of God, deadly fear, ultimate, absolute, complete fear."[19] This is the motive which determines Barth to consider that the understanding of the "Yes" in Scripture is correctly apprehended only when this "Yes" is included in "No." From this follows the understanding of grace, or the rejection of the law, as an awareness that all things are secondary — a preparation for final answers, which is consciousness of God. Overbeck calls this "the wisdom of death" (*Todesweisheit*), and it ultimately shows that the love of God is demonstrated in the sacrifice of Christ. The wisdom of death leads us to an understanding that the contemporary world does not have — that beyond it awaits a new world. This is the new creation (Rev 21:1), which is also the message of Easter. Resurrection is God's sovereignty; it means eternity, which is the goal of time. It means a new world, of which man is aware, that is founded and created by God (Rev 21:1–22:6).

Some Critical Considerations

In this last section, I would like to point to a few criticisms regarding Barth's understanding of Scripture and revelation. First, James Barr, during the 1991 Gifford Lectures (founded to support Natural theology),[20] criticized Barth for the mode in which he uses Scripture to support the christological concentration which characterizes his position. Barr maintains that the extreme position held by Barth is founded, in part, on his wrong approach to the Bible, because he did not start with exegesis; instead, it is philosophical-dogmatical in character.

Although Barr agrees with Barth that a "starting point" for theology could not be found in Natural Theology and he does not find the attempts to prove the existence of God very helpful either, he, nevertheless, holds that the Bible contains an implicit form of Natural Theology that is hard to avoid. In order to be able to reject the presence of this Natural Theology, Barth uses a selective method in the exegesis of Scripture which allows him to abandon such parts as: Paul's discourse in the Areopagus or the first chapters of Romans.

Barr thinks that Barth was too dependent on certain results from the historical criticism of the Bible, such as the conviction that the Gospels are not biographies and that no precise knowledge of Jesus can be obtained through historical research. The biblical scholars in Barth's time were more preoccupied with psychological aspects hoping to reach the "thinking" of the people of the Bible. Therefore, they were not interested in a Natural Theology, just as they were not interested in the apologetic aspects of the Scriptures. Natural Theology was also considered a result of Greek thought, and it became, thus, an enemy, because although the language of the NT was Greek the concepts in it were Hebrew. Barr disagrees with this position because he thinks that although Greek thinking is present in the Scripture, it accompanies but does not determine Natural Theology.

Barr also criticizes the rejection of Natural Theology on the basis of the uniqueness of revelation in Jesus Christ because the knowledge of God in the OT cannot be considered as being only through Christ—except by dogmatical construction in that exegetically this is impossible. Therefore, it means that the OT makes available an understanding of God anterior to the revelation through Christ, which would destroy Barth's argument.[21] "Why is it not possible," asks Barr, "that this knowledge of God before revelation in Christ also contains natural knowledge of God?" The obstacle is the "christological exegesis" of the OT through which Barth imposes the Christian understanding reaching the conclusion that Natural Theology is not possible as an alternative to the statement "Jesus is Lord."

A second criticism concerns the implications that Barth's theology has upon the understanding of God. Because of his christological concentration, the image of God proposed by Barth does not seem to be very "real." The question is: does Barth limit God's freedom when he considers that God reveals himself and does so only in Jesus Christ? In explanation, Barth sometimes forces the exegesis of the Bible. For example: in Judas's case, Barth insists on Paul's typology to demonstrate the possibility of a favorable verdict for Judas. By doing so he does not seem to do justice to the tragic verdict that the Gospel stories give to Judas; Barth does not only transform the realism of the story but seems to know more about God's purposes than the story itself is able to inform us. Therefore, the wonder that Barth shows for God's revelation of himself through an event determines him to absolutize that event and, at the same time, limit the possibilities for God to reveal himself in another mode.

Third, Barth's understanding of the inspiration of Scripture is often criticized. Although he supports an understanding of biblical inspiration, many theologians are not satisfied with the mode in which he qualifies this process—especially with his understanding that the biblical authors wrote with words in a way that was open to human limitations. Barth does not think that this makes the Scripture an inferior document. For example, in the preface to his *Commentary to the Romans* he claims that although Paul wrote as a child of his age, he addresses the Christians of all ages as prophet and apostle. He continues to say that if he had to choose between the historical-critical method of studying the Bible and the doctrine of verbal inspiration he would choose the second without hesitation, but he does not feel compelled to do so.[22]

The reason for which he can speak at the same time about the doctrine of verbal inspiration and about the historical-critical method when studying the Bible is because he introduces in his theology a distance between the Word of God, who he understands to be Jesus Christ, and the Scripture, which he understands to be the witness about him. Man hears the witness about the Word of God in human form, and this may not be perfect because it is only in that form that man can hear this message. But it is in this human word that God reveals himself in his freedom. The initiative remains God's—as the bridge between man and God can be built only by God.

Although this emphasis on the divine in the understanding of the Word of God is in accordance with the image of God in Scripture, the questions arise: "Must this priority in initiative be correlated with the human failure to reproduce inspired words? Could not God, in his freedom, choose a way of inspiration to leave us a text produced by God himself?" Barth's answer would probably be that God could have done so, but he chose not to because he revealed himself to man in a person, Jesus Christ, and did not have the intention to leave man a "paper pope." The act that guarantees the witness of the revelation is God's incarnation in Jesus Christ. The biblical text exists with unique importance for the Christian and for the Church because no analogy of Christ could be true if it does not conform to the image of Christ in Scripture. However this image can be true only in an analogical manner.

> The fact that [Jesus] lives, and what it means that He lives, are not things invented or maintained of ourselves. If we say them responsibly, our own responsibility is only secondary. We really draw on the biblical attestation of His existence. For in this attestation He Himself lives, certainly as its origin and theme, but even as such only in the mirror of the picture which is offered. It is He who lives, not the picture. But He Himself lives only in the form which He has in the picture. For it is not a picture arbitrarily invented and constructed by others. It is the picture which He Himself has created and impressed upon His witnesses. When we say that Jesus Christ lives, we repeat the basic, decisive, controlling and determinative statement of the biblical witness, namely, that He, very Son of God and Son of Man, the Mediator between God and man, the One who lives the life of grace, the Lord and Servant, the Fulfiller of the divine act of reconciliation, that He, this One, has risen from the dead, and in so doing shown Himself to be who He is. He lives as and because He is risen, having thus shown that He lives this life. If there is any Christian and theological axiom, it is that Jesus Christ is risen, that He is truly risen. But this is an axiom which no one can invent. It can only be repeated on the basis of the fact that in

the enlightening power of the Holy Spirit it has been previously declared to us as the central statement of the biblical witness.[23]

Revelation 1:1,17b-18, "The revelation of Jesus Christ, which God gave [John]. . . . 'I am the First and the Last. I am the Living One; I was dead, and behold I am alive for ever and ever!'"

John:

DIFFICULT TEXTS IN THE
BOOK OF REVELATION

LIVING OUT LOUD: THE WITNESSING CHURCH IN REVELATION 11:1-14

Jeff Snell

John's Apocalypse is noisy. From the initial blessing pronounced on those who heed what they hear (1:3) to the final canonical words of the risen Christ (22:20), the aural abounds.[1] Furthermore, John's own experience was profoundly but not exclusively visual; "I heard" (ἀκούω) is found almost 30 times and his 44 total uses of the verb are found in every chapter except 15, 17, and 20.[2] "Voice" (φωνή) is employed in 17 chapters; the 55 total occurrences almost equal John's 60 uses of "I saw" (εἶδον). Who or what he heard is sometimes difficult to determine, but it includes the Father (9:13; 16:1; 21:5), Son (1:8,10; 4:1; 11:12; 19:5; 22:7,20), Spirit (14:13), living creatures (4:8; 6:1,6), 24 elders (4:11; 11:17), angels (5:2; 7:2,12; 8:5; 10:3,8; 14:7; 15:5; 16:17; 17:7; 18:21), an eagle (8:13), Christians in God's presence (6:10; 7:10; 19:1ff); and God's opponents are heard as well: the dragon, beasts, and false prophet (13:5,15; 16:15), the kings and merchants of the earth (18:10,14,16,17) and others in allegiance with them (6:16-17).

John receives his commission and other commands aurally (1:10; 4:1; 10:7ff; 22:8,10). He also presumably hears unspoken sounds as God's judgment is portrayed through the unleashing of natural phenomena (11:19 and 16:18ff). On the other hand, Revelation can be described, like music, as planned silence. Amidst the clamor, the quiet is equally imposing and strategic (8:1; 10:4).

In light of these realities, perhaps a kernel of truth resides in Eugene Peterson's suggestion that no other biblical book has been wrenched so far from its roots in oral media.[3] These sights and sounds are presented in a unified narrative that would have been delivered orally and in its entirety to John's original recipients, thus "... the Apocalypse is not merely an argument, but an oral performance that generates an array of experiences and reactions, thereby to transform the social space inhabited by both performer and audience."[4] John doesn't merely teach truth; he evokes response, engaging the imagination through the mind's ear as well as the mind's eye, communicating creatively as he recounts his own multisensory experience. At first glance (or upon first hearing), Rev 11:1-14 is not one of the most deafening passages in the book.[5] In these verses, however, John compels his hearers to initiate and participate in the noisemaking. As they do, the nature and purposes of God are clearly articulated and evidenced on earth, just as they are celebrated in the heavenly anthems and enacted by heavenly agents. Furthermore, Revelation is a reminder that, since witness includes but transcends words, even deeds can be measured in decibels.

Revelation 11:1-14 in Context

A few observations regarding the overall structure of Revelation will provide the working parameters for the following reflections. First, we will adopt Hendrickson's position that Revelation is divided into two major categories (Rev 1–11/12–22), with the first section especially addressing the church's struggle on earth and the second especially addressing the spiritual realities behind that struggle. Each of the two major sections culminates with a portrayal of the world's end.[6] Second, the relationship between John's series of sevens (churches in Rev 2:1–3:22, seals in Rev 6:1–8:5, trumpets in 8:6–11:19 and bowls in 16:1-21) is crucial. The final three series are generally parallel chronologically (each covers the entire Christian era and portrays the end of the world), thematically (each addresses God's judgment through a series of similar images), and structurally (in each there is an interlude between the sixth and seventh element in the series that addresses implications for the church that relate to that particular series). Each section simultaneously contributes to an intensifying effect which produces a crescendo that climaxes at Revelation's conclusion.[7]

Within this overall framework, Revelation 10:1–11:14 forms an interlude between the sixth and seventh trumpets; it addresses the church's role and responsibility on earth during that era. Thus, the relationship between this section and Rev 8:6–11:19 warrants brief and focused consideration. First, both the overall series and the interlude within it focus on repentance (the overall section is bracketed by heaven scenes related to such and the interlude is bracketed by direct references to earth dwellers' failure to repent in 9:20-21 and 11:13).[8] Second, there are striking verbal and thematic connections (see below) between the plagues unleashed at the sounding of the trumpets and the results of the church's witness. This underscores that the role of such witness is to partner with God by creating on earth the realities declared from heaven. The church joins God in trumpeting His call to repent, and thus articulates and embodies the reality of, reasons for, and results of God's judgment.

Moving closer to our text, the relationship between Revelation 10 and Revelation 11 must be noted. Like the interlude between the sixth and seventh seals (7:1-17), this section contains two visions that are powerfully interconnected. In Revelation 10, John is commissioned by an angel with a voice as big as his body (v. 3); as a result, John presents a message (contained on the little scroll) linking the witness of the church to his own prophetic example and indeed to all who embody the prophetic tradition. In chapter 11, he continues the participation in his vision that began in 10:8-11 while also narrating a portrait that compresses a variety of OT images in order to describe the identity and activity of the church. In so doing, he locates each generation of Christians in a heritage of people who find their voices, though not their homes, in hostile territory.[9] Furthermore, he challenges each generation of Christians to embrace their moment on the stage of human history by choosing to live out loud.

111

Live Out Loud: Acknowledge the Reality (11:1-2)

Having received a prophetic commission in a manner reminiscent of Ezekiel (Ezek 2:9–3:4), John now unfolds and enacts the message of the bittersweet scroll he consumed (10:10). In so doing, he especially echoes imagery from Ezekiel 40–48, where the prophet records his vision of a temple in which God would dwell with his people forever. The nobility of living out loud for God can whet a believer's appetite; John simultaneously feeds and grounds such holy inclinations by introducing truths foundational to the remainder of this passage.

The Witnessing Church Is Protected

John's message for the church is sweet—not only because the message is from God, but also because it is encouraging for God's people. In a manner reminiscent of the angel in Ezek 40:3 and similar to Zech 2:1-5, John measures the temple (11:1). This measuring signifies God's watchcare over His church, to which the temple imagery, as a portrait of God's presence, refers (Eph 2:19-22; 1Cor 3:16; 2Cor 6:16).[10] It also anticipates Rev 21:15-17 (where an angel measures the New Jerusalem) and the full realization of a purified, protected, and complete community.

While the reality of God's protection is relatively clear, the scope of that protection is a matter of some debate. Most scholars contend 11:1 is an earth scene, showing believers are spiritually protected during their earthly lives though they may be physically harmed. However, temple imagery everywhere else in Revelation occurs in scenes presented from the perspective of heaven.[11] Notably, John's only other use of "temple of God" (ναὸς τοῦ θεοῦ) occurs only a few verses later (v. 19). Furthermore, in Revelation scenes frequently and relatively abruptly shift between heaven and earth. For these reasons (including the relationship between this verse and Rev 21:15-17) perhaps Rev 11:1 is a heaven scene, in which case John is affirming Christians are fully and finally protected once they are present with God upon death.[13]

The Witnessing Church is Persecuted

The bitterness of John's scroll is explained in verse 2. The outer court is still a reference to God's people (as is the holy city), but they are now exposed (though not abandoned).[13] Their witness places them at risk physically, economically, socially, and even, in a qualified sense, spiritually (since they dwell amidst forces that tempt them to abdicate or understate their identity). The NIV translation "exclude" (ἐκβάλλω) blurs an ironic wordplay, since the root word βάλλω (often translated throw, hurl, or cast) is frequently used in Revelation for activities related to God's judgment and in contexts addressing the persecution of God's people.[14] The two ideas coalesce here; because God's people articulate God's judgment, they are persecuted. God allows them to be "cast out" so they can communicate a message that all opposed to God will be eternally cast out. In the meantime, God's people are trampled upon for 42 months. The trampling imagery, drawn especially from Dan 8:13 and perhaps Zech 12:13, combines with the temporal designation to symbolize a limited period of time in which evil would be allowed relatively free reign and God's people would be oppressed and profaned.[15]

The paradoxical reality expressed in 11:1-2, then, is as follows: God's people are securely vulnerable. Their time on earth is dangerously purposeful. God's people suffer by God's permission for the accomplishment of God's purposes; He is ultimately in control.[16] Humanity's will to survive is remarkable and often noble, but for Christians it is subordinate to Christ's lordship and example. Self-protective insulation and isolation are actually at "cross" purposes with His example and agenda. Christians do pay a price; the language of "trampling" is strong stuff. However, though they are tempted to consider their suffering incompatible with their status as God's children, the reverse is actually true; mere earthly survival is beneath their dignity as God's "instruments" and their identity as Christ's body. This passage shows the church has something more important to do than survive.[17]

Live Out Loud: Embrace the Opportunity (11:3-6)

Building upon his previous emphasis on the presence of God as a source of paradoxical protection during the period of the church's witness, John next highlights God's presence as the means by which the church's witness is fueled. Suffering the indignity of being trodden upon is not burdensome compared to the possibility of being too puny for a divinely appointed task. John encourages Christians by reminding them they are more than sufficiently resourced for their role.

The Witnessing Church Is Equipped

The church is equipped to functionally succeed the OT prophets; she is endowed with authority and empowerment — both via the Holy Spirit.[18] This is especially communicated via allusions to Zechariah 4, in which the church is symbolized by the olive trees and lampstands; in Zechariah's night vision the trees provide the oil (often connected to the Holy Spirit in the OT) for the lampstand (a symbol related to witness in Rev 1:12,13,20; 2:1,5; 11:4). There, the olive trees refer to Joshua (the priest) and Zerubbabel (the king), who were anointed by the Spirit for the purpose of rebuilding the temple — despite opposition. More explicit is the direct statement in Zech 4:6, "Not by might, not by power, but by my Spirit says the Lord." When these verses are combined with the call to prophesy (Rev 11:3,6,10), this passage contains references to all three anointed offices in Israel. As a kingdom of priests, then, the church engages in her prophetic mission by the Spirit's power.

How one interprets the sphere of Christian witness (or the extent to which the sphere is limited or specified) is largely determined by one's understanding of the NT witness terminology itself (which is clearly prominent in Johannine literature generally and Revelation particularly).[19] Allison Trites has effectively argued that Revelation's use of witness and testimony should be understood in its primary forensic sense; in other words, he contends witness in Revelation occurs before Roman officials — perhaps especially those connected to the imperial cult.[20] This approach is especially poignant if John was himself exiled to Patmos for this reason (Rev 1:9). While witness primarily contains legal overtones, however, there is no reason to assume it exclusively does so. Faithful witnesses testify before earthly powers, but their faithful words and actions elsewhere land them before those powers.[21] Emboldened and equipped the church courageously tells the truth before earthly authorities and among all people on earth because she is confident her ministry is conducted before the Lord of the earth.

The Witnessing Church Is Effective

Like her predecessors who were similarly equipped, the church's testimony packs a punch (2Kgs 1:10-12; Jer 5:14). In this regard she echoes the ministries of Moses and Elijah. In the presence of Pharaoh, Moses lived out loud. His mighty words were accompanied by powerful acts of judgment, signified here by an allusion to the first of the ten plagues (Exod 7:17ff). Elijah confronted the Israelite king Ahab (1Kgs 17) and in the powerful convergence between his words and deeds, there was, ironically, a 3½ year drought (cf. Rev 11:2-3, also Lk 4:25; Jas 5:17).[22]

The church's effectiveness is clear if this passage is viewed in a vacuum, but the power of her partnership with God's trumpeting activity is especially evident when the results of her witness are compared with those paralleled by six trumpets. The judgments are referred to as plagues (8:12; 9:20; 11:6) which target earth-dwellers (8:13; 11:10). They are generated by agents with derived authority from God (9:3,10,19; 11:6). The results of these judgments include famine conditions (8:8-9; locusts in 9:7-10; 11:6a), killing (9:15,18,20; 11:5), and harming (9:10,19; 11:5). Fire proceeds from them (9:17-18; 11:5; also see 16:8-9), and water becomes blood (8:8; 11:6). The result of these plagues is torment for those who recognize their plight (9:5-6; 11:10).[23] These are not mere artistic brush strokes; they are how John portrays the church's success in fulfilling the call to live out loud.

The church's witnessing role, then, is a privileged opportunity. Apart from God's commission and command, she has no right to speak and nothing to say. Apart from God's empowerment, she has no reason for courage or optimism. Revelation 11 echoes the book of Acts, reminding us that God indwells His people to empower the successful accomplishment of His mission.

Live Out Loud: Accept the Hostility (Rev 11:7-10)

While God's presence empowers success, it does not guarantee safety. Jesus, the foremost faithful witnesses (1:5), is the ultimate evidence of this reality (11:8). The second faithful witness in Revelation is Antipas, who also died for his testimony (2:13). Most of this section doesn't deal directly with the attack; it addresses responses to the result. Even when other Christians are similarly treated, the church, collectively, has her say (11:7).

Faithful Witness Produces Confusion

Living out loud can be bewildering. As noted in the introduction to this essay, John reminds his audience that God's adversaries have a mouth, message, and platform. God's people aren't the only ones making an effort to live out loud. John is a marvelous artist, but in one sense, he only has two colors on his palette — black and white. His Apocalypse is not painted in hues of gray; allegiances are clear and so is the truth. His portrait is not one of relativistic confusion; rather, as noted below, it is more like the potentially disorienting confusion found in combat zones due to the convergence of competing and contradictory voices (11:6). Such confusion can produce tentative tongues and passive proclamation, so John steadies his hearers in the spirit of "forewarned is forearmed."

Faithful Witness Produces Conflict

In these verses the symbolism behind the images shifts almost entirely from God's people to God's enemies, in anticipation of the conflict in the following sections of Revelation (chapters 13 and 17 particularly). Drawing on a framework introduced in Daniel (7:3,17,18,27), John portrays the beast as earthly kingdoms at war with God's kingdom.[24] Its influence is portrayed through a painful collage of images/analogies. Like Egypt and Babylon (the great city according to Rev 18:10-21), Rome and her contemporary equivalents coerce with legal/political power and lure through cultural seduction, producing moral decay reminiscent of Sodom. No place is safe. Jerusalem lives down *to* the worst moments in her history (as experienced by the prophets, Jesus, and His earliest followers), rather than living those memories down. The opposition is comprehensive and extends through the entire earth (Rev 2, 9,

10).[25] God's adversaries mock (v. 9), and celebrate (v. 10) the apparent silencing of God's agents.[26]

Revelation portrays through imagery what 2Tim 3:12 declares more directly: when you represent God, people who are mad at God will take it out on you. With the shadows of Gethsemane and Golgotha looming over an Upper Room, Jesus reminded His disciples that a servant is not greater than his master (Jn 15:20). Perhaps God's enemies possess a stronger ecclesiology than many Christians do! Believers may be tempted to say to their adversaries, "If you don't like being tormented by truth, take it up with God." This passage reminds us that they are — by attacking the church, Christ's body and His presence on earth. Therefore, union with Christ invites suffering like Christ. In spite of the emphasis evangelical Christians place on "relationship with Jesus," self-absorbed, silent Christians attempt to avoid joining with Christ in the fellowship of His sufferings (Phil 3:20). In so doing, they miss some of the most intimate experiences of relationship with Jesus and with His followers.

John issues this reminder: when people tire of trying to shout the church down, they make an effort to shut the church up. And, sometimes they appear to succeed, but not for good or for long. Indeed, through their persecution of the witnessing church, they evidence hearts hardened toward God and thus seal their fate.

Live Out Loud: Anticipate Victory (11:11-14)

The sweetness of John's scroll is again evidenced; those who celebrate victory over the church do so prematurely. Echoing Ezekiel's vision of a restored Israel (Ezek 37-38) and with continued strong allusions to OT prophetic ministries, John declares God's ultimate upholding of His people and vanquishing of His opponents.

Faithful Witness Vindicates God's People

The language used to describe the resurrection/restoration itself is taken from Ezek 37:5,10 (notice also his description of Israel as slain by her persecutors in 37:9). During the Babylonian exile, Israel may have appeared abandoned by God; however, His deliverance vindicated them (and Him) and validated their mission as His witnesses. The same is true for the church (cf. Rev 20:7-10).[27] She is like Elijah, whose prophetic authority and identity were dramatically validated when he was taken up to heaven. (2Kgs 2:11). United with Christ, believers' experience is patterned not only after the life and death of Jesus, but also after his resurrection and ascension. The first reference to an audible voice in Revelation 11 is found in verse 12 as God vindicates His church in the presence of her victimizers—and the heavenly voice is loud! Those who speak for God and are empowered by God are now portrayed as taken up to God.

Faithful Witness Condemns God's Enemies

The opponents don't just witness God's vindicating activity—they are impacted as well, and they respond with fear (v. 11). John's description connects their response with the experience of the Egyptians, who similarly resisted God and His spokesman Moses and thus experienced the reality and the results of God's judgment.[28] Furthermore, it demonstrates the striking way God responds to the prayers of the martyred saints who long for judgment against their persecutors (6:9-11; 8:3-5; 9:13). In the seventh seal, the heavenly creatures are silenced and God listens to the prayers of the saints (Rev 8:1-3; cf. 6:13). He responds to those prayers with the judgments of the seven trumpets, which resemble the plagues poured on Egypt. As the church articulates this message of judgment, God uses the church on earth as one means by which He answers the prayers of his saints for vindication. As her opponents actively resist her message, they unleash the judgment of God upon themselves.

Conclusion

From this point on, the Apocalypse becomes a multidimensional presentation of the final triumph of good over evil.[29] As John brings us to the end of the world (Rev 11:15-19), both the sounds and the themes of this chapter crescendo to a climax. The declarative doxologies don't drown out the voices of the raging nations, for they are permanently silenced by God's judgment (which is symbolized by the loud cosmic phenomena that conclude Rev 19). God permanently rewards those who, whether great or small, find their prophetic voice and thereby make every deed a doxology and every syllable a means of service.

John invites us to listen in, so we may be strengthened to find our voices in the present. Since the church is the body of Christ, she is the mouth of Christ. In a climate opposed to God, it is tempting to whisper in prayer closets that which must be shouted from rooftops. Upping the decibels on our "Amens" and aggressively trumpeting the truth to those who already agree is of some value; after all, this is partly what John does in his Apocalypse. But, it is a limited and thus diluted description of what it means to find one's voice. May God strengthen His church to live out loud, so the sounds of heaven may reverberate on earth.

REVELATION 12: THE WOMAN AND THE DRAGON

Mark Scott

One of my favorite Bob Lowery stories is about the dragon and the manger scene. Bob's wife, Marilyn, had set out the crèche for the advent season. Bob found a miniature toy red dragon and placed it in the stable. Marilyn removed it. Bob put it back. Marilyn removed it again. Bob found it and put it back. However uncomfortable it might be for us, the story of the incarnation of Christ has an ugly unwelcome guest. Revelation 12 makes that very clear.

This chapter will have a very discernible outline. It is hoped that the outline will help carry the exegetical freight of the vision(s). "The Woman"[1] and "the Dragon"[2] are the two dominant images (players) in the visions. However Revelation 12 contains a kaleidoscope of other characters.[3] The text is Christian, apocalyptic, and poetic.

The Woman and the Dragon: The Promise at Risk and Preserved (1-6)

John's techniques of repetition, recapitulation, chiasms, and inclusio are all part of his "music."[4] By the time John sees the pregnant woman and the red dragon in chapter 12 he has *seen* the glorified Christ (1), he has *heard* what Christ thinks of the church (2-3), he has *witnessed* worship around the throne of God (4-5), and he has *watched* the seven seals and seven trumpets deliver the judgments of God on the world (6-11). Strategically placed in this last section are at least two (maybe three?) interludes (7 and 10-11). When the seventh trumpet finally sounds (11:15-19), we find ourselves at the end of the world once again.

The question may well be asked, "If Christ is sovereign, why does the church suffer so, and why is the world in such a fix?" The answer is found in chapters 12–14. They may well form the chiasmus of the book of Revelation. There is an unseen, though very real, enemy of the promise of God. This unholy trinity (dragon, beast from the sea, and beast — false prophet — from the earth) fights God and makes life miserable for those who "obey God's commandments and hold to the testimony of Jesus" (12:17).

A great sign[5] appeared[6] in heaven. The contrast between heaven and earth in Revelation cannot be overstated. While at times it seems only a membrane separates them (chapters 4–5), at other times they seem in different galaxies (chapters 13 and 21). It is this discontinuity that is emphasized in chapter 12. What is described in heaven in these first six verses seems worlds removed from the here and now.

The First Sign: The Woman (1-2)

The first *sign* in heaven John sees is a woman. The main hermeneutical hurdle in the chapter is, who is she?[7] Chapter 12 tells us several things about her. We read of her clothing (1), her latter stage pregnancy (2), her pain in childbirth (2), her birth of the male child (5), her flight to and preservation in the desert (6,14), her pursuit by the dragon (13), her wings like those of an eagle (14), her intended destruction by the dragon (15), and her other offspring warred against by the dragon (17). All these details must be regarded to rightly identify her.

Christopher Davis summarizes succinctly the possibilities.[8] First, the woman could be Mary, the mother of Jesus. This veneration of Mary is standard Roman Catholic doctrine. Tradition does indicate that Mary may well have served out her days in Ephesus, where John ministered.[9] One significant challenge to this interpretation is that the woman of Revelation has other offspring (17). Also even some Catholic scholars are hesitant to endorse this position totally.[10]

Secondly, the woman could be the church. This view has much to commend it. Her offspring are people who obey God's commands and hold to the testimony of Jesus (17). But did the church give birth to Jesus? Chronologically that is out of sync.[11]

Thirdly, the woman could be Eve, Adam's wife. This is based on Genesis 3:15 and the curse given to Eve, but the promise made in spite of her mistake. The woman's male child will destroy the dragon later, and that commends this view. However, in what sense is Eve a goddess who enjoys protection from God for 1,260 days?[12]

Fourthly, the woman is Israel. If the view is not to restrict the understanding to literal and physical Israel but would include spiritual Israel (the new Israel of the church), then this view is a strong possibility. Much of the imagery about how the woman is at first described (12:1-2) has parallels in the OT.[13]

Fifthly, the woman is Jerusalem. This view is admittedly close to the fourth view. Isaiah 66:7-13 does picture the famous Zion hill of Jerusalem as giving birth.[14] Later in Revelation the contrast between the cities, Babylon and Jerusalem, and the Harlot and the Bride intermesh.[15]

Sixthly, the woman is a literary device maybe symbolizing the people of God portrayed as a goddess. This is the position that Davis embraces.[16] It is also known as the combat myth in the ancient world. It cannot be denied that some of these myths and pieces of folklore are in the reservoir of the thinking of John's audience. Depending on how widespread these stories were, it would not be odd for John to baptize some of those stock images to make his point about the protection of God's people and the victory of the male child over the dragon. However, two questions remain: 1) Which myth or combat story should we choose?[17] Maybe the answer is none and all. Maybe John draws upon none of them in particular (though perhaps on some more than others) and all of them in general. 2) What did John actually see? If he saw God's people and the devil and used a literary device to communicate that, it makes good sense to say he specifically drew upon the mythology. If, on the other hand, he saw a pregnant woman and a dragon, then those images must be probed in the Bible first and most.

What is the real metanarrative in the Bible? Is it not "to get back what rightfully belongs to him"?[18] Is it not to destroy the works of the devil (1Jn 3:8)? Is John thinking of parallel worlds (evident in myths) or is he thinking of the primary struggle between heaven and earth (the biblical story)?[19] If chapter 12 is one of the more christological[20] chapters in Revelation, then shouldn't we expect some theology of promise connections? This is why the Eve option might need more press.[21]

There are three reasons why the woman might symbolize the holder of the promise: [1] The holder of the promise is a woman (Gen 3:15; cf. 1Tim 2:15; Gal 3:16). [2] Also in Pauline thinking Sarah and Hagar are real women but represent covenants (Gal 4:21-31).[22] [3] The woman/bride symbol in the OT (Isa 7:14; 26:17–27:1; 54:5; 66:7-11; Ezek 16, 23; Hosea 3) seems to represent God's people both compromised and real. When reading the OT, the question always needs to be, "What is happening to the promise of God?" So the woman symbolizes the holder of the promise of the Messiah and the community he leads.[23] The victory of chapter 12 is that the promise is not ultimately at risk. Rather the promise is preserved against a terrible enemy, who is now introduced.

The Second Sign: The Dragon (3-4)

The second *sign* in heaven is an enormous (μέγας)[24] red (πυρρὸς)[25] dragon.[26] Verse nine makes it abundantly clear who the dragon is. It is Satan. In this first heavenly vision we note first of all his knowledge and power. He is pictured with seven heads,[27] and each of these has a crown[28] on them (evil royalty). He also has ten horns indicative of his power. This power is further seen in verse four, where his tail sweeps one third (not all) of the stars out of the sky and flings them to earth. Typical for apocalyptic literature, we are not told when this was done. Was this before or after the battle with Michael described in verses 7-9? Time is not the point here. The point is power. He is vicious and angry and postures himself to eat the male child to whom the woman has given birth.

It is impossible to unread a text. A good Jewish reader would have thought of several conflicts with birth stories (Gen 21:8-21; 25:19-34; Judg 13:1-25; 1Sam 1:1-28). This is why many people think of Matthew 2:1-12 when they read this passage. The subplot of the visit of the Magi to Jesus is Herod the Great attempting to kill the young "child" Jesus. While Herod the

Great practically personifies evil, he is not the dragon of Revelation 12. He is small potatoes compared to the dragon. The point John may be trying to get his readers to know is that the unseen enemy attempted to do in the promise of God, and he will do what he can to disrupt their faith too (Rev 17; Jn 15:18-25).

The Promise Preserved: God's Care (5-6)

But as much at risk as the promise of God through the Messiah might be, God is at work in John's vision to show his preservation of the promise. This is the message of verses 5-6. The glorious woman gives birth to a male child. The power of the male child is mentioned as well as the provision for him and his mother. This male child is no small boy. The rest of the book of Revelation will give more attention to his magnificence. Here it is enough to mention his rule. He will rule the nations (not just Israel) with an "iron scepter." This image denotes royal power. But how that royal power is displayed is unique. He does it through "shepherding." The way of the male child in the world is love. His rule is love. This has huge ramifications. Jesus then, in Revelation, is not only the shepherd but also the lamb. What a strange way to save the world — i.e., through a child. What a strange way to conquer that world — i.e., through a lamb and the love of a shepherd. This underlines one of the major themes in the Bible, namely power through perceived weakness (2Cor 13:4; 1Tim 3:16).

God took care of the child and the woman. The child was snatched[29] up and taken to God's throne. This is the chief metaphor for the place of God's reign. While there would be nothing to keep it from being literal, it might be similar to the term "heaven," as the place of God's reign.[30] The woman flees into the desert and is provided for by God for a period of three and one half years.[31] The chapter begins with the glorious description of the woman, and it ends with the wonderful provision for the woman.

For the suffering saints in the seven churches, these six verses contain good news. Heaven acknowledges that the ugly enemy is vicious and hungry. He is knowledgeable, big, and powerful. But he can't do in the promise of God to save the world. God will preserve the promise of salvation by protecting the vulnerability of a woman and the innocence of a child. And, God will not only thwart the desires of the dragon, he will also defeat him in heaven, as the next section shows.

Heaven's Battle: The Promise Proclaimed (7-13)

This section begins with a battle and ends with a song — but the song is strange. It announces victory but also announces challenge. Verses 7-9 tell of the battle. Verses 10-13 give the lyrics to the song.[32] In the previous vision two signs appeared in heaven, a pregnant woman and a red dragon. In this vision there is a war[33] in heaven. In fact, literally it says a war "happened." In many ways 12:7-12 expands what we are told in 12:4-5.

The War (7-9)

To people in the West who are time conscious more than people in the Middle East who are more event driven, the natural question is, "When did this battle take place?" Was it previous to Genesis 1? Was it after the dragon failed to devour the male child? Was it in conjunction with Jesus' ministry (cf. Lk 10:18-19), particularly his cross and resurrection experience (Jn 12:31; Col 2:15)? Was it something that will yet take place? Sumney reminds readers that the verbs are passive.[34] The timing of the battle isn't the point. It is the telling of the story from a different perspective that John wants his readers to understand. It is part of the ongoing universal tension between God and Satan.[35]

This war was between Michael[36] and the dragon. John tells just enough in verse 7 to intrigue his readers but not enough to answer questions. John hastens to the result of the battle more than the timing and the nature of the battle.

While we would love to know more about Michael, we do not have to wonder about the dragon. As John does in other places,[37] he identifies the image. The dragon is identified in four ways: the ancient serpent (Gen 3:1), the devil (Mt 4:8), Satan (1Thes 2:18), and the one who leads the whole world astray (Jn 8:44; 2Cor

11:3). Here "serpent" (ὄφις) refers to the enemy of the faith (cf. Rev 12:9,14,15; 20:2; 2Cor 11:3).[38] There is much semantic overlap between the next three descriptions. Devil (Διάβολος) means slanderer[39] while Satan (Σατανᾶς) means accuser (an idea fleshed out in verse 10 and Job 1–2). The fourth description is in particip- ial form (the one who is leading the whole "inhabited" world astray). These four descriptions mark out his primary two func- tions, namely deception and accusation.

But the knowledge and power of the enemy was no match for heaven. The dragon was hurled[40] to the earth along with his demonic angels. This is cause for song. It may not seem so at first but to love the things that God loves means that one must hate the things that God hates. God hates wrongheaded identi- ty and deception. This would be a help to potentially seduced saints. They might be tempted to cave in morally, or believe wrong things about themselves, or shift their foundations. They do not need to do any of those things because heaven has won against their enemy.

The Song (10-12)

The loud voice[41] in heaven celebrates three attributes of God (salvation, power, and kingdom), and one attribute of Christ (authority). These attributes greatly overlap in their semantic domain. God rescues people through his supernatural power and establishes the social reality of his government on earth. He chooses to do that through the ἐξουσία[42] of his Son (Jn 5:22- 23). The main reason that heaven shouts is that Satan has been thrown down. His ministry of bringing "legal accusations" against the brothers[43] is over. Again, the time of that event is not as important as the event itself.

It would be tempting to take verse 11 to refer to Christians at all times, but in light of verse 12 indicating a time of praise in heaven, it is best to understand verse 11 as referring to mar- tyred saints. Heaven sings about faithfulness. Heaven sings about victory[44] by the people of God. The Christians overcame by two means: the blood of Jesus on the cross and the word (λό- γον) of their testimony. These could be viewed as the objective reality of the cross in human history and the subjective witness of the soul in the lives of the believers. It is the metanarrative of the gospel story and the petite narrative of the embrace of that gospel story. The last phrase of verse 11 is one of the most beautiful in Revelation that highlights the great faithfulness of the martyred saints. They didn't love their lives so as to shrink from death (literally, until death). They understood Matthew 16:24; Mark 10:45; and Acts 20:24. They understood living for something bigger than themselves. They were on an adventure of priorities.

Verse 12 calls the heavens (and those in her, namely the martyred saints) to rejoice one more time, but it sounds an ominous note[45] for the earth and sea.[46] The devil has come down to them. His "thermometer" (θυμὸν) is off the charts because he knows his specific time is very short. While John is not interested in giving any temporal details to the rest of this vision, he does for the devil. The enemy is on a finite eschatological collision course with the Creator. While defeated and already sentenced he will make as much trouble for the saints as possible as he marches off to the lake of fire.

The Dragon, the Woman, and the Offspring: The Promise in Struggle (13-17)

A vision from heaven can sustain saints in any trouble on earth. It's a good thing too. The enemy does not go to his lake of fire without yelling, kicking, and screaming all the way out of the courtroom. He will make life miserable for everyone who believes in the promise of salvation as long as possible.

The Dragon: His Pursuit and Attack (13,15,17)

The verses in this section alternate. Verses 13, 15, and 17 are about the attacks of the evil one. Verses 14 and 16 are about God's provision for the woman and her offspring. The dragon pursues[47] (13) the woman, he tries to drown the woman (15 and 16), and he makes war[48] against the offspring of the woman (17). How does this happen? Where does it show up? The text does not say specifically. It is hard to not read physical persecution into this symbolism. It might also include natural disasters. Creation is not totally redeemed (Rom 8:18-21), and the dragon is still the prince of this world (Jn 12:31; Eph 2:2). At times God allows the dragon to unleash his power through the natural processes of a fallen creation. In Jesus' day there was some belief about the watery depths being demonic. There is some OT in the backdrop here.[49] Both Moses and Israel knew something about "water world." Moses was to be drowned (Exod 1:22), and Israel had to be pass through the sea (1Cor 10:1). Both ran the risk of being destroyed. But by the power of God those situations became means of redemption. This would be great comfort to those who obey God's commands and hold to the gospel (17).

The Woman: Her Provision and Safety (14,16)

God was more than equal to counter the dragon's every move. When the dragon chased the woman, God gave the woman eagle's wings. Once again the OT backdrop is important.[50] Sometimes God cares for his promise/people by removing them from the danger. However, this does not happen all the time (Rev 2:13). Christ followers are not immune from trial. But sometimes God takes the danger away.[51] The woman is empowered to fly to the safe haven of the desert.[52] There she is taken care of for a limited, short duration of time.[53]

Sometimes God helps his people (and protects his promise) by enabling creation to come to the rescue. Here he doesn't take the danger away but enables his people to go through the danger and learn lessons of providence and gratitude. When the dragon spewed water (a river) at the woman, the earth[54] came to the woman's rescue and swallowed the river. The physical universe is at the command of God, as the miracles of Jesus show (e.g., Mk 4:35-41). The idea of God using the physical universe to do his bidding also has strong precedent in Scripture (Exodus 14-15; Numbers 16; Deut 11:1-7; Ps 106:17).

Conclusion

The male child has reinaugurated the reign of God (Genesis 1-2). The dragon has been defeated by God's angel, Michael. The dragon has been unable to thwart the promise of God and has only one place to wreak his havoc, the earth, where those who obey God and hold to the testimony of Jesus live (17). The dragon has been unsuccessful in attacking God's promise and promised one. So now he turns his attacks on the church through the instruments of government and false religion (chapter 13). John must tell his people the truth that the battle still rages, but they will see, in short order, that dragon will be destroyed forever (Rev 20:7-10). Without specifically mentioning the cross or empty tomb Revelation 12 is the apocalyptic fulfillment of Genesis 3:15.

Bob Lowery was correct in putting the dragon in the manger scene. He had accurately read Revelation 12. But Marilyn Lowery was also right to remove it. She had read accurately Revelation 20.

SIMPLIFYING THE NUMBER OF THE BEAST (REV 13:18): AN INTERPRETATION OF 666 AND 616

Shane J. Wood

Introduction

When Revelation 13:18 was originally penned by the Seer on Patmos, I doubt that he envisioned such wide ranging pandemonium over his numerical suggestion: 666. In this verse, John calls his readers to wisdom and insight in their interaction with the beast from the sea (13:1-10) that is heralded by the beast from the land (13:11-17) and their joint system of perpetuating the agenda of the Dragon, or Satan (12:3-9; 13-13:1). In this chapter of vivid descriptions of deceit, persecution, and calls to faithfulness, John concludes his cautionary tale by stating, καὶ ὁ ἀριθμὸς αὐτοῦ ἑξακόσιοι ἑξήκοντα ἓξ or "And its number is 666."[1]

Over the years, this number of tripartite sixes has both baffled and invigorated interpreters providing a multitude of elucidations. Some have suggested that the number points to a future computer chip placed in the foreheads and hands of the beasts' followers;[2] others have offered various words that add up to 666 — both meaningless words[3] and actual words,[4] and still others have used the number as an *ad hominem* — to slander the name of their earthly opponent.[5] Incredibly, these examples do not exhaust the usages for this enigmatic number — for some have suggested spiritual interpretations,[6] chronological interpretations,[7] "Roman Emperor" interpretations,[8] and still some have simply suggested that we abandon all hope of finding an interpretation at all.[9] More recent scholarship, however, seems to unite under the identity of the Emperor Nero as the key to unlock the number of the beast.[10]

Did John intend for this much confusion? Was the Seer on Patmos challenging his fledgling communities in Asia Minor to a battle of wits regarding cryptic mathematical computation? Was 666 supposed to be lost in the imagination of the prophet on Patmos — or is there a tenable explanation of all the evidence for this strange, unique symbol found in Rev 13:18? While at times the frustration of this cipher can elicit the desire to desert pursuit, I believe that John intended for his elusive number to be quite evident to his readers. Rather than playing mathematical games with his audience, he was actually presenting an easily discernible definition of 666.

In order to tender this "simple" option for 666, the argument in this chapter will progress as follows. Following a brief look at the use of "gematria" in the ancient world, the more commonly accepted solution by modern scholars for 666 (i.e., "Caesar Nero") will be examined. First, the "Caesar Nero" position will be explained — showing, in fact, that the moniker for this tyrant ruler does add up to both 666 and 616.[11] Second, a critique of the "Caesar Nero" position will show its inadequacy as a viable interpretation for the number of the beast. Finally, an alternative option will be presented that provides a simple solution for the 666 cipher and a lucid explanation for the emergence of the 616 textual variant tradition.

Cryptic Numbers in the Ancient World:
The Practice of Gematria

In the first-century-C.E. world, there was a widespread practice known as *gematria* in which names of people were reduced to a numerical value for a variety of purposes.[12] Adolf Deissman offers an example of such a practice from graffiti found by archaeologists on walls of the Roman city of Pompeii preserved by the volcanic ash that froze the city in time at the eruption of Mt. Vesuvius in 79 C.E. One "wall-scribbling" reads: "I love her whose number is 545" (φιλῶ ἦς ἀριθμὸς φμέ,).[13] This practice is found in Jewish contexts as well.

Genesis 14:14 comes in the midst of the record of the kidnapping of Lot (Abram's nephew) as a spoil of war against Sodom, where Lot resided. Verse 14 states that Abram, in an effort to rescue his nephew, calls upon men of his household numbering 318. In the Babylonian Talmud, Jewish commentary on this text explains the events in this manner:

> And he armed his trained servants born in his own house. Rab said, he equipped them by [teaching them] the Torah. Samuel said, he made them bright with gold. *Three hundred and eighteen*: R. Ammi b. Abba said: Eliezer outweighed them all. Others say, It [*sic*] was Eliezer, for this is the numerical value of his name.[14]

The name Eliezer (אליעזר), one of Abram's servants (cf. Gen 15:2), is suggested as the leader of Abram's household army as is communicated through the number 318, because, utilizing gematria, this is the number of Eliezar's name.[15]

Similarly, the Epistle of Barnabas, a Christian document from late-1st c. C.E. to the mid-2nd c. C.E.,[16] used gematria in regards to 318 in Genesis 14:14 (combining it with the circumcision of Abram's household in Gen 17:23) to point to Jesus and his redeeming cross in 9.7b-8:

> Abraham, who first instituted circumcision, looked forward in the spirit to Jesus when he circumcised, having received the teaching of the three letters. For it says: "And Abraham circumcised ten and eight and three hundred men of his household." What, then, is the knowledge that was given to him? Observe that it mentions the "ten and eight" first, and then after an interval the "three hundred." As for the "ten and eight," the I is ten and the H is eight; thus you have "Jesus." And because the cross, which is shaped like the T, was destined to convey grace, it mentions also the "three hundred." So he reveals Jesus in the two letters, and the cross in the other one.

Utilizing gematria, this author uses the numbers for 318 (ιητ in Greek) in order to point to Jesus from the OT account. The Greek name for Jesus is Ἰησοῦς (*ēāsoos*). Numerically, the first two letters of his name, as mentioned by the author, add up to 18 (10 and 8). From Genesis 14:14, the author points out that the remaining 300 is symbolized with the Greek letter τ, which is interpreted visually as resembling the cross.[17] Therefore, through gematria, the author shows that Abraham's covenant of circumcision pointed to Jesus and his method of redemption—the cross.

While many other examples of gematria could be explored,[18] these examples show that whether we are referring to a Roman, Jewish, or Christian audience, the use of numbers to refer to names and messages were prevalent before, during, and after John's use of 666 in the book of Revelation. With this in place, it should not surprise us when interpretations abound regarding the identity of the referent to the number of the beast, and most recently, scholars seem convinced the answer is found in the moniker "Caesar Nero."

"Caesar Nero": A Solution to 666 and 616

To explain, scholars take the Greek form of "Caesar Nero" and transliterate it into Hebrew[19] to get: *Qsr Neron* (קסר נרון).[20] When the numerical equivalents of these Hebrew letters are added together, the sum total is 666. At this point, this option does not appear much different than any of the other options seen above, but a textual variant for 666 in Revelation 13:18 bolsters the case for "Caesar Nero" as a more viable solution.

The number 666 is found in the earliest and most reliable manuscripts.[21] However, two other numbers emerge in the manuscript corpus: 665[22] and 616.[23] While the 665 derivation has been sufficiently dismissed through scribal error,[24] the 616 tradition is more difficult to handle for a couple of reasons. First, the evidence for the early emergence of this tradition is quite strong. In addition to the late 3rd c. C.E.–early 4th c. C.E. document known as p115 that displays 616,[25] Irenaeus, in his book *Against Heresies*, attests to the existence of this 616 tradition at the time of his writing around 180 C.E. After describing 666, Irenaeus writes:

> I do not know how it is that some have erred following the ordinary mode of speech, and have vitiated the middle number in the name, deducting the amount of fifty from it, so that instead of six decads they will have it that there is but one . . . Others then received this reading without examination; some in their simplicity, and upon their own responsibility, making use of the number expressing one decad. . . .[26]

Based on this description, Irenaeus claims that the number 616, although he thinks it is erroneous and spurious, has a strong tradition even at the time of his writing — which puts the tradition of 616 within about 80 years of Revelation's composition in 95–96 C.E. The manuscript evidence and the early attestation leads one scholar to conclude, "The reading 616 at 13,18 is, then, ancient and widespread."[27]

Taking this a step further, 616 becomes hard to explain based on textual critical rules. Specifically, a textual critical principle is to favor more difficult renderings of a textual tradition if it cannot be explained by paleographic errors and shares a similar time frame to the other options. The thought process behind this principle is that it is more likely that difficult texts will be simplified or smoothed out as time goes on rather than simple texts being made more difficult by later scribes. As a result, some have suggested that 616, being the more difficult rendering of the number in comparison to the smooth and logical 666, is actually the original number, since the tradition can be traced back to within a few decades of the original writing of Revelation.[28]

This assertion is bolstered due to the fact that a change from 666 ($\chi\xi\varsigma$) to 616 ($\chi\iota\varsigma$) and vice versa is not easily explained by scribal errors. While Irenaeus himself offers an explanation of possible scribal error,[29] scholars agree that his explanation and the attempts of others is lacking in parallel instances and logical deduction for such an error.[30] In other words, the shift from 666 ($\chi\xi\varsigma$) to 616 ($\chi\iota\varsigma$) or vice versa does not seem to be *accidental* but *intentional*.

So, what does all of this mean? Any option for 666 that cannot adequately explain the 616 variant as well should not be considered a viable option, because the tradition of 616 is, at worst, an early, widespread rendering of the number of the beast that appears to be an intentional variant. Therefore, it cannot be discarded with ease. The "Caesar Neron" option accounts for both numbers — 666 (as seen above) and 616.

If you take the Latin form of "Caesar Neron," it is rendered "Caesar Nero." As done previously, if this moniker is transliterated into Hebrew (קסר נרו), the numerical value of the letters equals 616.[31] So, "Caesar Nero" can explain both 666 and 616.

"Caesar Nero": A Critique of the Popular Option for 666 and 616

Nevertheless, the "Caesar Nero" option is inadequate for six reasons. First, there are *no* early church interpretations in any early church documents of "Caesar Nero" or even just "Nero" as an option for 666. In fact, David Brady suggests the emergence of this option "appears originally to have been suggested independently by four German scholars, each claiming priority."[32] These four scholars wrote from 1831–1837, making the development of this option quite late.[33]

Second, while there is early testimony of Nero being used as the cipher of 616, the methodology for Nero as 616 is drastically different than what is implemented today. In approximately 438 C.E., a document known as the *Liber Genealogus* suggests that the key to John's cryptic number, which is seen as 616 in this document, is to first add up the numerical value of the letters in the Latin word for "Antichrist," which equals 154. Next, the document suggests that the number should then be multiplied by four since Nero has four letters in his name.[34] The number acquired is 616. Even though it is accurate to say, then, that Nero was referred to as a solution for the 616 number of the beast at a somewhat early date (5th c. C.E.), the methodology which is implemented by the modern Nero option is drastically different.[35]

Third, while the "Caesar Nero" option offers an interpretation for 616, it does not explain why 616 (a more difficult reading) would occur later than 666 (a less difficult option). All it offers is another option, among many, that finds another name that through creative manipulation finds its way to the target number. There is no suggestion as to why a "Latin-name-for-Nero" interpretation (which equals 616) would arise so early in contrast to a "Greek-name-for-Nero" interpretation (which equals 666). Putting forth another interpretative possibility for 616 does not show why 616 would exist as a variant to begin with.

Fourth, why would John refer to "Nero" with the title "Caesar" — equivalent to the terms "emperor" or "king"? "Caesar" is not just a title of designation, but rather, it is a title that connotes power, honor, and dominion. After the first twelve chapters of Revelation in which John consistently pictures Yahweh and Jesus as the ruling agents over the world[36] and what happens in it (good or bad)[37] and even referring to them with regal language,[38] why would he now offer a comparable title for Nero?

Fifth, playing off of the previous point, why would John use this honorific title *in a cipher*? If he is offering a cryptic description of Nero that was not easily discernible, he could have called Nero anything that he wanted. So, why did he call him "King Nero" instead of "Infidel Nero," "Donkey Nero," or some other pejorative label? To find the honorific "Caesar Nero" in the number 666 or 616 would be counterproductive for the overall trajectory of the book thus far — not to mention the material that follows.

Sixth, identifying the number 666 and/or 616 with a Roman Emperor is assuming that the beast(s) is a symbol of the evils of the Roman Empire alone. Yet, the symbol is bigger than Rome; it is a symbol of systematic evil. The two beasts in Revelation 13 complete the unholy Trinity that has the red dragon of Revelation 12 at the helm of their evil operations. The workings of this tripartite evil manifests itself in various governments at various times, including Rome, but the image of Rome in Revelation, Babylon, does not emerge until Revelation 14:8. Following this line of thinking, when Babylon is pictured as a harlot (Rev 17:1-5), she is riding a beast (17:3), and yet she is defined as "the great city that rules over the kings of the earth" (17:18) after she is devoured by the very beast she was riding. Furthermore, after the destruction of Babylon in Revelation 18 (i.e., the picture of the destruction of Rome), the two beasts are still yet to be judged — this occurs in Revelation 19:11-21. What does all of this mean? Babylon/Rome is not a synonym for the beasts of Revelation 13. Instead, though Babylon is a puppet of the beast, it is not the beast itself — like the church is the body of Christ but the church is not Christ.[39] Therefore, to suggest that the "number of the beast" is equal to the name of an emperor is to reduce the symbol of the beast to just one of its many puppets.

In sum, while "Caesar Nero" does surface as a viable option in that it offers an explanation for both 666 and 616, it does not satisfy the evidence as John's likely aim for the number of the beast.

The Number of the Beast:
Simplifying the Solution to 666 and 616

The above conclusion begs the question: so what other options do we have that satisfy the evidence for this elusive number? The answer: I have only discovered one, and it drips with simplicity.[40]

Context: Revelation 13:17 and 15:2

First, an important clue is given in Revelation 13:17 and 15:2. Both verses contain the same phrase that sheds light on John's likely interpretation of the number of the beast: "the number of its name."[41] Revelation 13:16-17 describes the forced reception of the "mark" and then adds this clarifying statement about the "mark": "which is the name of the beast or the number of its name" (τὸ ὄνομα τοῦ θηρίου ἢ τὸν ἀριθμὸν τοῦ ὀνόματος αὐτοῦ). Similarly, in Revelation 15:2, John describes God's faithful witnesses standing by the sea (whence the first beast came) and holding harps. In this picture he describes them as being victorious over "the beast and its image and the number of its name" (ἐκ τοῦ θηρίου καὶ ἐκ τῆς εἰκόνος αὐτοῦ καὶ ἐκ τοῦ ἀριθμοῦ τοῦ ὀνοματος αὐτοῦ). Taken simply, these passages seem to suggest that the number of the beast is equivalent to the name of the (neuter) beast.[42]

So what "name" would fit the "neuter" requirements (neither male nor female) and also equal the number 666? The answer is simple: "beast." If the Greek word for "beast" — θηρίον (thārēon) — is transliterated into Hebrew — תריון (thārēon) — and added up using the numerical value of each Hebrew letter (i.e., gematria), the total is 666.[43] This means, then, that Revelation 13:17 and 15:2 were simply saying that the name of the beast, which is "beast," equals the number of the beast, which is 666.

Context: Revelation 14:1

This understanding of 666 fits well with the following context of Revelation 14:1, in which John looks upon the 144,000 from Revelation 7 who are now congregated on Mount Zion. The text says that the 144,000 have the name of the lamb and "his Father's name written on their foreheads." In order to demarcate who it is that the 144,000 worship and to whom they belong, they are marked on the forehead with the names of those whom they follow — the lamb and God.[44] In this context, then, the number of the beast is a distinguishing mark of the name "beast" to be put on those who choose to worship the beast (Rev 13:17-18), which contrasts the distinguishing mark of the names "lamb" and "God" to be put on those who choose to worship the Trinity (Rev 14:1). Therefore, 666, in context, is simply a cipher for "beast."

"Beast" and 616

Although the "beast" option for 666 seems to make sense in its surrounding context and certainly begins to simplify the meaning of the cipher, what can be said for the early and more difficult reading of 616 in the "beast" option? Before answering this question, it is important for us to establish that offering another possibility for a 616 interpretation does not help solve the problem of why the 616 tradition began in the first place. So the following answer will not just attempt to add up letters to equal 616, but it will also offer an explanation for the emergence of the 616 tradition as a whole.

If the 616 tradition was developed later than the 666 tradition, then there must be a compelling reason for a scribe to alter the smooth, easy reading of the symmetrical 666 number — especially in light of the fact that a "scribal error" does not seem to satisfy such a widespread and drastic alteration. I suggest that the 616 tradition originates as an effort from scribes to clarify John's intended meaning for the number 666 — "beast" (θηρίον).

In Revelation 13:18, the last time the word "beast" occurs before the verse concludes with the mention of 666, "beast" is in the Greek genitive form. In other words, the word "beast" (θηρίον) is actually written in the text with a different ending — θηρίου (*thārēoo*) instead of θηρίον (*thārēon*). This change in the ending allows the phrase to be interpreted "the number **of the beast**." Why is this significant? Because if you take the Greek word for "beast" with the genitive ending (θηρίου), transliterate it into Hebrew—תריו (*thāréoo*)—and add up the numerical value of the letters,[45] the total is 616.

Conclusion

So what is being suggested? The number 666, or the number of its [the beast's] name (Rev 13:17 and 15:2), should be interpreted as a cipher for "beast" due to the fact that the Greek word for beast, θηρίον (*thāréon*), adds up to 666 when it is transliterated into Hebrew (i.e., gematria). Even though it was likely that the audience would see 666 as the name of the beast contrasting the name of the lamb and God on the foreheads of their followers (Rev 14:1), some scribes may have encountered or foreseen early misinterpretations of 666. As a result, the 616 tradition developed shortly after the original writing of Revelation in 95–96 C.E. to point to the closest referent of the name "beast" in the text—the Genitive θηρίου (*thāréoo*), which adds up to 616 when it is transliterated into Hebrew. The mark of the beast, then, is not likely the name of a particular emperor, and even less likely a computer chip inserted into the foreheads of unknowing recipients. Rather, 666 and/or 616 is a cryptic way of referring to the name of the beast—otherwise simply known as "beast" (θηρίον).

THE BEAST AND THE PROSTITUTE IN REVELATION 17

Brian Lowery

A Subtle-Yet-Important Presence

The more I have studied Revelation 17, the more I have become convinced that the most important thing I must do as a student of this chapter is to look beyond the two characters I first lay eyes on to see the character resting just behind them. This ultimately is not the story of the beast, nor the story of the prostitute. It's the ongoing story of Satan, the age-old foe of the kingdom of God who was first seen as a serpent and now in Revelation as a dragon. Though he is not named and utters not a single word, he is peeking out from behind the curtain of images. This is no mere assertion I'm making, because two important chapters—Revelation 12 and 13—prove as much. They show the extent of the intimate relationship between the dragon and the beast (and thus the prostitute, who rides atop the beast in almost inseparable fashion).

In Revelation 12, a dragon appears and wages war in heaven against God and his kingdom. He is identified by John as "that ancient serpent called the Devil, or Satan, who leads the whole world astray" (12:9). Over the course of the battle, the dragon is hurled to the earth where he is left "enraged . . . off to make war against . . . those who obey God's commandments and hold to the testimony of Jesus" (12:17). At the start of chapter 13, we find him standing "on the shore of the sea," waiting, plotting his next move. Soon a beast emerges from the sea—a beast that has "ten horns and seven heads, with ten crowns on his horns, and on each head a blasphemous name"—and the dragon gives this beast "his power and his throne and great authority."

In Revelation 17, the same beast emerges once again. Its description in verse 7 is virtually a word-for-word match of the description offered in chapter 13, which means we're dealing with the same beast in both accounts—which means a dragon is lurking about in the shadows, always serving as the beast's sending agent, its enabler, the one who empowers. In other words, a working understanding of Revelation 12 and 13 tells us that the dragon does not have to be present in the sense of concrete imagery to be present in Revelation 17.

But then in some ways the dragon *is* present in concrete imagery. The Devil is in the details, if one is paying attention. Consider the color of both the beast and the garments of the prostitute: scarlet (17:3,4). This is significant not only because in Revelation scarlet and other forms of red denote evil and general opposition to God,[1] but also because this color seems to indicate an intimacy in identity between the dragon and the beast and the prostitute. The color match creates a scene in which one never really knows where the dragon begins and ends.

Consider also the source of the beast (17:8). He emerges from the "Abyss" (17:8), which in ancient times referred to the abode of the dead and the realm of the disobedient. Like its color, the beast's address also places him in close quarters with Satan, whose own source and destination is the Abyss (20:1-3). Again, where does the dragon begin and end?

Though the dragon is distinct from the beast and the prostitute, we mustn't embrace too much of a distinction. To do so would be to miss the fact that the dragon is really the chief antagonist of Revelation 17. In fact my contention from here on will be that the beast is really nothing more than a political servant of the dragon, while the prostitute is nothing more than its cultural servant, seductively wooing nations into the dragon's clutches. Because I hold this to be true, I have found that the interpretation of Revelation 17 is much more expansive than it is sometimes allowed to be, because it shows the dragon's willingness throughout history to embrace and just as quickly abandon multiple kingdom and cultural servants for his purposes.

The Dragon's Kingdom Servant

While the first character we encounter in Revelation 17 is that of the prostitute, attention will first be given to the beast on which she rides. There are two reasons why. First, when offering an interpretation of all the images that comprise the scene — beginning in 17:7 — the angel is initially concerned with the beast. If understanding the beast's identity and its many heads and horns seems paramount to the angel, it's probably best to begin there. But secondly — and more importantly — we will see that a proper understanding of the beast and its related imagery is the only way to understand the prostitute and her related imagery.

The beast and its heads and horns must be viewed through the lens of Daniel 7, the OT text from which the imagery of Revelation 17 is "borrowed." In Daniel 7, Daniel encounters four beasts — the fourth is a ghastly creature with ten horns — which represent "four kingdoms that will rise from earth" and wage war against God and his saints. When John's audience read similar imagery in Revelation 13 and later in 17, they would have caught the allusion to Daniel's vision, immediately recognizing that, like the beasts that populate Daniel 7, John's beast is representative of an evil kingdom that is setting itself up against God's kingdom.[2]

But what can be known about the beast's seven heads?[3] While we must once again turn to Daniel 7 for assistance, we are also aided by the angel's interpretation. The angel interprets the seven heads as both "seven hills" and "seven rulers"[4] (17:9-10). Pushing past the issue of the "seven hills" for a moment, the angel's interpretation helps us see that the seven heads represent seven political figureheads. This isn't a terribly surprising interpretation, given that in the Greek world, the head denotes that which is first or supreme — the "uppermost and most prominent feature of the human body [and] the very center of life" — thus making it the perfect symbol for a kingly figure.[5] Concerning why there are *seven* heads, as is the case elsewhere in Revelation and Jewish literature as a whole, the number seven is used to convey a sense of completeness. These seven rulers effectively represent in full all of the evil that will be present in the complete lifetime of this sinister beast (kingdom).[6]

Generally speaking, then, the beast is an antichristian kingdom, and its seven heads represent seven antichristian rulers. But does the text allow us to move past these generalities and talk specifics? Who exactly is the kingdom the beast represents and, in turn, who exactly are the seven rulers the seven heads represent?

We begin with the beast. Is it an allusion to Rome? When one considers both text and historical context, there is little doubt that the great empire is present in this symbol. While this might be proven true through some of the details of the scene—for example, some historical accounts say Rome began as a small settlement upon seven hills that rose from the banks of the Tiber River, leading more than a few commentators to suggest that the "seven hills" on which the woman sits is a reference to the geographical setting of Rome[7]—John's readers still would have identified the beast as Rome, if only because of the bigger picture set before them and the reality of their life situation. John's readers did not need a reference to seven hills in order to spot Rome because of Revelation 17's clear allusions to Daniel 7. As already noted, Daniel's beasts represented evil kingdoms populated by evil leaders who engaged in widespread persecution of God's people. Years after Daniel's dream, the Roman government fits that description. At the time of John's revelation, Christians were already feeling the early pangs of widespread persecution. While it was felt most in the social sector—believers were already being branded as atheists (because they did not engage in the Roman imperial cults), cannibals (because they spoke of eating "flesh" and "blood"), and even incestuous (because they called one another brother and sister and showed deep love for one another)[8]—political acts of imprisonment, exile, and even death had been taking place since the earliest days of the early church. So, the question is not so much "Is the beast Rome?" as it is "How could the beast *not* be Rome?"

If the beast is Rome, this means, then, that the seven heads are best interpreted as seven Roman rulers. But as for going one step further to try to identify who they might be, ultimately it's best not to play guessing games. While it's possible that John's readers would have been able to pore over recent history to figure out who's who as a Christian threat or even to determine a rough timeline as to when Rome's terrible reign would end, it's a fruitless agenda on our end. The big picture should suffice. John's use of the number seven proves as much. The fact that there are seven heads/rulers is simply to show that the rule and reign of these rulers will be lengthy, significant, *complete* (a beginning, a middle, and an end). As the angel points out, in this kingdom's complete lifetime, evil emperors have come and gone (the five who have fallen),[9] one currently rules (the sixth),[10] and there is yet another to come (the seventh).[10] The theological thrust behind the seven heads/rulers is to show the completeness of the range of evil influence given the rulers of the Roman Empire as a whole, and that the centre of that evil influence cannot hold, eventually meeting its demise.[11]

Armed with these conclusions, let's return to the issue of the beast — and also to my contention that Revelation 17 allows for a more expansive interpretation than it is usually given. Is the beast an allusion to Rome? Yes. But while it's correct to think the beast is Rome, it would be a mistake to think the beast can only ever be Rome. The beast represents both Rome and *any* kingdom that sets itself against the kingdom of God. There are two reasons one can reach this interpretive conclusion.

First, when determining the identity of the beast, the title given the prostitute — which by close association is loosely attached to the beast upon which she rides — is of great importance: Babylon. A short article in *The Dictionary of Biblical Imagery* sums up Babylon well. Throughout the OT and stretching on into the New, Babylon is "one of the dread images of the Bible" — the "mightiest of cities," the "famous counterpart to Nineveh," "Israel's captor, tormentor, devastator, and the location of her exile."[12] Because Babylon was an unparalleled antagonist in Israel's history, it became *the* example of an earthly kingdom that sets itself against the kingdom of God. When believers found themselves under the oppressive rule and persecution of Rome, they would have drawn comparisons to Babylon of old — so much so that the two could just as well share the same name. While Rome is not Babylon in a literal sense, they are one in the same in spirit.[13] This elevation of the spirit of Babylon, then, makes this text applicable not just for John's original audience, but an extended audience that even includes us. Its meaning and application can be transferred throughout time—effectively speaking into whatever time period the reader finds himself. These images can speak of any kingdom that bears the spirit of Babylon (i.e. any kingdom that sets itself against God).

Second, a more expansive view for interpreting the beast not only as Rome but *any* kingdom that sets itself against God is supported by another important characteristic of the beast that we have ignored up this point: the ten horns atop the seven heads (17:3,12-14).

The angel identifies these horns as "ten rulers" (17:12). Horns were symbolic of power or elevated status in social and political contexts, most often denoting political figureheads.[14] Because the angel says these ten horns "will receive authority as kings along with the beast," it is tempting to think these ten rulers are ten more Roman rulers to go with the seven rulers represented by the seven heads.[15] However, the fuller interpretation of the angel should not be lost in a rush to Rome. These ten horns are ten kings "who have not yet received a kingdom, but who for one hour will receive authority as rulers along with the beast." While these rulers are related to Rome, they are also set apart as distinct. They will move and have their being in the same spirit as Rome and Babylon, but they will be of a different empire (or empires) altogether that has yet to enter history's stage. Isbon T. Beckwith refers to the ten as "eschatological figures representing the totality of powers of all nations on earth"—of all the powers to come who will act in concert with Rome and Babylon of old.[16] In other words, after the seven Roman rulers have come and gone—along with Rome itself—there will still be ten rulers "waiting in the wings" to rear their ugly heads, all producing havoc for the saints of God's kingdom, all in the same spirit of Rome's kingdom.

This interpretation of the ten horns fits well within our interpretive lens of Daniel 7. In Daniel's vision the fourth beast possesses ten horns (7:7). Daniel is told that the ten horns are ten rulers who represent the fourth beast/kingdom that stands before him (Dan 7:24). However, Daniel soon encounters another horn — a boastful little fellow who eventually uproots three of the first horns of the beast. When Daniel seeks help in interpreting the message of the horns, he is told: "The ten horns are ten rulers who will come from this kingdom. After them another king will arise, different from the earlier ones; he will subdue three rulers. He will speak against the Most High and oppress his saints and try to change the set times and the laws. The saints will be handed over to him for a time, times and half a time." Like Daniel, the ten horns in Revelation 17 represent those who will (and always will) rise to power and set themselves up against God (17:12-13), if even for a little while (17:12).[17]

All of this brings us back full circle, really, to my contention that began this chapter. The beast should ultimately be seen as merely one more political servant of an evil — a dragon — that has long been roaming the earth. In OT times the servant was Babylon. In New, Rome. Today? That's a difficult discussion that can happen outside the pages of this book — but a discussion made possible by the fact that as long as the dragon is with us, so shall there be a beast (or beasts) as well.

The Prostitute: The Dragon's Cultural Servant

Now our attention turns to what we can know of the other major character in Revelation 17 — the prostitute riding atop the beast. Of the many images John encounters, it is that of the prostitute that most "astonishes" him (17:6). Just who is this woman? The title given her in verse 5 — MYSTERY, BABYLON THE GREAT, THE MOTHER OF PROSTITUTES AND OF THE ABOMINATIONS OF THE EARTH[18] — seems to give us our answer straightway: the prostitute is Babylon. But as we saw with the beast, the answer isn't always quite that easy. A more expansive interpretation comes about when we place the historical use of the image of prostitution alongside Babylon's history, and place our findings within the historical context of Revelation 17.

Prostitution, defined in the most general terms, is offering sexual intimacy for financial gain. But it appears the prostitution present in Revelation 17 is of a deeper kind—one that moves beyond matters of sexuality into the political and religious arenas. This is not the first time the reader encounters this "deeper" prostitution, having been referred to in a handful of critical OT texts.

While prostitution is most often spoken of in literal terms in prohibitive texts scattered throughout the legal literature of the Bible, the image of prostitution is also used in prophetic literature with regard to more spiritual matters. The two most important occurrences for our purposes are found in Isaiah 23:15-17 and Nahum 3:1-4, in which two godless cities—Tyre and Nineveh, respectively—are referred to as prostitutes. Tyre is described as a prostitute that "will ply her trade with all the kingdoms on the face of the earth," while it is said of Nineveh that through "the wanton lust of a harlot" she "enslaved nations by her prostitution and peoples by her witchcraft." These great cities are referred to as prostitutes because as superpowers, they woo other cities (including Jerusalem)— even nations (including Israel)—into intimate political and religious relationships, usually for purposes of economic gain and further superiority. But according to the description given in Revelation 17, along with the narrative arc of the OT as a whole, the whore-ish ways of Tyre and Nineveh pale in comparison to those of Babylon. According to Revelation 17, a survey of history assigns her the title "THE MOTHER OF PROS-TITUTES." Why such a seemingly over-the-top designation? Because as mentioned in the previous section, Babylon was the mightiest of cities, setting her up as a mistress for the ages.

While Babylon's devastating military campaigns throughout the ancient world certainly would have caused many people to consider an intimate allegiance with her, it was the financial security promised in her unsurpassable wealth that allowed her to woo nations like no other in history. Consider the many images of luxury associated with Babylon in Revelation 17. She "sits on many waters" (17:1). History records that Babylon sat upon many canals that found their source in the Euphrates, connecting her to many peoples and nations.[19] This afforded her great influence over the ancient world as *the* source of international trade — which afforded her staggering capital. More proof of Babylon's great wealth is found in the other details concerning her general appearance. In addition to wearing garments of scarlet, she is clothed in purple (17:3). Purple was a very expensive dye in its day, so its presence typically symbolized great wealth and even royalty.[20] Along with such extravagant clothing, the prostitute also adorns herself with numerous stones, gems, and other items of great value (17:4). All of this is punctuated by Babylon's vast economic wealth highlighted (and mourned over) in Revelation 18.

The unmatched economic system of Babylon allowed her to rule over "the rulers of the earth" (17:18), "intoxicating" them with "the wine of her adultery" (17:2).[21] In other words, she was able to use economic seduction to absorb nations and peoples into her evil empire — to get them to "fornicate" with her and her gods and goddesses, who were believed to have blessed her with an empire of luxury. Just as in John's time, Babylon was *the* example of an earthly kingdom that sets itself against the kingdom of God, so also was Babylon *the* example of the seductive power an earthly kingdom's economic-religious system can have over the world.

As this big-picture understanding of the prostitute and related Babylonian imagery emerges, it pushes us to expand our interpretation of Revelation 17 and its images. Borrowing language from my earlier conclusion about the beast, while it is correct to think the prostitute represents the seductive power of Babylon's economic-religious culture, it would be a mistake to think the prostitute can only ever represent Babylon. Since John's audience would have known the history of prostitution and Babylon as symbols, there is no doubt they would have made the appropriate connections to Rome and the allure of its mighty economic-religious culture. More specifically, it's hard to imagine they wouldn't have thought of the idolatrous nature of Roman trade guilds — organizations whose members sought economic prosperity in Roman culture. These members were expected to worship — i.e. "fornicate" with — the Roman gods and goddesses associated with the empire and her commerce, often in the form of a meal, in which members would eat and drink items offered in honor of the deities.[22] The allure of these guilds was great, not only because they were the chief means to good material standing, but because a refusal of membership could result in loss of employment or more general social rejection.[23]

But we mustn't stop with Rome in our interpretation. While it's correct to think the prostitute captures the allure of the great empire's economic-religious culture, it would be a mistake to think the prostitute can only ever be related to Roman culture. She ultimately represents any antichristian economic-religious culture that seeks to woo people away from the kingdom of God and into the clutches not just of the beast, but the dragon itself. It is critical to note that she is the "MOTHER OF PROSTITUTES" and "ALL ABOMINATIONS." While this is meant to show her authoritative side, Beale is right in his conclusion that this "also suggests she relates to harlots in the same way that the beast relates to his heads and horns. She expresses herself throughout the ages in ungodly economic-religious institutions and facets of culture."[24] Like the ten horns before her, she is an eschatological figure that takes many shapes and forms through the ages.

And so at this point, I cannot help but offer thoughts similar to those I offered when concluding the previous section on the beast — that all of this brings us back full circle to my contention. The prostitute should ultimately be seen as merely one more cultural servant of an evil — a dragon — that has long been roaming the earth. In OT times the servant was Babylon. In New, Rome. Today? Yet another difficult discussion that can happen outside the pages of this book — but once again, a discussion made possible by the fact that as long as the dragon is with us, so shall there be a prostitute (or prostitutes) as well.

"Come and See"/"Come Out"

Those who have studied with my father know that one of his working principles in teaching God's Word is to always identify the word of comfort and the word of challenge in a given text. Though space is limited, with all this talk of antichristian kingdoms and cultures, it seems fitting to close with both.

First, the word of comfort, which comes to us in the angel's invitation to John: "Come, I will show you the punishment of the great prostitute." The invitation betrays an underlying indicative—a statement that at some appointed time known only to God, the dragon and his minions through the ages will once for all be surrounded, battled, and defeated primarily by the Lamb of Christ and his saints (17:14), but also by evil's propensity to cannibalize itself in fits of internal jealousy and lust (17:12-18).

But with this comes our word of challenge—a word found within our text in subtle ways, but certainly within the wider context of Revelation 18: "Come out of her, my people." With the fall of the dragon and his servants certain and even imminent, a passionate summons to being set apart—a summons to holiness in the midst of rampant worldliness—rings in the ears of the reader. Revelation 17 and 18 serve as a stern reminder that kingdoms and cultures of evil are no place for a believer.

HISTORIC PREMILLENNIALISM IN THE BOOK OF REVELATION

Craig L. Blomberg

Introduction

The four major competing approaches to biblical eschatology are postmillennialism, amillennialism, historic premillennialism and dispensational premillennialism. The first and last of these have dominated for the shortest periods of time in church history, even if dispensationalism in some Christian circles is best known because it is newest, dating from around 1830, with the ministry of J. Nelson Darby and the rise of the Plymouth Brethren. With progressive dispensationalism today looking more and more like historic premillennialism and postmillennialism appearing increasingly like amillennialism, the main choice largely comes down to whether we accept this age as representing "as good as it gets" for God's people prior to the eternal state or looking forward to a separate millennial kingdom after the return of Christ and Judgment Day.

Critics of a discrete millennium, separate from "the church age," often charge its proponents with depending entirely on one chapter in the Bible—Revelation 20, the only place in which the actual words "a thousand years" appear in the context of a period of time in which believers reign with Christ. Two lines of reply immediately suggest themselves. First, how many places in the Bible does a given teaching have to occur before it is credible? Surely only once! Second, premillennialism is scarcely based just on Revelation 20. All of the OT passages that postmillennialists typically cite in support of the Christianization of the world before the end of *this* age (esp. Num 14:21;

Ps 2:8; 72; Isa 11:6-9; and Zech 9:10), make at least as much if not more sense on premillennialist interpretations. In the NT, Mt 19:28, Acts 1:6, and 1Cor 15:23-24 all seem as well to support a literal millennium after this present era of salvation history.

Historic Premillennialism and Revelation 20

Nevertheless, it remains true that Revelation 20 is the *key* passage that one must study in detail in choosing between amillennialism and premillennialism. Is it a flashback to Christ's first coming or some point thereafter in this present age, or is it heralded by the parousia? Robert Lowery defends a recapitulative view of Revelation, in which 17:1–20:15 is one of a number of sections that "returns to the point from which it began, but higher up, so to speak."[1] Lowery sees chapters 12–20 arranged chiastically, with their climactic center coming with the seven bowls in 15:1–16:21, which represent the "total judgment of creation."[2] Recapitulative views of Revelation usually are employed to bolster an amillennialist approach to the Apocalypse and are often combined with an interpretation that sees 20:1 as introducing a flashback to Christ's first coming.[3] Lowery does not indicate whether he wishes to move in either of these directions, but his overall sensitivity to Revelation as literature and his concern for its proper interpretation invite further attention to these questions.

The Preceding Context—Revelation 19:11-21
and the Second Coming of Christ

Revelation 19:12-21, by almost all accounts, depicts Christ's return at the end of this age. Verses 19-21 reintroduce two-thirds of the so-called satanic trinity, first described in detail in Revelation 12–13. This diabolical trio is depicted as a dragon — Satan — who acts as a parody of God; the Antichrist, also called the first beast or the beast from the sea; and the second beast, from the land, also known as the false prophet. The first beast, sometimes called just "the beast," provides a parody of Christ, God the Son, while the false prophet is a macabre imitation of God the Holy Spirit.[4]

When we read that "the beast and the kings of the earth and

their armies" are "gathered together to make war against" Christ "and his army" (Rev 19:19), we naturally wonder what the false prophet and the dragon are doing. The very next verse refers to the false prophet, as both the beast and he are captured (v. 20a). We learn that "the two of them were thrown alive into the fiery lake of burning sulfur" (v. 20b) and that the rest of those prepared to make war against the Lord were killed with the sword (v. 21). But what about Satan, the dragon? Our curiosity remains piqued to see if anything will be said about him. All we have to do is read two more verses.

Revelation 20:1 is one of the most unfortunate places in the Bible for a chapter break to have been inserted. The narrative continues seamlessly. An angel appears with a key to the Abyss and a great chain and seizes the devil. Satan is bound for a thousand years (v. 2). Amillennialists and postmillennialists alike have to interpret this verse as a flashback, usually to Christ's first coming, so that the thousand-year period or millennium can then be seen as concluding at the time of Christ's return. But there is absolutely no literary or narrative reason for doing this. Indeed, to return to any earlier time than Christ's second coming destroys the clear unity of 19:19–20:3 in describing the fates of the beast, the false prophet *and* the dragon *after* Christ returns.[5]

Revelation 20:1-3 — The Binding of Satan

To be sure, Jesus once told a parable about binding a strong man as an illustration of how his exorcisms were beginning to defeat Satan (Mk 3:26-27). Of course, he replied when the seventy (-two) returned from their mission that he saw "Satan fall like lightning from heaven" (Lk 10:18). It is a pervasive NT theme that the cluster of events including Christ's incarnation and ministry, his crucifixion and resurrection, and his ascension and sending of the Spirit at Pentecost inaugurated the kingdom of God and therefore likewise inaugurated the demise of the devil. But the same "already but not yet" approach to the kingdom's arrival that is almost universally recognized by NT scholars, amillennialists included, also applies to Satan's defeat. The decisive battle was fought on the cross, ensuring Satan's doom, as Lowery himself stresses.[6] But the interadvent period — the church age — represents the era of the devil's death throes. Like a snake with its head cut off, this serpent continues to slither out of control for a period of time, inflicting harm on anything in its way, before it collapses and expires altogether. Only with Christ's return will Satan be bound in a fully restrictive sense — thrown "into the Abyss," "locked and sealed," "to keep him from deceiving the nations any more" until after the millennium (Rev 20:3).

Indeed, for those inclined to see flashbacks to Christ's first coming in the book of Revelation, 12:1-12 is the obvious place to find one.[7] Most all historic premillennialists agree with amillennialists that the dragon ready to devour a male child about to be born, a child destined to rule the nations with an iron scepter (vv. 3-5), has to refer to Satan's preparing to attack Jesus. When the child is snatched up to God and his throne, we then have a reference to Christ's resurrection and exaltation (v. 6). The war that occurs in heaven between Michael, the dragon, and their respective angels leads to Satan being thrown down to earth (vv. 7-9), an even closer conceptual and linguistic parallel to Luke 10:18. Confirming our conclusion that the devil's defeat in the first century was only partial are verses 12-17. The devil "is filled with fury, because he knows that his time is short" (v. 12), so he proceeds to pursue and to make war against the woman who gave birth to the male child and against her other children also — God's people, now identifiable as Jesus' followers (vv. 13-17). Observe how dramatically this imagery contrasts with that of Rev 20:2-3. When Satan is seized and thrown into the Abyss, this prison is locked and sealed so that he cannot perform any of his dirty work for a very long period of time. Satan is bound far more decisively at Christ's second coming than at his first.

Revelation 20:4-6 — Christ and the Reigning Saints

If Revelation 20 introduces a millennium that begins after Christ's return, then why does it appear that only a small number of Christian believers participate in it? Verse 4 announces that John "saw thrones on which were seated those who had been given authority to judge." Apparently, these were those "who had been beheaded because of their testimony about Jesus and because of the word of God." Even most commentators who see only a small percentage of Christians in view here allow for the likelihood that "beheading" is a synecdoche for all those martyred for their faith.[8] But 1Cor 15:22 and 51-52 and 1Thes 4:13-18 anticipate the resurrection of *all* believers at Christ's return. How does the premillennialist explain this disparity?

The best answer emerges from a close look at the Greek text of Revelation 20:4. For the sake of breaking up an overly long and cumbersome Greek construction, the NIV and TNIV start a new sentence mid-verse: "They had not worshiped the beast or his image and had not received his mark on their foreheads or their hands." The Greek, however, uses no personal pronoun at the start of its new clause but the indefinite relative pronoun, οἵτινες ("those who were of such nature that"). Moreover, the clauses are connected by a καί. While καί does occasionally have ascensive force, meaning "even" or "namely," it would be very unusual to find it functioning that way connecting two long clauses like these. Far more probable is the translation of the NASB, NJB and RSV: "*and those who* had not worshiped the beast. . . ." In other words, John is generalizing in the second part of verse 4 from martyrs to *all* Christians. Everyone who did not receive the mark of the beast will exercise authority with him during the millennium.[9]

The final exegetical conundrum of verse 4 involves the aorist verb, ἔζησαν, from ζῆν ("to live") in the last clause. It is here that Millard Erickson finds amillennialism at its exegetically weakest point.[10] Normally, one would try a simple past-tense translation first: "and *they lived* and reigned with Christ a thousand years." But the identical verb form reappears in verse 5 with respect to "the rest of the dead," that is, unbelievers. To translate consistently, one would then have to render that verse as "the rest of the dead *did not live* until the thousand years was ended," which reads rather awkwardly. Of course dead people aren't alive! But imperfect and aorist tenses, in contexts in which the beginning of an action is indicated by a time change in the immediate context, are frequently inceptive (or ingressive) and should be translated so that a given action "*began* to happen." "Beginning to live" is well captured by almost all modern English translations with language like "they *came to life* and reigned with Christ a thousand years" and "the rest of the dead *did not come to life* until the thousand years was ended."

The amillennialist view has to understand the meanings of these two parallel uses of coming to life in quite different ways — believers come to life *spiritually* at Christ's first coming, while unbelievers come to life *physically* at Christ's second coming. But nothing in the actual context of Rev 20:4-5 would point to such a shift in meaning, so it is hardly the preferable exegesis.[11] Moreover, believers, especially if martyrs are particularly being highlighted, did not all come to spiritual life at Christ's first coming. People have been born again, and some of them martyred, throughout the whole church age. The description of these individuals as reigning with Christ could of course refer to spiritual reign during their Christian lives, as amillennialists insist. But it is less obvious how in ordinary Christian living they would be exercising their authority to *judge* from the thrones they are given, inasmuch as judgment in the NT is typically reserved for the end of the age. The imagery instead makes one recall Jesus' promise to his apostles that they would *in the future* sit on twelve thrones judging the twelve tribes of Israel (Mt 19:28) or Paul's prediction that even the immature Corinthian Christians would *one day* judge angels (1Cor 6:2). And amillennialists typically agree that at least these two verses depict what will not happen until Christ returns. Verses 5b-6 now refer to this coming to life and reigning with Christ as "the first resurrection." If this refers, as in amillennialism, to part or all of the church age, it is the only place out of forty NT usages of the term where actual "resurrection" language (ἀνάστασις; v. 6) is used for a merely spiritual event, that is, in which no physical bodies are transformed from corpses to living, embodied beings.[12]

Revelation 20:7-10 — Satan's Final "Battle"

The stronger part of the amillennialist case comes in the *rest* of Revelation 20. With verse 7, John jumps ahead to the end of the thousand years and portrays what verse 3 foreshadowed. For one last "fling," Satan is released from his prison and allowed to deceive the nations again. He gathers armies from all over the world to do battle against "the camp of God's people, the city he loves." But just as in chapter 19, the battle never gets off the ground. Fire comes down from heaven and devours God's enemies (vv. 8-9). Now the devil joins the beast and the false prophet in the lake of fire for eternal torment (v. 10). The chapter concludes with John's vision of the great-white-throne judgment of the dead who had not yet been resurrected. Judgment is meted out according to people's works, and those whose names were not written in the book of life are likewise thrown into the lake of fire along with the satanic trinity (vv. 11-15).

Here one can appreciate the strength of the amillennialist approach. Revelation 20:7-15 can appear to recapitulate, or present from a different perspective, the same events with which Revelation 19 ends and the same final, universal judgment that numerous other texts of Scripture depict (esp. Dan 12:2; Mt 25:31-46; Jn 5:24-26; Acts 24:15 and 2Cor 5:10).[13] After all, no other passage in the Bible separates final judgment into two stages with a long interval in between. Moreover, what is the point of Satan, finally chained and locked in the Abyss, being given one last chance to gain followers, only for him and them to be almost immediately destroyed? But if Rev 20:1-6 returns to Christ's first coming and if the thousand years represents the church age, then verses 7-15 *do* depict the Parousia and Judgment Day for all who have ever lived, causing no contradiction with any other text of Scripture.

On the other hand, if this millennium does take place after the second coming, as all the details of verses 1-6 suggest, then only believers would have received resurrected, glorified bodies. Unbelievers still alive would continue to live in their normal earthly bodies. But why give them another chance to rebel? If the unregenerate at the end of the millennium have *not* lived through the entire thousand years (because procreation among unbelievers continues), then one obvious answer would be to give them the same freedom that all people in earlier eras of world history have had. If they are, even in part, the *same* unbelievers who were alive at the beginning of the millennium (now enabled to live much longer because of paradisiacal conditions), it becomes one last chance for them to show their true colors. Intriguingly, on *anybody's* interpretation of the millennium, we have to account for how people who have experienced an unprecedented era of spiritual blessing, incontrovertibly attributable to Christ's beneficent reign, but given the chance to align themselves explicitly with Satan, choose to do so. If Rev 20:7-10 explains nothing else, it would appear to offer powerful support for the notion that those who wind up in hell would continue to choose their independence from God and its accompanying fate no matter how often heaven was offered to them.[14] Many of the difficult questions about the justice of eternal punishment may be answered in these verses. On this reading, a final "fling" for Satan to deceive the nations is no harder or easier theologically on *any* given millennial view, so it can hardly be used to swing the momentum away from the premillennialist interpretation that verses 1-6 already established.

What then of the parallels between Revelation 19 and 20? It *is* noteworthy that both chapters have set the stage with armies amassed for battle (for the background to Rev 19, see 16:16), which are then destroyed in an instant. But armies have been organized to fight God and his people countless times throughout Scripture. Two more such events rather than just one should scarcely cause much surprise. As for the immediate vanquishing, surely that is precisely what one would expect to happen when God is intervening supernaturally, demonstrating his utter omnipotence over all forces arrayed against him. Other than these two points, all the remaining details of the two pictures differ. Satan, not the kings of the earth, commands this rebellion. They gather not at the borders of the Euphrates (see Rev 16:16), the northeastern border of the Roman empire in the first century, but around God's holy city. Either Jerusalem itself is in view, or this is a metaphor for all Christians worldwide, corresponding to the worldwide origin of the armies. Christ does not appear with his troops to slay his opponents with the sword anywhere in Rev 20:7-10; fire falls from heaven to consume them instead. And Rev 20:10 clearly distinguishes this event from 19:20 by specifying that this time it is Satan who is hurled into the fiery lake, to join the other two members of his unholy trinity, who have already languished there since the previous rebellion. This closer analysis again appears to require that we separate the events described at the end of chapter 19 from those here in chapter 20, and that the former must precede the latter.[15]

Revelation 20:11-15 — The Final Judgment

How then do we account for there being no other biblical texts that describe two separate final judgments? Perhaps that is to ask the question the wrong way. It presumes that there *are* numerous texts throughout the Bible that clearly present the final judgment of all humans who ever lived *all at one time*. But are there any texts elsewhere in the Bible that unambiguously teach so comprehensive a final judgment? It is widely agreed that the only OT passage that *clearly* depicts a Judgment Day for all humanity, involving the resurrection of the wicked and the righteous, is Dan 12:1-2. The context matches what we have seen earlier in our survey of NT texts—an unprecedented time of tribulation or distress, followed by deliverance for God's people, described as "everyone whose name is found written in the book." Both Mt 24:15, with its "abomination that causes desolation" and Rev 20:15, with its opening of the book of life, looking for names written therein, allude to these verses, given the similarity of their wording in each instance. Dan 12:2 then declares, "Multitudes who sleep in the dust of the earth will awake; some to everlasting life, others to shame and everlasting contempt."

Without further clarification, it would be very natural to assume that the events of both halves of this statement occur at the same time, shortly after the end of the tribulation. But no words necessitating any chronology actually appear in the Hebrew, only the *waw*-consecutive ("and") introducing the verse and then again linking its two halves. NT students are accustomed to discovering Christian authors who assign juxtaposed prophecies in the OT to different periods of time.[16]

Indeed, Jesus himself sets a dramatically parallel precedent, early in his ministry, in his Nazareth synagogue sermon (Lk 4:16-21). In this message, he reads Isa 61:1-2a on the ministry of the Lord's Spirit in anointing God's spokesman to declare salvation for body and soul, but he stops mid-sentence just before the clause, "and the day of vengeance for our God." Commentators are largely agreed that this was deliberate because Jesus is about to announce the fulfillment of the prophecy he *has* read. Yet his first coming involved only salvation; his vengeance will be saved for his return. So he could not keep reading and declare the judgment element fulfilled. Indeed, the very concept of two comings of Christ is not clearly disclosed in the Hebrew Scriptures anywhere. Once a Christian allows for there to be *any* eschatological events predicted of the Messianic age that were not fulfilled in the first century when the other ones were, there should be no surprise if a NT author should choose to chronologically separate the positive and negative sides of final judgment as well.

In the NT, one looks in vain for a picture of final judgment in which every person who has ever lived appears. The so-called parable of the sheep and the goats portrays "all the nations" (or "peoples" or even "people") gathered before the Son of Man after he comes in his glory, with a separation between the righteous and the unrighteous (Mt 25:31-33). But there is nothing in this context at all about any of the *dead*, good or bad, being resurrected.[17] The same is true of 2Thes 1:5-10. Nothing precludes that information being supplied later, as in 1Cor 15:51-52. Yet what is fascinating about 1 Corinthians 15 is that it is entirely about Christ's resurrection and its significance for the resurrection of *believers*. The only place Paul *might* be generalizing is in verse 52, in which he explains that "the dead will be raised imperishable." But in context, "imperishable" is one of the adjectives predicated of resurrected Christians, contrasting with their perishable, mortal bodies. When Paul says, "we will all be changed," twice in verses 51-52, he is referring to himself along with the Corinthian *Christians*. Indeed, all of verses 35-58 deal with the issue of what resurrected, glorified, perfected bodies for believers will be like; there is not a word about the resurrection of unbelievers in this chapter.[18]

First Corinthians 3:10-15 even more clearly refers to the final judgment only of Christians.[19] Everyone in view here is building on the foundation which is Jesus Christ (v. 11). Some build with material that survives trial by fire; others do not (vv. 12-13). Those whose works survive receive a reward (v. 14); those whose works are burned up do not, "but yet will be saved" (v. 15). Obviously, no unbelievers are included in this vignette. Second Corinthians 5:10 similarly warns that "*we* must all appear before the judgment seat of Christ, that everyone may receive what is due them for the things done while in the body, whether good or bad." Without any further qualification, the logical assumption is that Paul is talking here about the only Judgment Day he has previously described to the Corinthians — in 1 Corinthians 3 and 15 — which involves all believers, dead and alive at the time of the Parousia.[20] Just as one can imagine adding without contradiction *resurrected* believers to the judgment scene in the parable of the sheep and the goats, one can envision supplementing Paul's teaching to the Corinthians on the final judgment of all believers, dead and alive, with *unbelievers* still living at the Parousia. But strikingly absent in all these passages are the *unbelieving dead*.

What then of Jn 5:28-29? Surely this text more resembles Dan 12:2 yet appears in the NT, without distinguishing temporally between the judgment of the wicked dead and the righteous dead? Here Jesus proclaims, "Do not be amazed at this, for a time is coming when all who are in their graves will hear his voice and come out — those who have done what is good will rise to live, and those who have done what is evil will rise to be condemned." To be sure, there is no temporal distinction introduced here. But the larger context of these words remains tantalizing. Just three verses earlier Jesus uses the identical words, "a time is coming" but then adds "and has now come," referring to the time "when the dead will hear the voice of the Son of God and those who hear will live" (v. 25). Here he apparently is referring to the opportunity for the spiritually dead to attain eternal life. [21] The era of the inauguration of the new covenant has begun, and will extend on into the future for a considerable period of time. During that entire period, spiritual salvation in Christ will be made available to the lost. Of course, Christ could not say in the same way that the time "has now come" for the resurrection of the dead; that event remains in the future. But should we be at all surprised if the same author of the Fourth Gospel, without any sense of contradiction, should later in his Apocalypse spell out that the era in which people will be physically resurrected also spans a long interval? The only difference is that then there will be two clusters of times for people to be physically resurrected, what John in Rev 20:5-6 calls the first resurrection and the second death, respectively, rather than the possibility of coming to life throughout the *entire* period.

Two final fascinating pieces of potentially confirming evidence for the premillennialist position appear in Rev 20:12-15. First, not a word is said about anyone being saved here, a striking omission if, with the amillennialist view, this is meant to depict Judgment Day for all who have ever lived. Verse 12 universalizes with respect to the dead, by referring to the "great and small" but not to the good and bad or to the believer and unbeliever. Second, there is no mention of judgment of *anyone* still living, good or bad, in this paragraph, but only repeated references to the dead, whether from Hades — the underworld beneath the land, metaphorically speaking — or the sea, presumably already an underworld of its own. To be sure the language of the books of these people's works being opened and all those whose names were not found in the book of life being condemned *allows* for the possibility that others were present whose names *were* so discovered. But it is unusual that no explicit mention is made of it.[22]

Second, the amillennialist view of Revelation, the one book whose genre and length make it the most complete depiction of end-times events, however literally or metaphorically they be interpreted, says absolutely nothing about *believers'* encounter with Christ on Judgment Day — not in 20:4-6 because this is taken to refer to Jesus' first coming and not in verses 11-15 either, even though it is thought to be presupposed here! On the other hand, if these are only the unregenerate dead who appear at the great white throne judgment, after a millennium that occurs after Christ's return, then John's language makes good sense. As these people's works are evaluated, it becomes clear that they cannot merit God's favor. As the book of life is opened to see if their names have been recorded, because notwithstanding their wickedness they repented and trusted in Christ for their salvation, they do not appear there either. God is thus shown to be completely just in pronouncing their final condemnation.[23]

Revelation 21-22 — The New Heaven and New Earth

The emphasis on *bodily* resurrection and glorification and on a renewed *earth* in a literal millennium after Christ's return provides the key to explaining why premillennialism is ultimately to be preferred and indicates what exactly is at stake in the debate. While the new heavens and new earth have at least some slight, unspecified form of continuity with this present universe, as shown by John's promise that "the kings of the earth will bring their splendor into it" (Rev 21:24),[24] what stands out are the discontinuities between the current heavens and earth and those still to come. Revelation does not speak of any fiery conflagration temporally separating the millennium from the eternal state. But there is no difficulty, logistically, in inserting one there, and 2Pet 3:10 indicates that we should. That the earth in that verse is "laid bare" suggests something short of total destruction, so that room remains for some things of the past to be carried over into the future and perfected.[25] But the emphasis clearly favors discontinuity over continuity.

The same is decidedly *not* the case with the millennium. A literal age of unprecedented godliness and goodness transforming *this* earth is what the millennium produces. God created *this* heavens and earth as good, and he will vindicate his purposes for *this* material world.[26] Without a millennium as premillennialists conceive of it, God in essence gives up on his current creation and just starts entirely over again, something he predicted he would never again do after the catastrophic flood of Noah's day (Gen 6-8). *With* such a millennium, all our activity related to *this* cosmos takes on incredible meaning and purpose. Just as our spiritual salvation and sanctification, personally and ecclesially, should model for a watching world, however imperfectly, what God's people will one day perform perfectly when they are resurrected and glorified, so too our relationship to the rest of the universe around us—whether "animal, vegetable, or mineral"—will make a difference, in unspecified ways, for the nature and quality of our millennial existence.[27] Neither in the material nor in the immaterial dimensions of his creation will God's purposes be thwarted. Because those purposes involved *this present* creation, he must demonstrate their complete fulfillment in this present creation, before passing to re-creation and the eternal state.

THE CHRISTIAN MILLENNIUM[1]

I. Howard Marshall

I n the NT the millennium is mentioned explicitly only in Revelation 20 and nowhere else. It is described there as the period during which Satan is kept bound and locked in the abyss while the souls of Christian martyrs come to life in the first resurrection and reign with Christ for this temporary period. Thereafter, Satan is released from his prison and proceeds to deceive the nations of the world who gather together for battle against the camp of God's people but are annihilated by fire from heaven, while Satan is cast into the lake of burning sulphur. This event is then followed by the judgment of all the dead before the great white throne of God and the punishment of those whose names were not in the book of life.

The Origin of the Concept

What made Christians think of this idea in the first place? Although the Revelation is presented to us in the form of a vision seen by John, who says "I saw" some forty or so times at regular intervals throughout the book, what he sees very often has parallels in the works of other writers. As with other writings that we call "apocalyptic," in that they all claim to be based on visions of heaven or visionary journeys and tours of the heavenly regions, the things that God enabled John to see and understand are expressed in a vocabulary and an imagery which were already known in the ancient world. Similarly, a preacher today might well claim divine illumination in the composition of a message, and might even get some inspiration from a dream or vision, but the language used and the imagery and the modes of thinking would be drawn from the preacher's experience, however much they are reshaped to give a fresh message. Something like this has happened with John, and therefore it is legitimate to ask what parallels there are to his vision here that may help us to understand it better.[2]

The main Jewish material is found in 4 *Ezra* (2 *Esdras*) 7:26-30 where an angel tells Ezra that the hidden city and land will appear together with God's Son the Messiah and his companions for a 400-year period, after which everybody including the Messiah will die, and the world will return to primeval silence for 7 days, and then the judgment will take place (cf. 4 *Ezra* 12:31-34). This is probably the closest parallel to Revelation 20 with the exception of the unusual period of time.

Similar material is found in 1 *Enoch* 91:12-17 and 2 *Baruch* 29-30. They follow a common pattern of a limited or temporary period of righteousness on the earth before the final judgment and the establishment of eternal righteousness and happiness. The Messiah may or may not be present. The passage in Revelation fits into this pattern, but of course is distinctive in what takes place.

Michael Gilbertson argues that the pattern arose as a result of the apocalyptic writers fusing together the OT prophetic hope of the earthly restoration of Israel and the later hope, which developed after the exile when this hope was somewhat eroded, of salvation beyond this age brought about by a decisive intervention by God: "there is in effect a composite hope, first for a renewal of an earthly Israel, and then for God's ultimate saving act, which will transcend earthly existence."[3]

Later Christian writers tended to accept the teaching of Revelation literally. Papias[4] prophesied the incredible fruitfulness of vines and grain on the basis of what the Lord had said to John, the disciple of the Lord. According to Eusebius, *HE* 3.39, Papias believed that there would be a period of 1,000 years after the resurrection while the Kingdom of Christ is set up in material form on the earth.[5] Similar teaching is found in many writers,[6] but a major exception was Origen who interpreted the millennium symbolically "of the spiritual growth of the soul which begins in this life and continues in the next."[7]

New Testament Precedents and Parallels

The teaching in Revelation 20 is unique in the NT. Only two passages can be brought forward as possible parallels.

1. In 2 Peter 3 the writer warns his readers that the present heaven and earth will be destroyed by fire on the day of judgment. But he cautions his readers, who wonder when it is ever going to happen, that with the Lord a day is like a thousand years and a thousand years are like a day, which is simply a way of saying that God has a different timescale from us. The new heaven and earth follow the judgment, as in Revelation 21, and there is no hint of any special period preceding the judgment. Nothing suggests that the use here of the term "thousand years" is derived from the concept of the millennium as it is found in Revelation; in all probability it is derived from Ps 90:4.[8]

2. In 1Cor 15:20-28 Paul refers to the resurrection of Jesus as the firstfruits of those who have fallen asleep. But the firstfruits precede and guarantee the main crop to be harvested. Although all will be made alive in Christ — i.e. all those who will be made alive will be made alive in Christ and not in any other way — there is an order to what happens. They will not be made alive immediately (as some of the Corinthian Christians may have mistakenly believed); only *then* when Christ comes (sc. again) will "those who belong to him" be made alive.

> *Then the end* will come, when he hands over the kingdom to God the Father after he has destroyed all dominion, authority and power. For he must reign till he has put all his enemies under his feet. The last enemy to be destroyed is death. . . . When he has done this, then the Son himself will be made subject to him who put everything under him, so that God may be all in all. (TNIV)

This extended quotation certainly refers to an ongoing reign of Christ until he has conquered all his enemies including death. The temporal sequence of "then . . . then the end . . ." has suggested that, just as there is a gap or period between the resurrection of Christ and his coming, so there is a period between his coming and the end when he hands over authority to the Father, and that this second period is identical with the millennium in

169

Revelation. However, according to F.F. Bruce, "the context suggests that the interval is short." Furthermore, the reign of Christ began for Paul at his resurrection and exaltation.[9] The evidence is perhaps not sufficient to exclude totally the possibility that Paul believed in it, but in the absence of the remotest hint that he did, we would be very unwise to credit him with the belief.[10]

The upshot of this brief examination is that for any unambiguous teaching about a millennium, we have no source other than Revelation 20.

Ways of Interpreting the Passage

We now face the question of the interpretation and significance of the text in Revelation 20.

1. We have already noted the early Christian evidence for a literal understanding of the millennium. This type of interpretation was taken up later in the church as *classical premillennialism*. The classification "pre-" refers to the relationship of the return of Christ to the millennium, and in this case the sequence is exactly that which arises from a literal, chronological understanding of Revelation 19 and 20 where the coming of Christ *precedes* the millennium, and the latter indeed presupposes it, since "they reign with Christ" on the earth.[11]

This early view had a renaissance after the Reformation.[12] In the nineteenth century a particular variant of it developed in the form of *dispensationalism*. This view is very much dependent on the literal interpretation of Scripture: the various prophecies in the OT, especially about the future of the Jewish people, must find a literal fulfillment, and this is to take place in the millennium.[13]

2. A *spiritual* or *allegorical interpretation* was dominant from the fourth to the eighteenth centuries, presumably along the lines developed earlier by Origen.

3. *Postmillennialism* holds that there will be a future millennium but it will precede the coming of Christ. This kind of view was developed by Joachim in the 12th century who held that there would be a third age, that of the Spirit. Similar beliefs were espoused by some Reformation and Puritan writers.[14] A leading defender is I. Murray, who gathers together the evi-

dence adduced by Puritan writers showing that biblical prophecies envisage a glorious triumph of the gospel in the last days so that the earth is ready to greet its king.[15] Passages from the Gospels which assert that the gospel must *first* be preached to all nations must find their fulfillment before Christ returns. This view starkly contrasts with the typical premillennial view that holds that things will only get worse and worse as evil takes an ever firmer hold on the world and the saints are martyred. According to Dodd, some postmillennialists hold that the millennium is already happening in the worldwide spread of the gospel.

4. To be carefully distinguished from the previous view is the one which argues that there is no specific millennial kingdom either after or before the return of Christ. This view is called *amillennialism*, and this title is appropriate if it refers to a parousia without the accompaniment of a millennium. However, those who hold this view do in fact generally believe in a millennium; for them the picture in Revelation is symbolical of the reign of Christ which began at his exaltation and is even now in progress. This view was developed by Augustine who held that the millennium takes place in the heavenly places to which believers have already been raised (Eph 2:6; Col 3:1), and therefore we are now reigning with Christ.[16] Most recently U. Schnelle writes: "John is not advocating a speculative 'chiliasm' . . . but is emphasizing that prior to the ultimate end, the present world too will be permeated by Christ."[17]

Bauckham includes as a later variant of this view that of the Protestant Reformers who believed that there had already been a period of 1,000 years during which the gospel had flourished but this was brought to an end by the rise of the mediaeval papacy; consequently they believed that the parousia was imminent.

5. Finally, some scholars claim that Revelation is inconsistent in its portrayal or that the writer is not attempting to develop a chronological scheme. This view would be found especially among nonevangelical scholars who are less tied to a literal interpretation of Scripture and argue that the symbolism in Revelation is to be taken seriously as *symbolism*.

But it is also held by evangelicals. For Bauckham the millennium is "a symbol, not of a period at all, but of the complete achievement of Christ's kingdom and his total victory over all at the parousia."[18] Similarly, McKelvey argues that the millennium is to be understood as one of the many symbols in the book for the vindication of the martyrs; it "is the disclosure of God's triumph over evil." Its limited duration is an indication that the struggle between good and evil continues while life on earth lasts but will terminate with God's victory. The millennium thus apparently remains a hope which we must strive to achieve by our witness to God's rule and our campaign to help those who are denied justice in this world. Yet the millennium cannot be historicised; it always remains an eschatological hope judging all our efforts. It follows that, although there are links between them, the millennium is not to be identified with the final city of God, which is a symbol for all the saints in God's new age to come. Nevertheless, it would still seem that the millennium is a symbol for that future hope which God will bring to consummation. The millennium thus resembles the picture of the Kingdom of God elsewhere in the NT in that it represents a hope that we must strive to bring into effect but that cannot be realised fully until God himself brings it about.[19]

It is impossible in a short paper to assess all of these various views. What I propose to attempt is to offer two different interpretations of the passage. The first is the interpretation worked out with infinite care by G.K. Beale.[20] The second is an idiosyncratic one of my own which I conceived some years ago.[21]

The Millennium as the Present Heavenly State of Deceased Believers

According to Beale, Rev 20:1-6 depicts the ongoing reign of Christ since the resurrection.[22] Beale is not happy with the concept of a future, temporary messianic kingdom preceding the end. He stresses the elements of symbolism and repetition in Revelation and argues that Revelation 20 is yet another repetition of the complete story line which begins with the resurrection of Christ and takes us right through to the end. The binding of Satan in the abyss takes place at the resurrection of

Christ. Satan is prevented from deceiving the nations to such an extent that individuals from them cannot believe the gospel, but his other activities continue. (Similarly in the Gospels, although he is apparently first defeated by Christ, his activity still continues in various ways.) But at the end of time he will be released full of fury to gather together the godless nations for a final onslaught against the church.[23] Thus the battle described at the end of chapter 20 is the same one as that in chapter 19. And the judgment described in 20:11-15 is the same event as that described in 19:11-21, only where the imagery in chapter 19 was that of battle, here it is developed into the picture of the judgment.

Meanwhile, in the period while Satan is bound, the saints of God, including but not restricted to the martyrs, are raised to life in the intermediate state and they enjoy their reign with Christ in heaven. So the millennial reign itself is not on earth, and we are wrong to assume that the earthly setting of 20:1-3,7-10 applies to 20:4-6 as well: John can change scenes with bewildering rapidity. The saints thus enjoy a foretaste of the heavenly kingdom, and here and now they live and reign with Christ, though presumably in a bodiless state—it is the "souls" that come to life. There is accordingly only one physical resurrection of the dead, that which takes place when Christ comes the second time, and not two separate physical resurrections. What is being described is the way in which the souls of believers are taken to heaven when they die, so that the so-called intermediate state is depicted as a conscious existence in heaven. The description is flexible, since we have another account of the same people in 6:9-11 where the souls of the martyrs are underneath the altar in heaven.

Beale thus takes forward the interpretation by Hendriksen and gives it a very detailed and largely convincing defence. On this view, the problem of the millennium disappears; there is no future millennium and the passage is simply another description of the present age between the first coming of Christ and the second.

However, there are some tensions in Beale's account. One of them is that the souls which are raised to life to reign with

Christ presumably reign for different periods of time over the whole stretch of time during which Christians live and die on earth, so that some get a longer millennium than others. Another problem is that here resurrection simply means that the souls come to life or continue in life, whereas resurrection is usually of the body rather than of the soul. However, Beale argues that the term can be used in different ways in different contexts. Again, both passages refer specifically to martyrs, but Beale argues, as I would also, that, although the martyrs are singled out for mention, in fact all Christians who died after a faithful witness are really in mind.

A greater difficulty is that Beale has to restrict the meaning of "deceiving the nations" to refer exclusively to Satan's prevention of their conversion, while still continuing his activity of temptation. Can a sharp line really be drawn between these two activities? Beale also has to argue that, although the devil is in the abyss, he is still present on earth in order that his other activities may continue. Although Beale argues that the binding of Satan fits in nicely with his being bound during the ministry of Jesus (Mk 3:27 and par.) and with his being cast out in Jn 12:31, it can be replied that the binding of Satan or his casting out in the Gospels is an anticipation of his final defeat rather than being identical with it.[24] Yet another problem is that on any reckoning a thousand years is a long time, and since John believed that Jesus would come soon and quickly, was he really saying here that the time gap would be of very considerable extent?[25] And, finally, as we saw, the Jewish apocalypses all thought of the millennium as a future reign by the Messiah rather than something present and heavenly.

The Millennium as a Symbol
for the Final State of Believers

Let me now develop an alternative view. I begin with five general observations.

First, the Book of Revelation certainly contains much symbolical language describing visions in which not everything is meant to be taken literally. Jesus appears in one vision as a fantastic man with a sword coming out of his mouth; then he appears as a lamb that looks as though it has been slain. We cannot take everything literally, because it is impossible in principle to do so. It would be strange if the millennium was exempt.

There is also much repetition; the same points are being made from different angles, or perhaps the same series of events are being described from different points of view. Every now and then we seem to get to a point that we have reached before, and then we go back and start again. W. Hendriksen's seminal work, *More than Conquerors*, is essentially correct, even if the details are debatable.

Second, the concept of a temporary kingdom is a very curious one. There is no obvious rationale for a temporary binding of Satan, the establishment of the reign of the saints, and then the undoing of all this in the release of Satan, the deceit of the nations, and their attack on the camp of God's people. There is a point in a series of successive judgments which are partial and incremental in order to warn people and urge them to repent, but there is no point in this temporary kingdom.

Third, the description of the millennium itself is remarkably undeveloped. The nations, presumably the non-Christian nations, continue to exist. Certain believers, especially including the martyrs,[26] are seated on thrones and reign with Christ for the thousand years, and Satan is not active to deceive the nations. But that is all we are told. Much is left to the imagination. Do the martyrs have to die a second time? Presumably not. Do the nations go on living as normal? We don't know. If they do, do they die in their generations while the resurrected martyrs remain alive? We don't know. Over whom do the martyrs reign and what effect does their reign have? Nothing is said. Do the nations (or the martyrs) sin if Satan is not able to deceive them? We don't know. Do the martyrs marry and have children? And where are the Jews in all this? (I answer that one with greater certainty: there is a thundering silence about them!) And so on. My point is that the description is fundamentally empty. There is merely a contrast between the saints' life and reign and the death and defeat of the beast and the false prophet.[27]

Fourth, this may suggest some kind of "spiritual" interpretation of the passage. But here the route taken by Augustine is simply not open to us. It rests on a confusion of categories between the description of the present spiritual reign of Christians in Paul's letters and what purports to be a description of the future reign of the martyrs after a resurrection. This latter can hardly be equated with the spiritual resurrection of those dead in trespasses and sins to share in the life and reign of Christ.

Finally, if our preliminary discussion is correct, there is no clear mention of the millennium as a temporary period of future blessing anywhere else in the NT. How could something so significant fail to be mentioned elsewhere?[28]

All this leads us to consider a different kind of interpretation, which is probably to be located in my earlier category 5 (symbolic interpretations).

▶ The picture of the coming of the Word of God in Revelation 19 symbolises his defeat of the powers of evil and culminates in the judgment of the beast and the false prophet. The devil also is seized. We would naturally expect the inauguration of the heavenly kingdom to follow. For the defeat in Revelation 19 looks rather conclusive! In particular, it does look as though all the nations have already ceased to exist, so that there is nobody left for Satan to deceive if a millennium now follows;[29] this difficulty has led some writers to postulate a physical resurrection of the people who were slain in 19:21.[30]

▶ The description of the heavenly city in Rev 21:9–22:5 would admirably describe the millennial city on earth (Rev 20:9), even though it is described as if it were separate from it and followed it.

▶ In Rev 19:6-9 we already have the invitation to the imminent (v. 7!) wedding supper of the Lamb, but if we have a consecutive chronological account the bride does not appear until at least a millennium later, in Rev 21:9. So the millennium is an awkward parenthesis.

▶ The millennium is certainly the occasion for the resurrection of the Christian martyrs. But nothing is said anywhere in this context about the resurrection of those who died in their beds or went down in the Titanic, unless this is the implied "second resurrection." But, even if that be so, the text would appear to imply that only the martyrs take part in the millennial reign, and there is no mention of any other believers who are still alive when the millennium starts and who share in the reign of the martyrs.[31] If we take the millennium account literally, and if we have not been martyred before it happens, then we may not be there to experience it when it happens.

▶ We have already seen that the concept of the millennium is a part of some Jewish apocalyptic writings of the time, so that John may have been constrained to use imagery that was already current to express what he wanted to say.

What then did he want to say? I fall in with those who see in the book of Revelation a symbolic account of the conflict between God and his people on the one side and the powers of evil on the other that has been raging ever since the coming of Christ. John throws every symbol that he knows into his account to comfort and assure his readers that, no matter how great be the force of evil, no matter how much it seems to get the upper hand, no matter how many believers are martyred, yet the victory is with God, and his people are to be faithful and valiant, assured that their God will share his victory with them, and that in the end there will be only his kingdom of peace, righteousness and love.

So John uses various traditional pictures to make his points; but he is an inspired genius and he is able to refashion them to tell his message. There are several pictures traditionally associated with the end. There is the concept of the new earth and the new heaven; there is the picture of the final battle; there is the new temple in a restored land of Israel; there is the resurrection of the righteous and the judgment of the unrighteous; there is the marriage and the marriage feast of the King's Son; there is the heavenly city; and so on. John picks up these images and melds them together as only a person with a poetic soul can do; we destroy their impact if we take his narrative to bits or interpret it as prose.

On this view the millennium period is yet another of these images of the glorious and final end which John has taken over;

what is described in Revelation 20 is thus an anticipatory vision of what is spelt out more fully in Revelation 21–22. The "thousand" in "a thousand years" is a symbol of the endless character of the kingdom of God.[32]

The imagery concentrates on the martyrs because they were a particularly potent symbol. They are the people to whom the opposition has done its very worst, and it wrongly thinks that it has won, but God will raise them from the dead and they will reign. The martyrs are thus representative of the people of God generally. The imagery of the city needs no explanation, based as it is on the concept of Zion as the place where God makes his presence known to his people, and it is developed fully in the garden-city in Revelation 21–22. It is still there in Rev 22:14-15 — surprisingly with the evildoers outside the gates (and not in the lake of fire).

The chief problem in adopting this interpretation, which says that the millennium is another picture for the heavenly kingdom, so that John gives us a preliminary sketch in chapter 20 and the developed picture in chapters 21–22, is that the *prima facie* reading is of *successive* events and of a *temporary* kingdom followed by a permanent one. "*After* that, he must be set free for a short time." "When the thousand years *are over*, Satan will be released. . . ." If on the first occasion he was bound in the abyss, on the second occasion he is put into the lake of burning sulphur where his confederates were already dispatched. The crucial question is whether these texts constitute an insuperable barrier to this interpretation. How far does a narrative which, as all interpreters must allow, contains symbolical material that cannot be understood literally, nevertheless retain some irreducibly literal elements?

Since elsewhere John uses the device of repetition, there is a case that it is present here also and that the temporal sequence is simply part of the imagery to convey truths that burst the limits of straightforward narrative.[33] Thus, if our interpretation of the structure of Revelation is correct, then we have a clear reference to the second coming of Christ to judgment in Rev 14:14-20 (note also the reference to the city in 14:20!), and other things are then said to happen *after* that. It may be then that we are not to press the literal significance of what looks at first sight like a temporal sequence.

We can indeed give a plausible reason why John followed this particular route. The nations who are deceived are named as "Gog and Magog." What is going on, then, is that at this point John brings in these symbolical end-time enemies of Israel who figure in Ezekiel 38–39 *after* the promise of resurrection and the establishment of the Messianic kingdom in Ezekiel 36–37 and *before* the establishment of the new temple and the new commonwealth of Israel in Ezekiel 40–48. This is the source of the material that John is using, and it may simply be the difficulty of incorporating it that has led John to use the device of the temporariness of the kingdom.

AN ALTER-IMPERIAL READING OF THE RELEASE OF SATAN (REV 20:7-10)

By Shane J. Wood

Introduction

Why *must* Satan be released? This question has plagued theologians for centuries, and it surely was on the hearts and minds of the original recipients of the Apocalypse as well. The tension felt in Rev 20:7-10 is built in Rev 20:1-3. A majestic picture of an angel from heaven binding the dragon for a thousand years (20:1-2) is compounded with the victorious image of "the ancient serpent, who is the devil,"[1] being cast into imprisonment in the Abyss, which is both locked and sealed in 20:3a to keep him from deceiving the nations. The jubilation from those hearing this message (1:3) can almost be heard two thousand years later, for the great persecutor that has wielded his army of evil against God's faithful witnesses finally receives his due—but the celebration must have been short-lived. The text continues in 20:3b with, "After that, he *must* be set free for a short time." It is at this point that the question emerges: Why *must* Satan be released?

Revelation 20:4-6 diverts the attention of the reader from the horror in 20:3b by depicting the souls of the faithful witnesses reigning with Jesus in heaven[2] and offering a beatitude for those who overcome the temptation to compromise or even abandon their faith.[3] This brief reprieve, however, dissipates in 20:7, "When the thousand years are over, Satan will be released from his prison. . . ." The dramatic tension of the anticipated events to follow once again prompt the question: Why *must* Satan be released?

Where Do We Turn? — Failed Interpretative Attempts

Throughout Revelation's history, interpreters have utilized two key trajectories to try to explain the images of Rev 20:7-10 — OT allusions and theological constructs. Given that the book of Revelation contains over 500 allusions to the OT in 404 verses, it seems probable that the OT would offer interpretative hooks from which we could hang a cogent explanation of the images.[4] Nevertheless, the OT helps only to establish some aesthetic symbolic referents like: "four corners of the earth,"[5] "sand of the shore,"[6] "fire from heaven,"[7] and "Gog and Magog."[8] While this helps with governing some of the images, the primary image of the passage — the release of Satan — has no OT referent whatsoever.[9] Recognizing this difficulty, scholars have traditionally turned to the second trajectory to explain the release of Satan: theological constructs.

Although coming to distinctly different conclusions, premillennial and amillennial interpreters have attempted to explain the release of Satan by forcing the image into their theological schemas.[10] On the one hand, premillennials,[11] who believe that the second coming of Christ (Rev 19:11-21) inaugurates a utopian reign on earth (i.e., the millennial kingdom), are presented with substantial difficulties with the events of Rev 20:7-10. Specifically, upon Satan's release he goes out and deceives the nations from the "four corners of the earth" and gathers them for battle (20:7) against the people of God (20:9). This evil army is as numerous as the "sands of the shore." But where did such a large number of evil come from? For a thousand years the world, according to the premillennial theological system, has existed in utopian bliss where the lion rests with the calf and the child plays with the vipers (Isa 11:6-8; 65:17-25) — complete peace and unity over all of creation.[12] So who does Satan deceive when he is released?

Premillennials answer this question by suggesting that there will be *some* in the "utopian" millennium who rebel even though Satan is bound.[13] However, this answer leads to further additions and difficulties for the theological system: the necessity of multiple bodily resurrections separated by the thousand years,[14] the rebellious *"some"* being nonresurrected persons born in the millennium,[15] and the army Satan gathers after his release being only those who were born after the year nine-hundred in the millennium — since nonresurrected bodies cannot live longer than one-hundred years even in the "utopian world."[16] Such theological alchemy can only be described as forced conjecture.

On the other hand, amillennials, who believe the "millennial kingdom" describes the time period between Christ's first and second comings, suffer in their attempts to explain the imagery of Rev 20:7-10 as well. Generally speaking, amillennials suggest the release of Satan points to a time of increased and widespread persecution of God's people right before Christ's final coming and the judgment of the world (Rev 20:10-15).[17] A significant difficulty for this interpretation, however, emerges with the opening phrase of 20:7a, "When the thousand years are over. . . ." If the thousand years is defined as the Church Age, according to amillennials, then the second coming has already occurred in 20:7, which would put the supposed persecution after the advent. So any interpretation that suggests a significant persecution by Satan right before the second coming of Christ based on this passage must omit the opening phrase of 20:7a, which places the events of Satan's release *after* the thousand years.

So if the OT does not allude to any governing imagery and the theological explanations prove contrived at best, then how do we answer the question: Why *must* Satan be released?[18] More to the point, where do we look for interpretative help for the imagery of Satan's release? What sources do we have to guide our explanations of this picture in Rev 20:7-10? This chapter will suggest that our inquiries into the OT allusions and theological explanations for the release of Satan prove futile because John was utilizing another key source common to him and his audience: imagery of the Roman Empire. A closer look at the text will show how this imagery begins to emerge.

Painting the Picture: Overlooked Anomalies

In Rev 20:1-3 and 7-10, there are important details used to paint the picture that are oftentimes overlooked or seen as anomalous — two of which point us in the direction of imperial parallels. First, Rev 20:1-3 describes two actions being done to Satan by the angel from heaven: (1) Satan is bound, and (2) he is imprisoned. Along with the key to the Abyss,[19] the angel from heaven holds the "great chain" that he uses to bind Satan. The term ἅλυσις ("chain") does not occur frequently in the Bible.[20] Nevertheless, based on Acts 12:7 where the ἅλυσις falls from Peter's hands, the picture painted shows Satan as a criminal being handcuffed with manacles in 20:2.[21] In a separate action, the angel imprisons Satan in the Abyss in 20:3. With these two distinct actions by the angel, Satan awaits his foretold release for a thousand years.

In Rev 20:7, one of these actions is undone while the other is not mentioned. The release of Satan is explicitly labeled in the text as being "from his prison" (20:7).[22] While the release from prison is appalling, it is important to note the picture that John is painting. The events that occurred in 20:1-3 are only partially reversed; the text never mentions that Satan is unbound. In other words, Satan is released from his prison still wearing his shackles.[23]

Second, as the previous description indicates, Rev 20:3b reveals that Satan does not escape or claw his way out of his prison but he is released by means of divine mandate. The Greek word *dei* (δεῖ), translated "*must*," is defined in contexts like this as a "Greek particle . . . which means 'it is necessary,' [and] was often used with the sense of 'divine destiny' or 'unavoidable fate'."[24] In other words, the *dei* indicates the divine necessity for Satan to be released — it is orchestrated by God, not by Satan.[25] This is emphasized by the passive "released" in 20:7, in which the action is done *to* Satan and not *by* Satan.[26] So although the text ostensibly shows Satan leading an escape and rebellion, between the lines the text discloses a divine guiding hand that is, instead, leading Satan — for purposes yet to be revealed.

In sum, the picture painted in Rev 20:1-3 and 7-10 shows Satan handcuffed by an angel from heaven and then thrown into prison. Due to God's purposes and plan, Satan is released by God from prison to march across the breadth of the earth — still bound with his manacles in place.

Why? What is John trying to communicate with these details? What is he symbolizing with this imagery? Put another way, "Why *must* Satan be released?" The answer does not surface in OT allusions or theological schemas; instead, the picture is found in imagery of the Roman Empire. Imperial ideology was communicated to a predominately illiterate empire through the use of symbols in architecture, coins, rituals, and other forms of nonverbal imagery in public arenas for all to see. These symbols flooded the streets of Rome's cities — including the cities of Asia Minor found in Revelation 2-3.[27] It is from this reservoir of images that John, an exile under the empire (Rev 1:9), borrows to construct his picture of Satan's release — specifically, the symbolic ritual of the Roman triumph.[28]

The Roman Triumph in the Roman Empire

S.J. Hafemann describes the Roman triumph as "the most important and well-known political religious institution of the period."[29] Recognizing that Roman triumphs were recorded over 300 times in Roman literature[30] and depictions of the events decorated the cities[31] and coins,[32] it is probable that elements of a Roman triumph were easily recognizable for those living in the Roman Empire.[33]

Although there is no set template for every triumphal procession, frequent repetition of certain features has led some scholars to see them as "key elements" of each triumph.[34] Regarding the victor celebrated in the triumph,[35] the emperor would enter the parade (usually last in succession) in a chariot pulled by four white horses,[36] sometimes with royal family riding in close proximity on single white horses.[37] Typically the emperor was dressed in a tunic ordained with palm designs and draped with a purple toga laced with gold thread.[38] The emperor also bore a crown upon his head[39] and key depictions of Jupiter to emphasize his divinity.[40] The emperor was surrounded by his army and various symbols expressing their victory.[41] The main attraction of the parade, however, was the enemy captives and their leader bound in chains marching in front of the emperor.[42] The final destination toward which the parade marched was to the steps of the temple of the god

Jupiter.[43] It is here that the audience waited in silence for the penultimate moment of the Roman triumph to commence.[44] Hafemann writes, "At the climax of the pageant, those prisoners and royalty who had been led in triumph and were not destined to be sold into slavery were executed in honor to the victor as the ultimate sign of his conquest and in homage to Rome's deity."[45]

The purpose of these triumphal processions was to give a public display of the sovereignty and glory of the Emperor by presenting him as both their god and savior.[46] In addition, the parade was intended to shame the conquered nation into submission. As a result, the triumphal procession was both the climax of honor for Rome and the climax of humiliation for Rome's enemy.[47]

The Roman Triumph in Revelation 19:11-21

Recently, building upon the suggestion of David Aune, David Andrew Thomas has argued persuasively for the Roman triumph as the driving imagery behind key symbols in Revelation 19:11-21.[48] Summarily, in Revelation 19:11, Christ enters the scene on a white horse and is labeled in 19:16 as the "king of kings and lord of lords," or the emperor over all emperors. He is described as wearing a robe dipped in blood in 19:13, which echoes the ceremonial dress of the emperor and depictions of their victory.[49] Furthermore, the army that surrounds Christ is dressed in "fine linen, white and clean" in 19:14 like the onlookers of a Roman triumph.[50] Revelation 19:12 describes Christ as being adorned with "many crowns," referencing the crowns obtained in battle and celebrated in the triumph. Finally, all of the language describing the magnificence of Christ is reminiscent of God himself, similar to the emperor being depicted as the god Jupiter. All of the key elements are present in Rev 19:11-21 except two significant omissions – (1) the chief enemy leader marched in chains to his execution, which precedes (2) the emergence of the emperor on a chariot concluding the procession.

While Jesus contains significant elements of the royal family in the Roman triumph, it is remiss to assume that he is depicted as the triumphing emperor. First, he does not ride in on a chariot pulled by four white horses.[51] Although there were rare exceptions to the presence of the four white horses,[52] numismatics and architecture show that the quadriga had become an essential feature of the imagery of the Roman triumph by the time of Domitian's reign.[53] This point suggests that Jesus is not being depicted as the triumphing emperor, but instead, he is presented as a part of the royal family that is being celebrated in the triumph.

A significant parallel to this point is in the Roman triumph in 71 C.E. for Vespasian and Titus that celebrated the Roman victory over the Jewish rebellion that resulted in the destruction of the temple in Jerusalem. In this event, seared in the minds of Jews and Christians alike, Vespasian, the newly inaugurated emperor, rode in the quadriga with his son Titus — who was a key general in the victory. Domitian, the emperor at the time of Revelation's composition, rode on a *single white horse* in close proximity to his father (Vespasian) and brother (Titus) — both of whom were being celebrated with divine overtones pointing to Domitian as "a son of god."[54] This striking parallel suggests that John depicts Jesus in Revelation 19:11-21 as the beginning of the triumphal procession of his Father in which "the son of god" rides on a single white horse in close proximity to the emperor.

Second, the triumphal procession climaxed with the triumphing emperor in the quadriga — *after* the procession of the spoils of war, depictions of victory, and most importantly the bound enemy captives.[55] This suggests not only that Jesus is not the triumphing emperor but also that the procession is not over — but just beginning. These observations beg the question, "Who, then, is the triumphing emperor?" The answer is given in Rev 21:1-8 where John portrays the majestic procession of the "one on the throne" descending to earth.[56] If Jesus begins the triumphal procession in Rev 19:11-21 and the "one on the throne" concludes it in Rev 21:1-8, then how does Rev 20:1-10 fit into the Roman triumph? The answer to this question is also the answer to the question that began this chapter, "Why *must* Satan be released?"

The Roman Triumph in Revelation 20:7-10

Although Rev 19:11-21 omits the key element of the triumphing emperor, Rev 21:1-8 offers the missing piece with the procession of the "one on the throne." Likewise, Rev 20:7-10 submits the other key element of the Roman triumph excluded from Rev 19:11-21 — the chief enemy leader marched in chains to his execution.[57] David Andrew Thomas summarizes the significance of this event:

> The most important element of [the Roman triumph] was the parading of live prisoners, especially enemy commanders, princes, and kings. Their eventual sacrifice at the Capitol reveals that the triumph was meant to be more than just a celebration of a past victory or even a means to relive it. The triumph was an act of *consummation*. The victory for the triumphator was not complete until his hated foe was no more, and the triumph was the ordained means to realize this crucial final detail. . . . Until the triumph, therefore, the matter was officially and deliberately (if not essentially) left open.[58]

As mentioned earlier, while Satan was released from prison in 20:7, he was *not* released from his shackles.[59] Through the *dei* in 20:3b and the unseen hand that released Satan from prison, God is pictured in Rev 20:7-10 as sovereignly leading Satan, the single bound captive, to God's intended destination — Satan's execution. In the midst of God's city, which is his people, the climactic moment of the triumphal procession is achieved — Satan is executed in the lake of fire.

Like depictions of the Roman triumph, single bound captives were not at the beginning of the triumph (e.g., Rev 19:11-21) but put on display as the climactic "spoil of war" preceding the triumphing general (Rev 21:1-8).[60] So here, Satan, the chief enemy leader, follows Jesus' appearance in the triumphal procession but precedes the "one who sits on the throne" (i.e., the triumphing emperor). So, "Why *must* Satan be released?" From this perspective, Satan is released so that he can participate in God's triumphal procession, which is the climax of both honor and humiliation in the eyes of the audience.

The Roman Triumph in Asia Minor

Although all of the indicators point toward affirming this interpretation, would John's audience in Asia Minor recognize the Roman triumph imagery? Was the triumphal procession symbolism prominent or even evident in the cities of Asia Minor?[61] First, as described above, the pervasiveness of the Roman triumph imagery infected virtually every facet of Roman society. Mary Beard, a leading Roman historian, describes the Roman triumph as "embedded in the day-to-day political, social, and cultural world of Rome, with innumerable links and associations, both personal and institutional, to other ceremonies, customs, events, and traditions."[62] After meticulously proving this point throughout her book on the Roman triumph, Beard concludes her work by saying, "I have come to read the Roman triumph in a sense that goes far beyond its role as a procession through the streets. Of course it was that. But it was also a cultural idea, a 'ritual in ink,' a trope of power, a metaphor of love, a thorn in the side, a world view, a dangerous hyperbole, a marker of time, of change, and continuity."[63] In other words, the power of the Roman triumph went far beyond a mere one-time parade through the streets of Rome; instead, it was a defining element of the existence and dominance of Rome that perpetuated its glory and defined its sovereignty — a message that would symbolically adorn the entire empire, including Asia Minor.

A specific example from the chief city of Asia Minor — Ephesus (see Rev 2:1-7) — offers evidence for both the existence of triumphal procession imagery in the cities of Revelation and the imagery of the single bound captive of the Roman triumph in Rev 20:7-10 suggested above. Steven J. Friesen has argued for the overwhelming influence of the Roman imperial cult in the city of Ephesus and Asia Minor as a whole.[64] Simply stated, the imperial cult is defined as the worship of the Roman emperor as a god. Imperial cult worship intensified in its reach and zeal later in the first century C.E. under the reign of Domitian.[65] In Ephesus, in particular, the city's architectural landscape and civic allegiances were bombarded with the unabashed deification of the Flavian dynasty while Domitian was still living and

189

reigning as emperor—an audacious act only replicated by the psychosis of the emperors Caligula and Nero.[66]

As a result, a magnificent temple dedicated to the worship of Domitian as a god was erected at the apex of a main city road that led to the market past the frequented bath houses, public restrooms, and even the local Jewish synagogue.[67] The foot traffic passing by the temple in such a key location could hardly be measured—similar to the pervasiveness of the smell of burnt sacrifices offered in worship to the emperor on the altar just outside of the temple. It is this "open-air" altar at the temple of Domitian in Ephesus that offers an important key to the imagery seen in Rev 20:7-10.

As can be seen in the museum of Ephesus today, this altar, a key cultic tool of the imperial cult temple, is made up of imagery depicting a Roman triumph.[68] On the far left end, the altar shows a bull next to an altar, designating the animal as a sacrifice, with laurel décor lining the top—a specific symbol of Roman triumphs. At the opposite end of the altar two large shields are depicted, which follows the motif on the front side. The front panel contains a conglomeration of foreign weapons, armor, and booty—symbolizing the spoils of war that are marched in a triumphal procession. Significant for our purposes is the center panel. All of the spoils of war from both sides direct the attention of the passerby to the two figures in the middle: one standing in Roman military garb raising a weapon and looking down at the second figure, a single bound captive sitting down awaiting his execution.

Conclusion

Why is this significant? In addition to the pervasive imagery of Roman triumphs throughout the cities on coins, architecture, and other forms of propaganda, the Christians of Ephesus, in Asia Minor, would have encountered the temple to Domitian on possibly a daily basis due to its central location. The altar sitting in front of the temple, closest to the road, would carry the smell of death from the sacrifices burning in worship of the Emperor as god and savior of the world. The smell and the temple remind the onlooker of the dominance and sovereignty of Rome, both of which are celebrated in the ritual of the Roman triumph. The imagery on the altar reiterates this imperial message with a triumphal procession at its climactic moment frozen in its stone depiction — the single bound, chief enemy leader is about to be executed. It would be fitting, then, if John, speaking to the cities of Asia Minor, would borrow such an image to communicate his message of victory celebrated in God's triumphal procession.

Therefore, the release of Satan is the climactic moment of the alter-imperial triumph that began in Rev 19:11-21 with the appearance of the "son of God" on a white horse and culminates in the procession of the "one on the throne" in 21:1-8. The depiction of a single bound captive released from prison and marched to his execution would have made his readers feel right at home, but now the picture that reinforced their oppressive position under the rule of the Roman Empire is transformed into a victorious promise of their liberation at God's triumphal procession.

Every Grain of Sand:

APPLICATION AND THE
BOOK OF REVELATION

IMAGES OF JESUS
IN REVELATION

Mark E. Moore

Revelation begins and ends with a shout out to Jesus: "The revelation of Jesus Christ" (1:1) and "Come, Lord Jesus" (22:20).[1] All too often our interpretations of Revelation fail because we blow past Jesus to the blows of the church. Our anthropocentric interest in "The Tribulation" or end-times chronology blinds us from the very vision designed to sustain us in those times of trial. This essay, therefore, will concentrate on Jesus, specifically the three portraits John paints in chapters 1, 5, and 19. Rather than asking "What will happen?" we will attempt a different and more important question: "Who is *HE*?"

In essence, this is a study of the Christology of Revelation but done in an idiosyncratic way.[2] We are not delving into the titles of Jesus.[3] Rather, we are looking at his portraits and asking how they function in the overall narrative of the book. From the rise of the first curtain, Jesus is center stage, standing in the spotlight with his coauthors, God the Father and the Sevenfold Spirit (1:4-6). Here he bears three titles: Faithful Witness, Firstborn from the Dead, and Ruler of the Kings of the Earth. These three titles represent the three portraits which punctuate Revelation. The Colossal High Priest of chapter 1 is the *faithful witness* to the seven churches. The slain lamb of chapter 5 stands in the midst of God's throne as the *firstborn from the dead*. And the Rider on the White Horse *rules the kings of the earth* in chapter 19. Hence, from the opening doxology, Jesus stands center stage as the lens through which the rest of Revelation's Christology will be read.[4]

The Heavenly High Priest, Revelation 1:12-18

The first portrait of Jesus is so striking that it knocks John to the ground (1:17). The portrait is drawn from the well of OT imagery. As the following chart shows, it is a composite of the visionary figures of Daniel 7:9-14 and 10:5-6:

> The Ancient of Days took his seat. His clothing was as white as snow; the *hair of his head was white like wool*. His throne was flaming with fire, and its wheels were all ablaze. . . .there before me was one like a *son of man*, coming with the clouds of heaven. He approached the Ancient of Days and was led into his presence. He was given authority, glory and sovereign power; all peoples, nations and men of every language worshiped him. (Dan 7:9,13-14)

> I looked up and there before me was a man *dressed in linen*, with a *belt of the finest gold* around his waist. His body was like chrysolite, his face like lightning, his *eyes like flaming torches*, his arms and legs like the gleam of *burnished bronze*, and his *voice* like the sound of a multitude. (Dan 10:5-6)

The figure has the accoutrements of a priest (robe, sash, and candlesticks)[5] but the face, eyes, hair, and voice of Yahweh.

Image from Rev 1	Old Testament Source(s) of the Image	Attribute of:
Seven Lampstands (cf. 1:20; 2:1)	Num 8:2, the seven lampstands gave light in front of the temple	Priest
	Zech 4:2, describes an apocalyptic lampstand with seven lights directly connected to the olive tree.	Priest
Son of Man	Dan 7:13-14, He approached the ancient of days and was given all power and authority and was worshiped.	Man
Robe (ποδήρης)	The Linen Ephod of the High Priest: Exod 25:7; 28:4,31; 29:5; 35:9; Zech 3:4; Wis 18:24; Sir 45:8.	Priest
	Ezek 9:2,3,11, an apocalyptic harbinger of the city's destruction. With his writing kit he marked those in the city not to be destroyed.	Angel
Golden Sash	High Priestly Vestments: Exod 28:4,39,40; 29:9; 36:36; Lev 8:7,13; 16:4 [אבנט].	Priest

Hair white like wool	Dan 7:9, "the hair of his head like pure wool"	God
Eyes of fire (cf. 2:18; 19:12)	Dan 10:6, "His body was like beryl, his face like lightning, his eyes like flaming torches, his arms and legs like the gleam of burnished bronze, and the sound of his words like the roar of a multitude."	Angel
Feet like glowing bronze (cf. 2:18)	Dan 10:6 [see above], also the four living creatures of Ezek 1:7.	Angel
Voice like rushing water (cf. 1:10, "like a trumpet")	Dan 10:6 "his words like the roar of a multitude"; God's voice is like many waters (Ezek 43:2) and like thunder (Job 40:9). The voice of the four living creatures is also like thunder (Rev 6:1) and the mighty angel has a voice like a lion roaring (Rev 10:3).	God/Angel
Right hand held seven stars (cf. 1:20; 2:1; 3:1)	It may refer to the seven stars of the constellation of Pleiades (Amos 5:8, KJV).	God
Double-edged sword (δίστομος, cf. Rev 2:12; Heb 4:12)	"The word of God is living and active, sharper than any two-edged sword" (Heb 4:12).	Prophet
	In the OT it was both literal (Judg 3:16; Ps 149:6) and metaphoric (Prov 5:4; Sir 21:3).	Prophet
Face shining	Moses' face shone from God's presence (Exod 34:30,35; 2Cor 4:6); in a similar fashion, Jesus' face shone at the transfiguration (Mt 17:2/Mk 9:3/Lk 9:29).	Prophet
	2Esd 7:97 (cf. 7:125), the 6th of 7 levels of exalted souls have shining faces.	Saints
	Zion allegorically appears as a woman with a shining face (2Esd 10:25).	Saints
First and Last (cf. 1:8; 21:6)	Isa 44:6; this is a title for Yahweh, which Jesus assumes in 22:13.	God
Living One (cf. 4:9; 10:6; also 7:2; 15:7)	A title for God in 1:4,8; 4:8 (c.f. Deut 5:26; Josh 3:10; 1Sam 17:36; 2Kgs 19:4; 3Macc 6:28; Acts 14:15; 2Cor 3:3; 6:16; 1Thes 1:9; 1Tim 3:15; 4:10; Heb 3:12; 9:14; 10:31; 12:22).	God
Keys of death and Hades	The sole prerogative of God (Deut 32:39; 1Sam 2:6; Tob 13:2; Wis 16:13). They were not given to any delegate according to the Rabbis (b. Taan 2a) or any creature (PesiqR 42.7, 178a).	God

197

In one sense, this looks like other appearances of mighty angels (e.g., Dan 10:4-6; Ezek 1:4-28, 9:1-11; *Apoc. Ab.*; 3 *Enoch, b. Sanh.* 38b) but never was an angel granted equivalent status with God.[6] As the chart above points out, several attributes of the celestial figure could be applied to a mighty angel. However, the white hair, grasping stars, first/last, ever-living one, and possessing the keys to death and Hades are the exclusive properties of Yahweh.[7] Thus we have an apocalyptic figure of a celestial being that takes on the appearance, authority, and titles of Yahweh.

One would naturally assume, therefore, that this is a theophany (an appearance of Yahweh) except for the fact that he is introduced as one "like a Son of Man." This was a popular term in the OT[8] and in the Gospels[9] but after that it only shows up four times (Acts 7:56; Heb 2:6; Rev 1:13; 14:14). What does it mean? In Ezekiel it is God's designation for the prophet. Otherwise, it is a general term for humanity with a particular emphasis on human frailty.[10] It's not necessarily an insult but no one would brag about this title either.

Hence, here in Revelation 1, "Son of Man" suggests this theophany is a human figure. Now that's odd. However, this paradox has a precedent. In Daniel 7:13-14 one like a son of man was affiliated with God's majesty on high and promised adoration on earth. Only Daniel's heavenly "son of Man" can explain John's use of this term.[11] Thus, we have a conflation of deity and humanity in this opening vision of Jesus as a heavenly High Priest.

The Crucified Lamb, Revelation 5:5-6

Our second portrait is a mere snapshot compared to the first. Two simple verses promise a majestic lion but wind up offering a bludgeoned lamb. At first blush this would appear to be an egregious case of false advertising. As it will turn out, the power promised in the King of the Beasts is wrought through the weakness of the Lamb.

The action takes place in the throne room of God which opened back in chapter four. These two chapters are deliberate parallels:[12] both open with John looking (εἶδον) at the throne

(4:2,9; 5:1,7,13) which is surrounded by four living creatures (4:6,8; 5:6,8,14) and twenty-four elders (4:4,10; 5:5,6,8,11,14). They fall down in worship (4:10; 5:8,14) with all of creation (4:11; 5:13) because God and the Lamb are "worthy" of praise (4:11; 5:2,4,9,12). In short, John put an equal sign between Yahweh and the Lamb. For those steeped in Christian traditions this is not nearly as scandalous as to one wearing a yarmulke or a toga. For the Jew, this would be a bodacious, even blasphemous claim.[13] For the Roman it would smack of anti-imperialism and an assault against the burgeoning Emperor Cult in Asia Minor.[14] The scandal resides in the throne, the scroll, and the songs.

The Throne clearly belongs to Yahweh but it is shared by Jesus. He stands in the midst of the throne.[15] He was not *being* enthroned (as the mythical Son of Man of *1 Enoch* 69.26-29); he belonged there. His "standing" is reminiscent of Acts 7:56 when Jesus was seen standing at the right hand of God. Both Acts 7 and Revelation 5 hearken back to Daniel 7:13-14 where the Son of Man receives divine honors.[16] Thus, Jesus standing is not a sign of subordination to Yahweh; rather it is evidence that the one slain is alive and well.

The Two-Sided Scroll has been the subject of a good bit of speculation. One theory that fits not only the description of the scroll but the theme of the vision is a Roman Testament. "In accordance with the Roman custom of preparing and sealing a testament in the presence of seven witnesses, John sees a 'scroll' (*biblion*) 'having been sealed with seven seals'."[17] Jesus is receiving his inheritance. That's why he alone is worthy to open this scroll. As Unnik demonstrates, the word "worthy" is used with particular reference to one who has passed a test or achieved a victory and thus earns access to divine mysteries.[18] The Lamb has the bloodstains to prove he is worthy to stand as the Lion.

The Songs of the Elders (vv. 9-10) and the angels (vv. 12-13) afford the Lamb the same status as Yahweh, "To the one seated on the throne and to the Lamb be blessing and honor and glory and might forever and ever!" (v. 13b). Both Yahweh and the Lamb share eschatological judgment (6:15-17), both are the Alpha and Omega (1:8; 22:13), and both share the same name

(14:1), the same throne and the same servants (22:3).[19] This is all the more astounding since even the mighty angel in Revelation refuses adulation from John (19:10; 22:8-9). This is the kind of adulation which flowed freely around the throne of the Emperor, particularly the megalomaniac Domitian. "John's description in Revelation of the heavenly ceremony practiced in the throne room of God bears such a striking resemblance to the ceremonial of the imperial court and cult that the latter can only be a parody of the former."[20]

What makes this image particularly striking is that the one worshiped was not the Lion, but the Lamb. One can understand the Lion's being exalted. That beast had long been a figure of the Messiah (Gen 49:9-10; Isa 11:10; Ps 76:1[2]; 2Esd 12:31).[21] But the lamb was a symbol of weakness. This particular word for "lamb" (ἀρνίον) is used thirty-one times in the NT and thirty of those are in Revelation. They all refer to Jesus (except 13:11 where the beast tries to imitate him), and it all starts here in 5:6. No other title for Jesus in Revelation comes close to the Lamb in prominence or dominance. Jesus, throughout the Revelation, is the lamb. His weakness is not a passage to greatness; it is not the means by which he becomes the Lion. The weakness of the Lamb *is* his power; it is the blood of this vicarious martyr which makes him the victorious savior of the saints.

Some have attempted to rehabilitate the lamb by calling him a ram[22] and pointing out the power he has in his horns (cf. Dan 8:3-12; 1 Enoch 89.46; 9:6-19; T. Jos. 19.8).[23] This misses the point of the metaphor. The Lamb doesn't transform into a powerful beast. He doesn't wash his wounds and grow fangs. He ever remains the bloodied lamb, for it is in his weakness that his strength lies. There is no question that he is a mighty warrior (17:14; 19:7,9). However, his sacrifice is what vanquished his enemies; his blood disarmed the devil (12:10; 13:8; 14:4; 21:27). He becomes the model martyr for all those who will soon follow.[24] As Blount puts it, Jesus was "Wreaking Weakness":

> Unbelievably, God apparently believes this strategy will win the eternal day and transform human history into a reality where the dragon is dead and God dwells directly and securely with God's people. According to John, God's victorious way is the

slaughtered way; it not only describes the path God's son took, it prescribes the path God's people will take on their way to the new heaven and new earth their combative effort will help God create.[25]

The Conquering King, Revelation 19:11-16

This final image of Jesus as a conquering warrior is, at the same time, the most invigorating and the most troublesome. It is the most invigorating because, alas, all beleaguered believers are rescued by our mighty redeemer. It is the most troublesome, at least for those who wince at the image of a violent and despotic deity. It should be clear, however, that this portrait does not stand alone. It is part of a collage of Christ in Revelation and must be viewed in coherence with the Son of Man and Slain Lamb.

There is simply no getting around the fact that Revelation 19:11-16 plays off the image of the Divine Warrior in the OT and other Ancient Near Eastern texts but particularly Isaiah 63:1-6:[26]

"Who is this that comes from Edom, from Bozrah in garments stained crimson? Who is this so splendidly robed, marching in his great might?" "It is I, announcing vindication, mighty to save." "Why are your robes red, and your garments like theirs who tread the wine press?" "I have trodden the wine press alone, and from the peoples no one was with me; I trod them in my anger and trampled them in my wrath; their juice spattered on my garments, and stained all my robes. For the day of vengeance was in my heart, and the year for my redeeming work had come. I looked, but there was no helper; I stared, but there was no one to sustain me; so my own arm brought me victory, and my wrath sustained me. I trampled down peoples in my anger, I crushed them in my wrath, and I poured out their lifeblood on the earth.

Here in Revelation 19:11-16 Jesus comes astride a white horse with a robe that is paradoxically both bloodstained from battle and clean white linen. In his hand is an iron scepter and from his mouth juts a double-edged sword. "He will tread the wine press of the fury of the wrath of God the Almighty (*Pantokratōr*)" (v. 15) and invites the birds of the air to consume the carrion of his slaughtered enemies. This is NC-17 stuff for sure. Because of such images, Friedrich Nietzsche slandered Revelation as, "the most rabid outburst of vindictiveness in all recorded history."[27]

Revelation can, and has been, read this way, rendering a portrait of Jesus antithetical to that of the Gospels. This is not likely John's intent. The following observations suggest that John is subverting rather than adopting the Divine Warrior motif.

1. The entire scene is prefaced with the "Halleluiah" choruses culminating in a **wedding feast** (v. 6-9).[28] The emphasis is not exclusively, and perhaps not even primarily, on the destruction of God's enemies but on the rescue of his people. The original recipients read this letter first and foremost as an exhortation to those inside the church as opposed to a threat to those outside the church. Our emphasis, therefore, should be on God's promise to believers rather than his warning to the world.

2. Jesus slays with a **sword** coming out of his mouth, obviously a reference to his words, not a literal weapon. The sword aligns with Jesus' appellation "Word of God" (v. 13).[29] Christians are familiar with this metaphor from Hebrews 4:12; Jews were familiar with it from Isaiah 49:2 (cf. Isa 11:4b). This is not physical violence but legal declaration (cf. Jn 5:22-30).

3. The most troublesome description is the **blood-soaked robe** in conjunction with treading the winepress of God's wrath (v. 15; cf. 14:20). The image is rather gruesome. Human enemies are thrown into a giant vat where colossal feet pop their bodies into a bloody libation staining the garments of God. That may work with Isaiah 63:3 but it breaks down in Revelation 19:13,15. Jesus' robe is dipped[30] in blood *prior* to coming to the battlefield. These stains were from a previous battle, ostensibly 12:11, "They have conquered him [the devil] by the blood of the Lamb and by the word of their testimony."[31] Jesus is not a *bloody* warrior but the *bloodied* one. While there is a lot of blood in the book, virtually all of it is Jesus' (1:5; 5:9; 7:14) and his followers (6:10; 16:6; 17:6; 18:24; 19:2). This blood-soaked garment, far from supporting the Divine Warrior motif, subverts it. This is

not merely the message of Revelation 19, this is the consistent portrait of Jesus throughout the book of Revelation.[32] It is the same Jesus we encounter in the Gospels who lays down his life for his sheep.

4. There is, surprisingly, **no battle**. Chapter 19 poises the global armies for war, yet no shot is fired, no bow drawn, no missile launched. Why? Because the unassailable weapons of Jesus are his sacrificial death and his divine declarations of judgment. The fact is, there are precious few direct confrontations between Yahweh and his enemies and most of those are either in the passive verb tense or arbitrated by angelic mediators (e.g. 14:20, the single mention of the blood of God's enemies).[33] In fact, the most direct violence in the book of Revelation is 17:16, "The ten horns that you saw, they and the beast will hate the whore; they will make her desolate and naked; they will devour her flesh and burn her up with fire." This violence was of the wicked destroying their own (albeit by the sovereign will of God).

Conclusions

All this leads to two decisive conclusions. First, the portraits of revelation present Jesus as God but in an unexpected way. He lays down his life as the lamb. It is his self-abnegation and sacrifice that wins the galactic battle. This Christology shares the same basic contours of that found in Paul and the Gospels.

The images of Jesus point to a second conclusion not heretofore mentioned. Namely, each of these images precedes a terrible tribulation. The heavenly High Priest stands before the seven churches of chapters two and three. In fact, each of the seven letters begins with a snippet of the vision of chapter highlighting one of the attributes of Jesus. These churches under duress, often due to their own sin, must fix their eyes on Jesus if they are to survive the onslaught of the evil one. The Lamb, likewise, stands before the great tribulation when all hell breaks loose (chapter 6–9). In order to survive the dragon, the saints had better look to the Lamb. Our survival and triumph is directly due to his blood and our faithful witness of a slain savior (12:11). Finally, before the final battle stands the King of

Kings, a victorious warrior with unassailable strength. True enough, the bound beast is released for a short time in chapter twenty. He will wreak havoc but only on those who lose sight of the Rider on the White Horse. In face of an uncertain future, it is the image of a coming king that sustains the saints through the thick side of suffering.

These images are not merely aesthetic or theological. They drive the narrative in Revelation. They are the foundational images John offered a church in crisis. Without a clear picture of Jesus, we will lose our way. What Revelation reveals is not our future but our savior.

SUFFERING AND HOPE IN REVELATION 2–3

Carmen Trenton

"'In this world you will have trouble. But take heart! I have overcome the world'"

—Jesus (Jn 16:33b NIV)

Introduction

Today's airwaves are filled with accounts of disasters devastating human lives: earthquakes, tsunamis, hurricanes, fires, floods, and the ravages of war, all taking their toll in human suffering. Headlines report world economic and financial dangers, political upheavals, and hazards to general health. They decry the physical pain, suffering, and death, all the while mostly ignoring the worsening spiritual blight on the human condition. Our country, and many others around the globe, has for decades gone about removing God from the public arena. Our media glorify immorality and our churches often look not all that different from the outside world. Christians have gone from being respected to being ridiculed and sometimes despised. Even lives are in jeopardy with worldwide persecutions on the rise.

With such real physical, mental, and spiritual need, how does the church bear Christ and nourish hope in such a time? I believe the book of Revelation gives us guidance—in particular, Jesus' words to the seven churches in Asia Minor. The churches were suffering from persecution and spiritual malaise. Jesus' message to them in Revelation 2 and 3 includes praise and rebuke, encouragement and counsel, warning and promise. Threaded throughout is a message of encouragement and hope for those suffering.

In this essay I will show: (1) there is a NT warrant for suffering with Christ; (2) Romans 5 shows that Christian suffering leads to hope; (3) the seven churches vary in their willingness to suffer for Christ, affecting hope; and (4) Jesus' self-introductions and concluding promises form a basis for both present and future hope.

New Testament Warrant for Suffering with Christ

The NT confirms our call to suffer with Christ. The Suffering Savior we serve calls us to deny ourselves, take up our cross daily, and follow him (Lk 9:23). Paul told the Philippians it had been granted to them "not only to believe on [Christ], but also to suffer for him" (Phil 1:29). Paul also said he wanted to know "the fellowship of sharing in [Christ's] sufferings" (Phil 3:10). Peter said, "But if you suffer for doing good and you endure it, this is commendable before God. To this you were called, because Christ suffered for you, leaving you an example, that you should follow in his steps" (1Pet 2:20b-21). Finally, Paul said that we are "heirs of God and co-heirs with Christ, if indeed we share in his sufferings in order that we may also share in his glory" (Rom 8:16-17). This witness of Scripture has been borne out in the suffering of saints for two millennia. Christians who follow Christ in a fallen world will suffer for him.

Romans 5

> And we rejoice in the hope of the glory of God. Not only so, but we also rejoice in our sufferings, because we know that suffering produces perseverance; perseverance, character; and character, hope. And hope does not disappoint us, because God has poured out his love into our hearts by the Holy Spirit, whom he has given us. (Rom 5:2b-5).[1]

Paul turned upside down popular notions of suffering. While citizens of a broken world may claim it leads to despair, Paul says that, for Christians, suffering leads to hope.

Hope. Christian hope has both a *now* element, placing our confidence in Christ, and a *future* element, the eager expectation of dwelling with Christ for all eternity with an end to suffering. Christian hope, then, is confidence in the sustaining presence of Christ and the sure fulfillment of biblical promises.

Suffering Produces Perseverance. By allowing us to suffer, God tests us and gives us opportunity to shore up our confidence in him. He wants us to rely on him completely, as Jesus did (Jn 8:28-29). Suffering often places us in situations beyond our control where we must rely on God. As we do, we build endurance[2] to bring us through our next test (1Pet 5:10).

Perseverance Produces Character. Dr. Lowery likes to quote: "Sow a thought, reap an act; sow an act, reap a habit; sow a habit, reap a character; sow a character, reap a destiny."[3] Habit is key. As we endure suffering, we make it a habit to rely on God. That develops character—the complex of traits marking a person.[4] We are marked by our reliance on God. It has become habitual. James supports this notion, saying that testing develops perseverance that leads to maturity [character] (Jas 1:3-4).

Character Produces Hope. As we find God dependable in our tests, we shore up our hope that he will continue to be dependable. Enduring is what we do. Character is who we become—one who habitually endures. Enduring suffering yields the maturity that dares to hope.

Heart-filled Love. Romans 5 grounds this hope in the love that the Holy Spirit pours into our hearts. The Spirit is a little piece of heaven, a down payment on other promises. Since we feel God's love in our heart and see the Spirit working within us, we have assurance that Christ has claimed us and will bring us into his eternal kingdom.

A recent news broadcast interviewed a US Navy Special Forces recruit: "They pretty much took me through everything possible, mentally and physically . . . . That's when you know you can do it."[5] Endurance alone shows what *we* can do. Endurance relying on God's love and strength shows what *God* can do. God can meet us in our suffering and bring us to hope.

The Seven Churches: Suffering and Hope

In Revelation 1, Jesus instructs John to write to the angel of each of the seven churches in Asia Minor. These letters are in chapters 2 and 3. Revelation 1:9-20 prepares the reader for the messages Christ gives to the seven churches.[6] Specifically, Revelation's human author, John, identifies himself with the suffering churches by his own suffering (1:9). Jesus identifies with the churches through the description of his exalted appearance (1:12-20). He selects relevant elements of that description for each of his self-introductions to the churches, shoring up the church's present hope.

The seven letters have a parallel structure: Jesus' self-introduction, praise and rebuke, command, warning or encouragement, and a final promise meant for all of the churches. Not all churches have all elements. Smyrna and Philadelphia receive no rebuke, Laodicea receives no praise, and Sardis gets an honorable mention. Below, I look at the suffering of each church and its basis for hope.

1. Ephesus (Rev 2:1-7)

Acts 19 records the apostle Paul bringing word of Jesus to the Ephesians. They received the Holy Spirit, spoke in tongues, and prophesied. Paul did "extraordinary miracles" (19:11) and "the word of the Lord spread widely and grew in power" (19:20). This threatened the cultic worship and business enterprise surrounding the goddess Artemis and a riot ensued (19:23-41). Unharmed, Paul warned the Ephesian elders: "Savage wolves will come in among you and will not spare the flock. Even from your own number men will arise and distort the truth in order to draw away disciples after them. So be on your guard!" (Acts 20:29-31a).

Jesus' praise in Rev 2:2-3 shows the church had heeded Paul's warning by not tolerating wicked men, exposing false apostles, and hating "the practices of the Nicolaitans."[7] He commends their hard work, perseverance, and enduring hardships for him. This implies anguish, even in hating wicked practices. The besieged church is suffering.

Despite their worthy deeds, Jesus rebukes them: "You have forsaken your first love." He tells them: "Repent and do the things you did at first." Otherwise, Jesus will remove their lampstand. Since "lampstand" refers to the church (1:20), Jesus is threatening the church with extinction.

"First love" is better rendered "the love you had at first."[8] Beale urges that "first love" means their Christian witness, citing Christ's self-identification: "him who . . . walks among the seven golden lampstands" (Rev 2:1).[9] Lamps give light, which implies witness. This is true, but Jesus mentions *both* love and action. The love in view is for both God and neighbor. If love is there, witness will follow. Jesus wants their light to shine again (Mt 5:16). Their lamp is flickering, but it does not need the wick turned up; it needs more oil.

The oil that the Ephesian lampstand needs is love, like they had at first. Romans 5 says that suffering leads to hope, through perseverance and character, grounded in love. The church is suffering, and persevering, but is no longer properly grounded in love. Paul said they had been "rooted and established in love" (Eph 3:17). To restore hope they must restore that love. Jesus, who "walks among the seven golden lampstands," has power to remove or refresh their lampstand. His command to repent is an act of love. If they do repent, he will grant life to their church and their suffering can again lead to hope, grounded in renewed love.

Jesus' final message to each church is to the *individual* "who overcomes." Here the final message is for all of the churches, not just Ephesus. Jesus promises that the overcomer will "eat from the tree of life, which is in the paradise of God" (Rev 2:7). Just as Jesus implies *continued life* for the church that repents, he promises *eternal life* for the one who overcomes. Amen!

2. Smyrna (Rev 2:8-11)

Smyrna was a picturesque port city on an Aegean Sea inlet, with beautiful buildings and temples to pagan Gods. Politically aligned with Rome, it was a center of the imperial cult, which worshiped Roman emperors as divine.[10] The large Jewish population in Smyrna was exempt from emperor worship. Christians no longer enjoyed that protection, and Jews were not reluctant to inform against them to authorities. Jews also opposed Christians on religious grounds, considering "worship of a crucified criminal" as blasphemy.[11]

At the time of the Revelation 2 letter, the church is enduring poverty and persecution, yet Jesus says they are rich. He offers no rebuke of Smyrna or Philadelphia. They have remained faithful in the face of opposition, including slander by the Jews. The Smyrna church's poverty could have resulted from being marginalized as nonparticipants in the emperor cult. The nature of the Jewish slander is not given, but Jesus seems to say that Christians are the real Jews. The so-called Jews, those slandering Christians, "are a synagogue of Satan," hardly a description of true Israel.

Not only are the Christians suffering now, they will suffer much more. These are Romans 5 sufferers. They have continued to suffer in poverty, but Jesus calls them "rich." They are rich spiritually. When Jesus tells them not to fear upcoming imprisonment, a test of the devil, Jesus expects they can do it. They are mature and maturing.

Jesus says they will be persecuted and should "be faithful, even to the point of death." If they are, they will receive "the crown of life." Everlasting life is their future hope. They can believe it because of who said it: the one who is "the First and the Last, who died and came to life again." Because he died and lives, so can they—whether by martyrdom or natural death. But Jesus gives one more promise to all who overcome: they "will not be hurt at all by the second death," the lake of fire for unrepentant sinners (Rev 20:14; 21:8).

The church in Smyrna heeded Jesus' message. Half a century later, Polycarp, for some time the bishop of Smyrna, was martyred. When they tried to burn him alive, the fire would not burn him, but instead, formed an arch around him. Eventually, they killed him with a dagger. He would not deny Christ, but instead said, "Eighty and six years have I served Him, and He never did me any injury: how then can I blaspheme my King and my Saviour?"[12] Amen!

3. Pergamum (Rev 2:12-17)

Pergamum was Asia's oldest city and provincial capital. It had temples to the Roman emperor and several gods, including Zeus and the serpent god Asclepius, god of healing.[13] Roman influence extended to emperor worship and a resident Roman proconsul had "the power of the sword" to inflict capital punishment.[14]

According to Jesus, Pergamum is living "where Satan has his throne" (2:13). This might mean worshiping pagan gods or the Roman emperor, or it might address the entire idolatrous and immoral community. The church is resisting while suffering persecution, evidenced by their faithfulness even when Antipas was martyred, probably by Roman officials. Yet, Jesus rebukes Pergamum for tolerating heretical teachers who encourage immorality and "eating food sacrificed to idols" (14). He tells them to repent [of their neglected discipline] or he will come and fight the teachers himself.

Looking at Romans 5, the church has clearly been suffering and enduring trials, but noncompromisers have not persevered enough to reach to the solid character that exercises discipline. Hope is in jeopardy. The compromisers fall down at the first step, unwilling to suffer for Christ. Jesus addresses only the noncompromisers, expecting their discipline to address the problem of the compromisers.

Jesus' self-identification as "him who has the sharp, double-edged sword" shows his power over both Rome and the compromisers. This shores up the church's present hope. If they trust Jesus and exercise discipline, they will be producing the character that leads to future hope. Jesus also gives future hope in his promise to overcomers: they will eat true spiritual food (not offered to idols) and receive a new private name on a white stone, a new identity in him. Amen!

4. Thyatira (Rev 2:18-29)

Thyatira was situated on key trade routes, which gave rise to numerous trade guilds (trade unions) for all types of merchandise. They worshiped pagan gods and required participation in festivals and temple gatherings where members ate meals and engaged in sexual promiscuity. Those who did not participate, such as Christians, faced limited employment opportunity and social isolation.[15]

Some in the church may be suffering due to nonparticipation in the guilds. In Jesus' list of praises, the only hint of possible suffering is "perseverance," perhaps indicating resistance. In any case, Jesus rebukes the church, much like Pergamum, for tolerating compromise with the culture. He singles out Jezebel and those she is misleading into sexual immorality and idolatry. She is giving them a way out of suffering. Claiming to be a prophetess with "dark secrets," she appears to be persuading vulnerable church members that their sinful indulgences (through the guilds?) are approved.

Jesus issues judgment on the compromisers. Those who are sinning with Jezebel will face intense suffering, unless they repent. Jezebel's opportunity is past; her judgment is certain: Jesus will cause her to suffer and even "strike her children dead." As to the noncompromisers, they are to hold on to what they have, with no other burden imposed.

How does Romans 5 play? As with Pergamum, Thyatira's failure to exercise church discipline means the church has not endured enough to produce mature character. Compromisers fail at the outset by avoiding Jesus' example of suffering. Unless they repent their path to hope is aborted.

Jesus' self identification, having eyes "like blazing fire," echoes in his words that he is the one "who searches hearts and minds." His coming as a judge can actually bring hope to sufferers. Jesus' promise to overcomers here alone adds "does my will to the end," telling us how and how long they are to overcome. They must persevere, but Jesus gives hope: they will reign with him in his coming messianic kingdom. Beale says both the Psalm 2 excerpt (v. 27) and "the morning star" point to the messianic kingdom.[16] Jesus will reign in his kingdom long after the idols have crumbled. Amen!

5. Sardis (Rev 3:1-6)

Sardis was both an elevated fortress and a fertile valley community. The latter was situated at the crossroads of two important trade routes, fostering commerce and attendant wealth. Idol worship was pervasive with temples to many pagan gods.[17] Gold from the Pactolus River contributed to Sardis's prosperity and they were the first to strike "gold and silver coins."[18]

Jesus gives no leading praise to Sardis. They are reputedly alive but are actually dead. Their deeds are incomplete. Evidently they are neither servicing their members nor witnessing to the community. Jesus tells them to wake up, shape up, and repent. If they do not, he "will come like a thief."

Is this church suffering? Jesus mentions no oppression from outside forces, no heretics from within. They appear to be oblivious of their plight and are not explicitly suffering. Jesus does hint as to what is going on when he says some "have not soiled their clothes." Evidently the majority have. They have perhaps so assimilated into the surrounding pagan culture's values and practices that they look no different. There is no persecution because there is no threat. In Thyatira, Jezebel gave the conscienced compromisers a rationale. Sardis does not need her; they do not see a problem.

As to Romans 5, Sardis is stuck at the starting point: the majority are not suffering for Jesus, so they are not persevering. Their only hope is to heed Jesus' call to repent. If their Christian witness resumes, they must be willing to suffer in the midst of their pagan community and persevere, leading to maturity and hope.

Jesus gives a special promise to noncompromisers: they will walk with him "dressed in white," a reference to Jesus' coming kingdom. This shores up their hope now and for the future with Christ. To all overcomers he gives a like promise and adds that he will acknowledge the overcomer before "my Father and his angels." This is every overcomer's future hope. Amen!

6. Philadelphia (Rev 3:7-13)

Philadelphia was a prosperous city with temples and festivals dedicated to various gods. Located on a confluence of trade routes between Asia and Europe, it became known as "gateway to the East."[19] Although this gave it commercial and cultural importance, its size was somewhat constrained by earthquake activity. After the large quake of A.D. 17, many citizens moved to the countryside. There was also a subsequent name change to Neocaesarea, which stood for several decades.[20]

How is the church at Philadelphia doing? It is very much like Smyrna. Leon Morris gives this general summary: "Both receive no blame, only praise. Both suffered from those who called themselves Jews and were not, both were persecuted it would seem by the Romans, both are assured that the opposition is satanic, and both are promised a crown."[21] Keener finds it likely that the Jews excluded both Smyrna and Philadelphia churches from the Jewish synagogue.[22] This may be why Jesus says he "holds the key of David," has sole control over opening and shutting, and tells them, "I have placed before you an open door that no one can shut." The Jews may shut the synagogue door, but Jesus opens the door to the heavenly kingdom. He will make the Jews admit that he has loved the Christians.

These are words of hope for the Philadelphian church. They have suffered, endured patiently, kept Jesus' word, and not denied him. They are Romans 5 Christians. Because of this, Jesus promises to keep them from the coming "hour of trial." He commands them to "hold on to what you have [faith, endurance], so that no one will take your crown."

Jesus closes with hope for the overcomer. He will be a pillar in God's temple and never leave it. Kistemaker sees significance for those who suffered from earthquakes: instead of flimsy shelters, the temple has solid pillars; instead of dislocation, they will never have to leave the temple. They will also receive new names, as the city had.[23] The greater significance, however, lies in Jesus' promises: overcomers will dwell with their God in the new Kingdom and they will never *ever* be shut out. Amen!

7. Laodicea (Rev 3:14-22)

At the time of the Revelation letter to Laodicea, the city was quite wealthy and prospered as a center for banking, wool products, and medicine. Their water was remotely supplied and became tepid as it flowed through the aqueduct.[24] A mostly pagan community, their patron deity was Zeus but they had temples for a veritable panoply of gods.[25]

How is the church suffering? Evidently it is not. They are stuck at the starting point of Romans 5: unwilling to suffer for Jesus. He criticizes their "deeds" as lukewarm, possibly a wordplay on the Laodicean tepid water, which was good for neither bathing (hot) nor drinking (cold) and was also unpalatable.[26] Accordingly, Jesus, who introduces himself as "the faithful and true witness" wants to spit the tepid, faithless nonwitnesses out of his mouth.

Laodiceans boast of their wealth and self-sufficiency, but instead are "poor, blind, and naked." They are *spiritually* poor, blind to their condition, and nakedly exposed as shameful. He counsels them to buy "gold refined in the fire." As refining gold burns off impurities, so he invites them to purify themselves in the crucible of persecution, by refraining from their present compromising practices (1Pet 1:6-9).[27] Getting "white clothes to wear" means they will keep themselves from the sinful aspects of their culture. By applying eye salve, they will gain spiritual discernment of their fallen condition.

Jesus, by way of encouragement, tells them that he rebukes and disciplines those whom he loves. By asking them to repent, he is giving them another chance. Only by being willing to suffer for him will they return to the path that leads to hope.

Jesus saves one of his most encouraging and hopeful promises to last. It is not just for Laodicea, but for "anyone." Jesus is knocking at the door. If anyone opens it, Jesus will fellowship with that one — now, during suffering, and into eternity. His final promise is to overcomers: they will sit with him on his throne, as he overcame and joined his Father on his throne. Let all who overcome say, "Amen!"

Conclusion

The seven churches of Revelation succeeded or failed at various points along the path from suffering to hope. Sardis and Laodicea failed at the starting point by refusing to suffer. Pergamum and Thyatira endured somewhat but fell short at character. Ephesus failed in the undergirding love. Only Smyrna and Philadelphia followed faithfully.

The seven churches' call is also our call. In troubled times, our Suffering Savior, the Lamb who was slain, calls us to follow him in the path of suffering. Dietrich Bonhoeffer captured it: "When Christ calls a man, he bids him come and die."[28] We die to ourselves that we might live for Christ. Our suffering will not cease until God's kingdom fully comes and He wipes every tear from our eyes (Rev 21:4). But our Suffering Savior rose Triumphant as Conqueror of all suffering, sin, and death. His promises to the seven churches are our promises and they lead to our hope as well.

The word *hope* occurs nowhere in the book of Revelation, yet hope abounds: in the letters to the seven churches, in the heavenly worship scene, in the New Jerusalem coming down from heaven, and in Dr. Lowery's favorite passage, the Wedding Supper of the Lamb, beloved by him for its celebration, intimacy, community, and love. This is our hope.

How do we live and nourish hope in our own troubled times? We persevere with Jesus:

> Let us throw off everything that hinders and the sin that so easily entangles, and let us run with perseverance the race marked out for us. Let us fix our eyes on Jesus, the author and perfecter of our faith, who for the joy set before him endured the cross, scorning its shame, and sat down at the right hand of the throne of God. (Heb 12:1b-2)

Christ paved the way. He endured, so we can endure. He conquered, so we can conquer, but only through him. No present trial cancels his love for us or his promises to us. Through him we endure every tribulation:

> Who shall separate us from the love of Christ? Shall trouble or hardship or persecution or famine or nakedness or danger or sword? As it is written:
> "For your sake we face death all day long;
> we are considered as sheep to be slaughtered."
> No, in all these things we are more than conquerors through him who loved us. For I am convinced that neither death nor life, neither angels nor demons, neither the present nor the future, nor any powers, neither height nor depth, nor anything else in all creation, will be able to separate us from the love of God that is in Christ Jesus our Lord. (Rom 8:35-39).

Come, Lord Jesus, come. Amen!

WHAT CHURCH OF REVELATION DO YOU LOOK LIKE?

Paul E. Boatman

Introduction

Seriously, how can you, or any person, look like a church? It is a suggestion that would have Nicodemus tilting his head and wryly asking, "Can I somehow transform myself into looking like an entire congregation of people? Old, young, tall, short, fat, skinny, handsome, ugly . . . all at the same time?" And perhaps the author of these messages to the churches would declare simply, "I tell you the truth. You already DO look like at least one of these churches." And in light of the fact that we are reflecting on a biblical genre that is replete with symbols, images, and figurative concepts, perhaps it is not stretching it too far at all. Maybe I CAN look like a church.

Actually, I have long known that it works both ways—a church can look like a person and a person can look like a church. For thirty years, I have been asking students in my developmental psychology class in the Seminary at Lincoln Christian University to write a paper on "The Personality Development of a Congregation." Using the lens of developmental psychology, each student takes a careful look at a local congregation, asking such questions as, "What were the factors that brought this church into being?" "Who were the parental figures that nurtured the church into being and toward maturity, and what was their nature?" "What critical formational crises molded the church in its maturing?" "Have there been points of rebellion—regression, or digression from the church's essential nature?" "What alliances has this church formed that have influenced its character?" "Has this church birthed other congregations, and what do those churches look like?" In every paper submitted in response to this assignment, the students identify some strong personality whose influence has been stamped on the face of the congregation. Sometimes, it is an influential preacher who imbued the church with its sense of mission. It may be a faithful elder or mature woman who guided the church through periods of surviving a string of feckless preachers. It may be someone who so negatively dominated the church that, when the congregation chose to move toward maturity, it vowed, "Never again will we let ourselves act like that leader acted."

It would be fascinating if we could raise the questions in the previous paragraph for each of the seven churches. We do know something of the early development of the Ephesian church through Luke's report of the activities of Priscilla and Aquila, Apollos, and, especially, Paul in Acts 18–20. This lively segment of history, along with Paul's epistle to the Ephesians, gives enlightenment to the Spirit's challenge in the letter in Revelation 2. For example, who in Ephesus would not know about the time, several decades earlier, when the number of disciples was growing so rapidly that the craftsmen who made idols saw their trade threatened and stirred up a riot with the fear that the majestic deity, Diana, along with the stunning Temple of Diana was in danger. The huge amphitheater, still nestled today into the side of Mount Pion, was filled with such insane shouting that the city clerk intervened to rescue the city from self-destruction. He, perhaps inadvertently, rescued the disciples who were in danger from the mob. The Ephesians *knew* that the church was a force to be reckoned with.

Beyond Ephesus, however, we have no firm history of the other six churches. Lydia, whom Paul met in Philippi, was *from* Thyatira (Acts 16:14), and one might conjecture about her possible return to her hometown, but such conjecture lacks substance. The church at Laodicea is mentioned several times in Paul's letter to the Colossians, with implied familiarity and even an allusion to another letter that has never been firmly identified. But, again, there is no substantial indication of the origin of this church. Only in the example of Ephesus can we see clear influence of a particular personality upon the nature of that congregation. When it was holding fast to its "first love," the Ephesian church may well have "looked like Paul" or one of his colleagues.

However, as we turn the viewfinder in the opposite direction, we may begin to see among us some distinctive identifying characteristics of some of the seven churches. This may not be a comfortable exercise, but the rather free-ranging figurative style of Revelation almost invites us to wonder and conjecture about nonliteral parallels and applications. How might you, or congregations that you know, look like one of these churches? Even to consider the question is a bit intimidating. None of these churches has survived to the present day. Most received sharp critique from the Spirit. One received no commendation at all! Do we even want to risk seeing how we might look like one of these churches?

Identifying Our "Look-alike"

The title of this essay implies that some of us may have enough similarities, that if we were walking alongside one of the seven churches, a keen-eyed observer might grab a candid shot to amuse the press. But how does one person happen to look like another?

In some instances, genetics are a powerful factor. When I am in a setting where my late father was well-known, I have no anonymity. My physique, physiognomy, and hair (or hairless) style are remarkably reminiscent of Dad. It may be fortunate that we have no physical images of these churches. The wonders of archeology have unearthed elements of the contexts in which these churches existed. We learn much about the economy and culture of the ancient communities, but there are no identified structures or images that say clearly, "First Church of Ephesus, Smyrna," etc.

We may indeed share the spiritual genetics of one or more of the churches, but there are additional factors that enhance identification with one another. For example, identical or similar

219

environment produces a recognition. People traveling outside of their home geographic setting are often recognized by their accents. We develop contextualized ways of behaving that cause us to "remind" people of someone else who behaved similarly. Shared participation in critical incidents may contribute to identification. People who survived Hurricane Katrina or the earthquake in Haiti will have one experience that always links them. Long-term fellowship in the same life-influencing institutions creates a mutual recognizability. Preachers who are graduates of certain schools get "lumped together," for good or ill. Understudies of influential architects, artists, teachers, and politicians are often seen as reminiscent of their mentors.

Readers of Revelation in the late part of the first century would not have seen these seven churches with the awe or mystery ascribed by twenty-first century readers. In fact, this listing of seven churches may have been the most tangible part of the whole book. In the midst of Scrolls, Seals, Angels, Trumpets, Plagues, Bowls, and the Woman on the Beast, these geographic realities would have provided assurance that the outpouring of imagery was tied to reality. These were specific, extant congregations in identifiable locations. It would be reasonable to infer that the Spirit is aware of and concerned about the nature and character of congregations.

In interpreting Revelation, it is more typical of western cultural perspectives to emphasize the Spirit's interest in individuals, rather than congregations of people. The letters to the churches speak, for the most part, of collective faith, and collective reward and punishment. Yet, a few references single out those who have been exceptionally faithful or unfaithful. We may safely infer that the Spirit clearly desires to speak to whomever has ears to hear. Unless we assume a radical difference in the manner of the Spirit's function and style, the Spirit's concern for us today is parallel to that which is shown in this segment of Revelation.

The goal of this essay is not to give new insight into the true meaning of this section of Revelation. The intent is to allow the richness of the Spirit's message to reach beyond the first recipients to speak to the joys and pains, hopes and anxieties, confidence and sins of Christians 20 centuries later. In plumbing the depths both of the scripture and our own life experiences we should be able to "hear what the Spirit says to the churches" . . . and to us.

The Messages to the Seven Churches of Asia Minor

Notice the way in which Jesus encounters the churches. Each encounter is distinctive as Christ introduces himself in each letter and addresses each congregation in a unique fashion. By his message he gives evidence of knowing the churches better than they know themselves. In talking to them regarding their life "issues" he never singles out anomalies, but rather addresses the persistent life patterns each congregation exhibits. While some of the patterns are more entrenched and alienating than others, Jesus still addresses each congregation with hope, a message of what the most alienated body needs to do in order to experience Christ's victory. The parallel of Christ's personal interest in us is inescapable: His desire for our redemption, insight into our personal predicaments, grace that surpasses our violations, concern for our covenant consistency, and hope for our redemption even when we are at our worst . . . only Christ cares like this.

In the reflections that follow, we shall be looking at each church individually, in the order in which Christ addressed them. The reader is encouraged to let the exegetical efforts, the intensive hermeneutical assessments, and other scholarly pursuits hover in the background. This is not to disparage such pursuits, but rather to let your scholarship serve as both a foundation and a tether for creative application of scripture, allowing you to look inside yourself, as you look into scripture.

Ephesus

Look at the church in Ephesus. This was a highly respectable church, rich in history, steeped in apostolic lore. By the time of this letter, most of the Christian world would have heard of such events as the rebaptism of some disciples of John the Baptist, the wild story of a demon-possessed man beating up the presumptuous seven sons of Sceva, the converted sorcerers burning their scrolls, the amazing growth of the church in and beyond Ephesus, and the craftsmen's riot. The stories would have been told and retold as Christians passed along the good news of how the gospel had brought transformation in a major city. The wider circulation of Paul's Ephesian letter would have further enhanced the reputation of this church.

Jesus addressed the church with compliments: these people worked hard at pursuing the right things and persevering even under stress. They apparently exhibited spiritual maturity, being able to distinguish between genuine and phony spirituality. They even showed the courage to challenge and reject those who persisted in their allegiance to evil. This was no small task, in that the evil alliance is named and likely well-organized. If this were the end of the story, we would be unmitigatedly impressed. But there seems to be more.

Some churches have such storied pasts that they are spoken of as "the historic church at _____," a description that reflects awe of the past, but often looks askance at the still existing, less vibrant congregation. Ephesus was so notable and had such wide impact, that near the end of the first century A.D. it could have been referred to as "the historic church at Ephesus." But in the core of this assembly was ominous danger of an infection that could undermine all of the positive influence. It was not an easily identified risk factor, because the leadership of the church seemed to be as solid and faithful as ever. Yet Jesus offered a stark critique: "You have forsaken your first love!" This offense was so serious that the church was called to collective repentance, with a warning that failure to do so would lead to the removal of the "lampstand." . . . Christ would reject them. To suggest that this was a simple problem of lost passion seems to oversimplify the problem. The church was faithfully carrying on "business as usual" while church culture was under serious threat. Those very Nicolaitans that were put out of the fellowship may have been in position to have the last laugh as the church experienced the inevitable stagnation resulting from inattentiveness to the primary relationship that made them Christ's body.

Analogies to congregations we know may be safe and a bit too easy. The riskier analogy is the personal one: Are there ways in which you or I may be at risk of the Ephesian infection? How would we look? We would probably look quite respectable. We might even be called upon to help others with their spiritual challenges. Our history may be widely communicated as a testimony, a reference letter that announces, "You can trust this person. Look at the track record." Yet in some key areas we may have "gone soft." Losing our first love, may relate to zeal, but it may be more content oriented. We may have ceased the kind of study that once kept us sharp. We may have developed a blasé spirit about issues that were once important. In short, we may simply not be finishing well.

It would be a mistake to assume that this problem would erupt only in those who are well-known or aging. A young preacher seeking to gain acceptance in a more prestigious placement may choose to adjust his image for the sake of career advancement. A worship leader, having wearied of the battle to keep congregations focused on truly Christ-honoring worship, may have decided to just give in, let the worship service gravitate more toward narcissistic entertainment. A spouse, after many years of experiencing the awesome reality that good marriage always involves ongoing investment of time and energy, may announce that "I'm tired of always giving. I want to spend some time receiving."

To the extent that we resemble the Ephesian church, our redemptive need is identical: Repent! Recapture those values, convictions, behaviors that were central to our faith and practice when we were clearly strong and in a healthy relationship with Christ.

Smyrna

The church at Smyrna may have had a significant self-image issue. Christ addressed the church with a clarification of his own identity and durability. He had personally been down the road that they were traveling. The existing predicament was a depreciation of self, noting poverty and affliction. However bad they may have been feeling about their present circumstances, things were soon likely to get worse. The persecution was already underway, and was soon to intensify, not just in brief moments, but for an extended time. In the short run, this is almost a bad news/worse news story. Yet in the face of the difficulty, Christ had encouragement in his evaluation of the church: "I know your afflictions and your poverty, yet you are rich!" Further, he offers no chastisement. Instead of "Repent!" he urges, "Remain faithful." Even those who die in faithfulness were promised the crown of life.

When we look around us, we may see Smyrnas in a variety of manifestations. There are churches that have carried out effective ministry in community, only to see their surrounding community change—economically, ethnically, socially. Other churches give up by disbanding or relocating. But a few have sensed a divine calling to ministry in a locale, assuming that the previous generations that established the church and erected the building were giving the resource as a beachhead for ministry when the next generation of residents moves in. Hence Englewood Christian Church in Indianapolis has found its distinct ministry in its same old, but radically changed locale. First Christian Church in Chicago has a different look from the old days, but provides a vital witness to its ever-changing environs. On a larger scale, the church in China appeared to be destined for annihilation when the Communist Revolution took over the land in 1949. The Christians were impoverished and persecuted. But a faithful remnant found their 20th-century equivalent of the catacombs and the "underground church" flourished. As the second decade of the 21st century dawns, estimates put the number of Chinese Christians as high as 100,000,000—more than in any other nation. I recently witnessed a Chinese government official commending the Chinese Christians for their good works in Chinese society.

On a personal level, the parallels to Smyrna need to be suggested carefully. There are some who may be physically or spiritually impoverished as a result of their failure to act responsibly. But I know of some persons who have clearly been abused—some by family, some by society, and some even by the church. I know faithful elders who continue in small congregations, caring for the flock when there is frequent heartache and no glamour. I have witnessed ministers who, having endured demoralization at the hands of unfaithful congregations, nonetheless remain faithful to their calling. One such man lives modestly, but still occasionally serves as my mentor. The church at Smyrna, in some very positive ways, lives on.

Pergamum

As Christ addresses the third congregation the letter opens with a more polemic tone. Jesus presents himself wielding a sharp, double-edged sword. There is good reason for this change in flavor. The battle being waged in Pergamum is of a different nature than that in the first two churches. The city was the most "Roman" and likely the most pagan of all seven cities in which these churches were placed. Polytheistic contexts developed a finely honed style of tolerance. The competing deities and loyalties maintained a truce with one another through acceptance of differences that may parallel our present-day fan loyalties to athletic teams. Each group may have been convinced of the superiority of its deity, but there was no battle as long as each deity was granted a place in the pantheon. The tolerance ended abruptly, however, when anyone made an assertion of the superiority of a particular god. This predictably made targets of those faithful to the Lord God Omnipotent who reigns over the whole universe as King of kings and Lord of lords. No pantheon can be built to contain that God, and He leaves no room for the petty imposters. This radical contrast may have sparked the persecution that led powerful people in this center of emperor worship to make an example of the Christian leader, Antipas by (according to tradition) roasting him in a kettle. Jesus commended the church for remaining faithful to his name, even in the face of such brutal intimidation.

So what was the problem? Apparently the infectious spirit of compromise that maintained balance in the society had intruded on the practice of the church. This congregation apparently held allegiance to the Name, but little sense of the distinctive value of Christian faith. An indulgent ideology inevitably led to indulgent behavior. Following patterns of

225

weak faithfulness dating back to the days of Moses the applied creed seemed to be: "Affirm your faith, but behave according to your impulses." When the church acts in this way, its surrounding society celebrates, because such indulgence in the church affirms the secular indulgence. To this sloppy and overly tolerant church, Christ again calls out, "Repent!"

Parallels to the cultural environment of Pergamum abound. Satan's Throne may be a major example of a "Sin City," or it may be a more subtle withering away of distinct Christian values. Las Vegas and Lone Prairie may each call for Christians to compromise both their convictions and their ethics. Our personal contemporary challenge is to decide on which side of the repentance call we are going to stand.

Thyatira

The church at Thyatira presents some similar scenarios. The city's commercial prominence may have been hinted at in Acts 16 when a businesswoman who became a disciple at Philippi was identified as from Thyatira. The manufacturing guilds were more than just unions; they provided a collective life pattern that called for joint beliefs and behaviors, all centered around the pagan idolatries. "Jezebel" may have been an influential woman who invited the same kind of compromise as occurred at Pergamum . . . with predictably similar results of immoral behavior and ultimate destruction. However, Thyatira had a core of Christians who were persistent in their Christ-like behavior, even to the extent of doing Christ-like deeds—good works that exhibited before the world the nature of Christian love. Christ's two-edged challenge is particularly striking. For those who consorted with Jezebel, the time for repentance seemed to have passed. Christ now gives only a warning: She and her ilk were to be subjected to intense and deadly suffering as an example to all the churches. On the other hand, those who had not engaged in her pollution were called upon to hold steady until Christ comes.

I have seen churches that are as internally divided as Thyatira, who still choose to present a united façade to the community. Those who focus on tolerance and indulgence deride those of simple trusting faith. The people of purer faith and practice, however, cannot seem to find a voice to challenge the disciples of Jezebel. As this book goes to press, major American denominations are facing this dilemma. They are already divided churches. The divisions are typically rooted in perspectives on the truthfulness and authority of scripture, but the flashpoints that facilitate the denominational fragmentation are such subsequent issues as homosexuals in church leadership and affirmation of homosexual marriage. Those who oppose such actions are often vainly hoping that prudence will prevail and repentance will come. It may be that Christ is saying to such churches, "I have given you time to repent."

Which portion of the Thyatira church you look like may depend upon what kind of price you are willing to pay for the image you choose to project to the world.

Sardis

The message to the church at Sardis is a loud wake-up call. There was little evidence of a major aggressive corrupting force here, yet the once lively church seemed to have died without even noticing the decline. It is of note that those who still found Christ's approval were described as not having "soiled their clothes." It may be that a weak, fruitless faith is parallel in offensiveness to blatant, aggressive unfaithfulness.

I have visited congregations where the buildings are well cared for, the people are friendly, at least to one another, and they have a schedule of "churchy" activities. Yet as I left, I found myself asking, "Why would anyone choose to be a part of the church?" The faith was not presented winsomely, the worship had an air of lifeless ritual, and the whole experience was most akin to visiting a family museum. Sardis has its small parallels.

I have visited large cathedral-style church buildings in North America and Europe. There is sometimes no more than a remnant congregation, hinting at what was once a setting for collectively expressing a vibrant faith. But the building may have literally become a museum, with the church more focused on a former glory than an ongoing commission. Sardis has its sad grand parallels.

I have visited with persons who speak wistfully of the joy they once had when they were active in their practice of Christian faith. They indicate they still hold the same faith, they articulate a religious vocabulary, but little of their lives would support an accusation of being Christian. Sardis has its very personal parallels. For each counterpart to ancient Sardis, the message would be the same today, "Wake up! Get back to work."

Philadelphia

No Christian person or agency would likely be offended by being compared to the congregation Christ addressed at Philadelphia. This body seemed to be finely attuned to the mind and mission of Christ. Beyond their own strength, they were faithful in pursuing Christ's cause, keeping Christ's word, and upholding Christ's name. Because of their consistent identification with Jesus, they were promised a participation in the blessings of his victory, and protection as the enemy attempted to test them.

I witnessed a parallel to this church in Central Java in Indonesia. The church was frequently harassed and threatened by the leader of the nearby mosque. Yet the church continued its ministry of good works in the community, providing education and medical care to the Muslim children, and even opening a cottage industry to the Muslim women in the community. As the Imam became more aggressive, his adult son watched the outcomes of the two faith groups and chose to become Christian. The church exhibits strength beyond its apparent resources.

When I first met Pat, she was a soft-spoken woman with no flashy talents. But she believed that her understated giftedness in arts and crafts could bring glory to God. She approached the leaders of her church with the then-unheard-of notion of a church-sponsored craft fair/autumn festival that would raise money exclusively for an agency that provides disaster relief through missionaries. Two decades later over $1,000,000 has been raised for hunger and disaster relief through the Harvest of Talents at Lincoln Christian Church.

God still rewards the faithfulness of Philadelphia-like Christians, allowing them to share in his victory. To them he says, "Hold on to what you have."

Laodicea

No Christian person or agency would likely be compliment-
ed by being compared to the congregation Christ addressed at
Laodicea. This church had no appearance of division; it collectively showed itself as smugly successful people who had
acquired such wealth that they needed nothing. Physically and
shortsightedly they may have been right. But from the stand-
point of faith, their narcissistic self-satisfaction left them desti-
tute and disgusting. Jesus' rejection of them in their complacent
confidence was unique among the churches, roughly, "You
make me sick." They had earned and spent themselves into a
position of being insensitive to the challenges of Christ, and perhaps to the plight of those who lacked their wealth. Christ's call
is to respond to his loving rebuke with a total reorientation of
their values. He approaches them not as a close colleague, but as
a loving outsider who wants to enter in and engage them.

Where have you seen the Laodicean church? Every congregation that tastes financial success is on the verge of this mala-
dy of becoming tepid. Any church that thinks it can leverage its
financial resources to assure its collective well-being is substi-
tuting fiscal standards for faith. Few American churches are
immune to this ailment.

Similarly, all but the most impoverished individual
Christians are vulnerable. Even the relatively poor can set
themselves up for this difficulty by a dependency that suggests
that if they had the money/things they wished for, life would
indeed be good. Christ's admonishment to the Laodiceans is
parallel to his sweeping statement, "Life does not consist in the
abundance of one's possessions" (Lk 12:15).

Conclusion

Do you see yourself in any of these churches? Do you find
yourself a bit disheartened by the intrusiveness of any parallel?
Are you encouraged by any of the comparisons? Whatever
your reflective observations are, the intent of Christ for you is
the same as the intent of the entire book of Revelation: Take
heart! Hold fast! Be faithful to the end! Receive the crown! and
whenever or wherever appropriate, REPENT!

FROM THE CAGE TO THE CITY: TRANSFORMATION IN THE BOOK OF REVELATION

Tony Twist

Life in the Cage

We didn't have a prayer. Stumbling blind with no hope. In a cage mocking momentum by spinning around. Grappling with shadows. For so long we knew nothing else. Insanity became normal. Passions degraded. With souls so polluted that septic soup tasted delicious.

It hurts us and we fight back. At the shadows because evil lurks there. At the light because it rattles our cage. Even at ourselves because we don't have a prayer.

From a dimension beyond the cage we perceive an impulse. A voice urging us to look upward. Still in the cage, but less of it. Calling us into glorious light and life.[1] A way of being that can, in time, convert our cages. So, frightened and not really knowing how, we begin to follow.[2] To get us going, He places His right hand upon us (Rev 1:17).

We process in the lamplight of those who have prayed before.[3] Listening for perspective and gaining from experience.[4] Waiting for Him to tabernacle among us. And, when He is ready, the cloud rises above the camp. We're being invited to be transformed into His glorious life in our heart's true home.[5]

So, as His called out ones, we hesitantly respond. Awaiting insight, love, formation and direction.[6] Letting the relationship unfold as He wills. But, He awaits us to open the door.[7] Going through life's tasks in His powerful and sustaining Presence, mindful of our heritage and destiny. Life then becomes a "process of being conformed to the image of Christ for the sake of others."[8] And, responding to His invitation to "come up here" (Rev 4:1),[9] we seek to become more prayerful.

Prayer and Perspective from Above

But, let's be honest. From the cage, don't we sometimes find our service of prayer a bit boring? Yes, we do look up and see the throne in heaven. Another dimension. Dazzling lights. Twenty-four elders dressed in white with crowns of gold. Flashes of lightning, rumblings and peals of thunder. The seven blazing lamps and sea of glass. The four living creatures covered with eyes in front and back. Even with eyes under their wings. Night and day they never stop saying: "Holy, holy, holy is the Lord God Almighty, who was, and is, and is to come" (Rev 4:8). But frankly, doesn't that job look a bit confining and repetitious? Not nearly as glorious as a good adventure or football match?

What if, however, our vision is faulty? What if the throne room is in reality the epicenter of all that exists? From whence comes all love, family, ideas, galaxies, creatures, salvation, re-creation and more than we can begin to understand. From their vantage point, the living creatures are the first to feel each new impulse coming from the throne. They first saw, see, and will see each new initiative coming from the mind and heart of God Himself. Brushed by His breath, they experience more glory in a millisecond than most adventurers would have in many lifetimes of travel. *Kairos* without *chronos* slowing it down. And even all those eyes can't take in the full texture of everything streaming from God's throne. What if they are the most truly alive creatures in the entire universe?

Looking through their eyes, even we cage dwellers can begin to glimpse His glory. And, with halting speech, to join the chorus. With Revelation's rhapsody[10] vibrating the bars of our cages, we listen up. And the formerly strange and otherworldly becomes more familiar. We join up. And acknowledge the truth: "You are worthy, our Lord and God, to receive glory and honor and power, for you created all things, and by your will they were created and have their being" (Rev 4:11). Giving glory to the Lord God Almighty puts us in harmony with the deepest impulse of creation. It joins our voices to the heavenly chorus. It begins to orient us to ultimate reality. And, as we glorify His holy name from the cage, our sights are raised.

Prayer, like a sense of humor, requires perspective. Hallowing His name brings us closer to reality. Our eyes clear. Then, as they adjust in His light, we begin to participate for real. Transfiguration whiteness begins to work its deep power, even in our cages. But, darkness continually pushes back. Relentless. Requiring us to continually refocus. And, on a harrowing journey with an ever steeper path before us. With much yet between us and our New Jerusalem.

One moment the cage seems so real. Bars of steel. Totally grounded and firmly settled. A safe place to hide. But, in a flash of glory, time's true face is "demasked by the eternal."[11] No longer the illusion of self-sufficient safety. From all sides eternity begins to press upon us. "Mounting from the depths and plunging from the heights."[12] An entirely new form of reality rattles our cages.

We become unglued. Our Lord opens His glorious Word to us. And, as we look up, the seals are lifted. Looking from above, our center of gravity begins to shift. Reality no longer revolves around our little cages. Moving toward the Holy City involves transformation according to God's vision for us. As we live through the lifting of the seals, we experience more and more of His sovereignty.

He goes forth as conqueror with a bow and crown (Rev 6:1). We welcome our ruler. When war breaks out, we welcome our protector. When we are in want, we welcome our provider. When we face death, we welcome our deliverer. When we are martyred, we pray for justice. When the earth is being destroyed, we move ever closer to the safety of His throne. When all creation is being re-created, there is nowhere else to go. The foundations are being destroyed. Our cages provide no foothold to secure us from His complete restoration of all creation to Himself. A restoration that works from the subatomic to the vast reaches of the universe in the complete expulsion of evil. And in dimensions of reality that we cannot even begin to comprehend.

The Cycle of Transformation Begins Again

After a period of silent waiting, the process repeats. As Bob Lowery points out in *Revelation's Rhapsody*, God uses repetition and recapitulation throughout His Word as a way to reinforce His message and make it clearer.[13] Perhaps because our transformation is often cyclical in nature. Sin's tentacles run deep. Wheat and tares are rooted in the same bedrock. We find a measure of growth as God cleanses, heals, and brings fruit. But in the next season, we often find the same sinful tendencies at work. Even deeper. Thus the need to revisit on a deeper level. Allowing for deeper demolition on His part.

Perhaps because the city is a place where glorious light and life are possible only with complete transparency. No longer any place to hide even the slightest root of imperfection. And our best gifts are often held hostage to deeply hidden impulses which, if carefully removed over time, would allow our gifts to emerge robust and entirely useful. If the entangled evil is too quickly dissolved, it might take some of our best with it. Only the Great Physician has the skill for this kind of surgery.

So, His Word gradually becomes unsealed in us. And the trumpets announce that there is more that must be done. His cleansing fire burns up a third of our world. A third of our sea. A third of our water. And a third of our sky. All hell breaks loose and a third of us dies. So that, with loud voices, we can proclaim after the second woe has passed: "The kingdom of this world has become the kingdom of our Lord and of his Christ, and he will reign for ever and ever" (Rev 11:15). We cannot proclaim such a family reunion without a thorough house cleaning.

The Final Transformation

But, there is still more. Perhaps because there is even more to us. We are, after all, created in His image. There are depths and dimensions to us that we cannot yet even realize. We were created, are created, and will be created to be like them — in eternal community. Like the living creatures who ride the winds of the glory pulsating from the throne. Living in the bright supernova love flowing between the Father, Son, and

Holy Spirit. Proclaiming to all that exists that such bright glory is simply the radiance of holiness. A Trinity of Holiness. Calling upon all creation to look upward and see the glory. The Father giving away all glory to the Son. The Son returning all glory to the Father. The Spirit flowing between Father and Son, surging and increasing the glory. Brighter than light itself and more powerful than any Love that can be imagined.

So, deeper must the cleansing go. The bowls of wrath are poured out. Disease. Death. Blood. Fire. Darkness. Armageddon. And, with the seventh bowl, thunder, earthquake, hailstones, and the fall of Babylon. Evil rooted out so deeply that it is finally obliterated. Forever and ever. The rider on the white horse, with blazing eyes and crowned with many crowns, strikes down the enemy. He captures the beast and false prophet and throws them alive into the fiery lake of burning sulfur (Rev 19:20).

At long last!!!

No more will His little children suffer hunger and danger.[14] No longer will creation be subjected to futility (Rom 8:18-23). No longer will we be imprisoned in terrible solitude, groaning and waiting for the liberation from bondage to decay into "the glorious freedom of the children of God" (Rom 8:21). No longer unable to find expression for our deepest desires, loves, and dreams.

The bride is finally prepared for her new home. A home found in a new heaven and new earth. But, she does not just live in the Holy City. She is the New Jerusalem. Its heart and soul. The passion and love pulsing through its streets. The grace of its politics, beauty of its art, and character of its culture. The dearly beloved bride of Christ. Fully prepared in every way for such a time as this.

No longer an isolated cage. Now there is a new set of physics at work. Transformed by resurrection chemistry, her bars have been refined through suffering into a great high wall. Her tiny floor is now part of twelve foundations. She has literally become part of the most holy place. A glorious temple in which her King and Lord can abide forever. A radiant jewel. The smelting pot of war, famine, and epidemic has been used to transform a forgiven collection of corrupt cages into the beautiful and loyal bride of Christ. What Dallas Willard calls the "revolution of Jesus"[15] has taken place. A revolution in which heart, soul, mind, and spirit have been transformed. Not by imposing outer forms or even good orders of life on us. But by changing us from within through His ongoing relationship with us. We allow His transforming love to shine through our cages.

Hidden nakedness gives way to radiant adornment. The wounds and scars morph into precious stones. We are free to show the full extent of love. Not hampered by fear, insecurities, pride, and hideous dark soul spots. His transfiguring radiation melts away all such disease so we can come into His glorious light. Free to finally love all His family freely and openly. With a love deeper than anything earthly possible. Completely pure. Transparent to His entire family with all evil forever banished.

No longer full of darkness and death, but filled with the pure water of life and living fruit. Instead of stagnant cesspools between the cages there is now a pure river flowing from the throne of God down the middle of the great Holy City street (Rev 22:1-2). Instead of disease and curse, there is healing and blessing. Instead of shadow boxing with evil phantoms, there is glorious service face-to-face which ever more enlightens and brings new life. We are home. Embraced within this loving relationship we call the Trinity. The heritage and destiny of all who pray "our Father."

From Birth to New Life:
Transformation Now and Not Yet

For it was this loving relationship which birthed you and me (along with all else). I love my parents and will be eternally grateful for family, teachers, friends and adversaries who helped form me along the way. They were midwives and mentors for a season. They all participated (and still participate at times) in His conception of me. But, there comes a time to leave home and cleave fully to our eternal soul mate.

God's strong, right-hand Word formed us from frail dust, while His powerful, left-hand Spirit energized us into being.[16] We are now sons and daughters of Abraham, called out of

Egypt, given the Law and Prophets, the Incarnate Word, the Written Word, martyrs, trailblazers, guides, friends, and witnesses all though the ages.

And that's not all. Formed by His many beams of love,[17] we are now being transformed into Him (2Cor 3:18). We're being re-created to live in our heart's true home: This eternal relationship of love which painted the first supernova, smiled at the first sunrise, and now cleanses away every spot so that He can finally welcome His bride home.

Knowing where we came from and where we're headed makes all the difference when we feel caged in life's wilderness. The desert can become a place of instruction rather than destruction. A place where, as we draw life from Him, we grow up. Listening deeper. Feeling healthier. Thinking clearer. Doing better. Loving more.

Through abiding, we are being re-created. When quiet before Him, His Word reaches transforming fingers into our hearts, this inner chamber from which we live.[18] From which thoughts and feelings emerge. He brings order into this vast restless heartland which no psychologist can reach. We find soul food by abiding in the True Vine (Jn 15:1-17). Willing to follow in spite of distracting thoughts and feelings.

It is a journey with no perfect roadmap. Simply a commitment to becoming more cultured by our Father through His Spirit to become the bride of His Christ. But, we must remember. With our vows here taken, from His perspective, WE ARE ALREADY HIS BRIDE.

When we first fall in love with Him, we journey with Him anticipating the sunrise. Abiding begins here and now.[19] We speak tenderly to each other. Listening attentively. Reading carefully all verbal and nonverbal cues. Even enjoying the silence. Our communication extends to all levels and involves our entire being. We read each other, not for information alone. But attentively for relationship. Heart waiting, like a moist field receiving life-giving seed. In love, we receive and then slowly meditate upon the Word He gives.

Then we respond to Him wholeheartedly, right-mindedly, entire soul and strength. Awaiting insight, love, formation, and direction.[20] Letting the relationship unfold through times of adoration, confession, thanksgiving, and intercession. Before long, as we all know, the journey gets complicated because cage life intrudes.

The Mysterious Almighty and Our Journey

Thanks be to the Ancient of Days that He wants to share ALL of our journey.[21] However, He will not come uninvited. So, we just say "yes" (Rev 3:20). Inviting Him to form the relationships that form us and those we love. Turning to Him when sleep eludes us in the night. Observing His reaction as He watches television with us and goes along to the movies we consume. Fasting, for His sake, from ball games, shopping, food, friends, vacations, or anything else that intrudes between us. Faithfully keeping the morning, afternoon, evening and/or late night appointments with Him. Having and forming His children. Taking care of His little ones.[22] The more we obediently share life with Him, the better we become. The better we become, the more we want to be with Him.

As our relationship with Him develops, its health is seen in our deepening love for Him and others (Mt 22:34-40). We do this by journeying alongside and toward the Ancient of Days. The One who brought Adam into existence. Who led Abraham out of Ur in search of a place to really live. Who spoke to Moses face to face.[23] Who sent His Son to reveal Himself (Jn 14:8-9). Who gives His Spirit to make us whole. He alone is our eternal abiding place (Jn 14:1-4). Our roots go deeper and deeper into His eternal family.

And, in the autumn of life, we look forward still. Still journeying with Him even as the sun sets. Still speaking tenderly to one another after all the years. Hearing deeply beneath the few words being spoken. Knowing verbals and nonverbals without even looking at each other. Libraries of love back and forth, especially in the silence. Looking back on the fruit of a life of love together. While looking forward with the One Who keeps us ALWAYS living.[24]

Even so, we will not now fully understand the process of becoming the bride of Christ. Why it takes such drastic measures. What is happening with the unsealing, trumpet, and bowls. How His process of restoring all things to Himself works. Somehow turning dead steel cages into living, radiant jewels which, when joined together through a physics we can't yet understand, form an eternal, interconnected family which will never perish, spoil or fade.

Conclusion

We also cannot fully understand why it takes so long. Why it seems to us that God works so slowly throughout history. Taking ages to bring about incremental change. Progressively revealing Himself throughout time. Or throughout a lifetime. Doing quiet, deep inner work through the slow march of moments we call life.

Yes, transformation is difficult to understand. And undergo. But, from His eternal perspective, He is coming soon. With everything ready for the wedding feast. Our place fully prepared. We are the dearly beloved bride of the King of kings and Lord of lords. He has prepared us for life at court, formed in us His noble character, clothed us with the culture of Christ, and welcomed us into His glorious Kingdom of light and life.

A marriage such as this is worth more than everything to an unworthy bride like us. What a glorious life. And incredible future. We have indeed "married up." So, whatever it takes, let's get ourselves ready!

FROM "HAUNTED HOUSE" TO WELCOMING HOME: TEACHING REVELATION IN THE LOCAL CHURCH

Matt Proctor

When I interviewed for my first preaching ministry at age 23, I told the pulpit committee that I absolutely believed in the power of God's Word to transform lives. I told them I was convinced that "all Scripture is God-breathed and is useful for teaching, rebuking, correcting and training in righteousness" (2Tim 3:16).[1] I affirmed for them my commitment to proclaim "the whole counsel of God" (Acts 20:27 ESV).

That wasn't 100% true.

That commitment was 65/66 true, but at that point in my life, there was one book of the Bible I didn't preach, one part of "all Scripture" that I avoided, one portion of "the whole counsel of God" that I didn't proclaim.

The book of Revelation.

Staying Away from the Haunted House

Revelation just didn't seem "useful for teaching." Apparently I'm not the only preacher who has avoided Revelation. Fred Craddock says that preaching through the NT is like walking down the street. The Gospels are first, and they are well-lit, a familiar neighborhood. Next comes Paul, still friendly territory, but as you move through the epistles, the shadows grow deeper, the houses more neglected. . . . Second Peter, First John, Third John, Jude. Then suddenly at the end of the street, shrouded in darkness, stands the frightening, haunted house of Revelation.[2]

Not many preachers want to go in there.

The reasons for staying out of Revelation are many. First of all, *the book is just flat hard to understand.* The church father Jerome said, "Revelation has as many mysteries as it does words." Martin Luther said the book of Revelation ought to be kicked out of the Bible because it doesn't reveal anything. Let's face it: bizarre images of strange creatures, a beast with ten horns and claws of bronze, stars falling from the heavens, a great red dragon with seven heads, 666, bowls of sulfur, people eating scrolls, bottomless pits, the four horses of the Apocalypse, war, pestilence, famine, and death aren't normal water cooler conversation. This is strange stuff. So, early in my ministry, I just stayed away.

Another reason preachers ignore Revelation is because *it's been so abused.* No other book in the Bible has sparked more obsession, strange teaching, and wild speculation than Revelation. When I started Bible college in the fall of 1988, everyone on campus was talking about Edgar Whisenant's *88 Reasons Why Jesus Will Come Again in 1988*, which predicted Jesus' return in mid-September. (Mt 24:36 says we can't know the day or the hour, but apparently we can know the month and the year!)

I read about another preacher who claimed that "the literal building blocks for the new temple in Israel have been constructed and numbered and are being stored in the basements of K-Marts all over the United States until they can be shipped to Israel and used to build a new temple."[3] (Seriously? K-Mart? If there's a new world order coming, everyone knows it's going to be Wal-Mart.)

Revelation seems to attract wild-eyed, delusional characters, prompting G.K. Chesterton to remark that "though St. John saw many strange monsters in his vision, he saw no creature so wild as one of his own commentators." I certainly didn't want to be lumped in with those guys. To avoid guilt by association, I avoided Revelation.

A final reason I didn't preach Revelation was what I'll call *job security.* In my first ministry, an elder's wife loved the book of Revelation and taught a women's Bible study on it . . . from a vastly different perspective than mine. I liked having a job, and if this book was so controversial and divisive, why should

I stir up trouble? After all, I heard the true story of a preacher in Ohio who was teaching on Revelation, and when he finished, somebody shot him. I thought, "I'm 23 years old. I'm too young to die. I'll just stick with the Psalms."

Tom Long notes that I'm not the only preacher who has shrunk back from this last book of the Bible: "'Apocalyptic,' Ernst Käsemann once announced, 'is the mother of all Christian theology.' If there is any truth at all in that statement, then it is also true that most Christian preaching has become at least slightly embarrassed by its mother."[4]

Reclaiming Revelation

This chapter is intended as a call to get over that embarrassment.

Simply put, preachers must not leave Revelation for others to explain. Let's admit, preacher, that our people are getting teaching about Revelation elsewhere — hotel conference room lecturers, TV prophets, bestselling novels — and not all such teaching is helpful. The folks in our congregations deserve our help in learning to read this book wisely.

A turning point came for me when I enrolled at Lincoln Christian Seminary during that first ministry. I took a class on Revelation by Dr. Robert Lowery, and in those sixteen weeks, my eyes were opened. Sitting in Dr. Lowery's class, I began to see that my church needed a strong dose of apocalyptic literature. My imagination was captured by Revelation's images of the reality of the spiritual battle, the insidious influence of the Enemy in the surrounding culture, the harshness of the coming judgment, the imminence of Christ's return and the need for clear-eyed, uncompromising perseverance. I saw that all this needed to be preached because, as Eugene Peterson reminds us, we all too often suppose that our lives are "so utterly *ordinary*. Sin-habits dull our free faith into stodgy moralism and respectable boredom."[5]

I suddenly realized that, "with the vastness of the heavenly invasion and the urgency of the faith decision rolling into our consciousness like thunder and lightning, we cannot stand around on Sunday morning filling our time with pretentious small talk on how bad the world is and how wonderful this new stewardship campaign is going to be."[6] Revelation was a clarion call to live each day in light of the high stakes of eternity, and my people needed to hear that call. *I* needed to hear it.

It was time I reclaimed Revelation in my preaching.

Teaching the Church *How* To Read Revelation

A preacher's job is not just to teach his congregation God's Word; it is also to teach them how to read God's Word for themselves. If this is true for the first 65 books of the Bible, it is truest of the 66th book. So, preacher, begin by giving your people a few hermeneutical tools to help them read Revelation rightly.

The Setting of Revelation

First, help them understand the historical setting of Revelation's original readers. The apostle John writes to seven churches in Asia Minor near the end of the first century who are facing two threats. The first threat is persecution. The Jews targeted the "heretical" Christians, and while Roman persecution of Christians is not yet empire-wide policy, it's real and rampant nonetheless — especially for those who refused to participate in emperor worship. Believers who declined to say their Roman "pledge of allegiance" by offering a pinch of incense and pronouncing "Caesar is Lord" were viewed as treasonous and could lose their friends, jobs, even their lives.

So the believers in Ephesus have endured hardships for Christ's name (Rev 2:3). Those in Smyrna have been slandered and will be put in prison (2:9-10). In Pergamum, Antipas has already been killed (2:13). John himself is in exile on the prison island of Patmos (1:9). It is true that this book speaks to those who face life-and-death struggles.

In building the applicational bridge from the original audience to your audience, then, the sermon must deal with issues of true suffering, "not minor daily trials or inconvenient obstacles. The first-century believers to whom Revelation was addressed were facing martyrdom, not flat tires."[7] John's book addresses those in deep despair — "when the police dogs are being released toward the marchers on the bridge into Selma, when the knock of the secret police is heard at the door and the church is hiding an attic full of Jews, when the diagnosis is melanoma and there is nothing more that the physicians can do."[8]

But the second and greater threat John's readers face is cultural seduction. They are tempted to conform to the priorities, values and lifestyles of the culture around them. If the Enemy cannot destroy the believers through open conflict, he will dilute them through subtle compromise. Why push them into the electric chair when the easy chair will do? If they will just relax their obedience a bit to "fit in," then the devil's job is done. They will be "lukewarm — neither hot nor cold" and God will spit them out of His mouth (3:16).

Revelation is written to a comfortable church in an immoral culture, and the applicational bridge to contemporary American Christians is clear. Ronald Sider's book, *The Scandal of the Evangelical Conscience: Why Christians Are Living Just Like the Rest of the World* cites surveys showing that Christians aren't living much differently than the culture — percentages of spousal abuse, giving habits, cohabitation, divorce, racism, addiction to pornography are almost the same as those among non-Christians.[9] John writes to challenge his readers — there are 72 second person imperatives in the book — not to give in to the world. This book is not a crystal ball but a megaphone in John's hands — a trumpet call to faith and endurance and radical holiness of life. When your people understand the historical setting, they'll see the relevance.

The Structure of Revelation

Next, help your congregation understand the structure of Revelation. Give them a portable outline for the book so they can make sense of what they're reading — so they can get the big sweep of the book. One friend said a simple outline of Revelation is Things Are Bad, Things Are Going to Get Worse, We Win. That's not bad for starters, but keep pushing for more specific labels. Chapters 1–3 might be *Jesus counsels the church*, while chapters 4–5 might be *Jesus controls the universe*, as we see the Lamb on the throne with the scroll of history in

His hand. Chapters 6–11 with the seven seals and seven trumpets of judgment might be *Jesus condemns the earth*. In chapters 12–20 the conflict deepens and moves from the earthly sphere into the heavenlies where Christ is ultimately victorious, so a label might be *Jesus conquers Satan*. The book climaxes with the New Jerusalem coming down out of heaven like a bride beautifully dressed for her husband, so chapters 21–22 might be *Jesus consummates His long-awaited marriage*.

A special note: while we can appreciate the natural organization that the three sevens of judgment (seals, trumpets, bowls) provide, help your people see that they are not necessarily in chronological order — like some 21-point timeline. In fact, John is likely employing repetition. Like a song returns to its chorus, John's book returns to the same event three times. In each of the sevens of judgment, he brings us to the end of the world, intensifying the degree of evil and God's resulting judgment with each progressive "seven." Notice also that an interlude appears between the sixth and seventh of each group. The interlude in 7:1-17 stresses the saints' security. 10:1–11:14 stresses the saints' witness. 16:15 stresses the saints' vigilance.[10]

When you teach the structure of Revelation, you help your people see that, in the midst of all the mind-blowing noise, visuals, and special effects, there's a powerful story — an understandable plot that drives the whole book.

The Symbols of Revelation

Then help your people understand the symbols of Revelation. In an attempt to convey the incredible vision he is given, John ransacks the Greek language for all the metaphors he can find. He pillages the OT for images — over 500 OT allusions in 404 verses — as he pushes language to the breaking point trying to capture what he's seeing.

As the one teaching Revelation, you'll want to help your people interpret these symbols in two ways. First, help them understand the historical associations of the symbol. Rather than reading twenty-first-century connections into the text, point them to the first-century connections. In a Revelation series at Willow Creek Community Church, John Ortberg wanted to teach his listeners to interpret the symbols as the original readers would have. He asked them to imagine reading the following paragraph on the sports page of the Chicago Tribune in the winter of 1999:

The bull which once ruled the earth for 72 months has suffered a mighty fall. For at the end of the 72 months, the great right horn of the bull—whose number is twenty and three (let the reader understand)—departed, and so did the great left horn of the bull. Then the third horn of the bull, which was pierced in many places and dressed like a woman, likewise departed. Then all the beasts of the earth—the hornets and timberwolves—came and devoured the flesh of the bull, and the glory of the mighty bull was laid low.

If you lived in Chicago in the winter of 1999, you would know that the sport the writer was talking about was . . . basketball, of course.[11] The point was clear: we must not rip Revelation's metaphors out of their historical context, like the teachers who see modern-day Apache helicopters flying through John's apocalypse. Instead, we must seek to understand what the first readers would have understood.[12]

Second, help your congregation understand the emotional associations of the symbols. The fact is: metaphors paint pictures that conjure powerful emotions. A Lamb is innocent and vulnerable, a Lion is fierce and noble, and a Dragon is frighteningly large and evil. These images are meant to stir something in our hearts, but sometimes in our attempts to explain a symbol, some of its evocative power can be lost. Overexplaining can "unweave the rainbow." Instead, we as teachers must seek to recreate the original effect of a metaphor by finding parallel modern analogies.

At the end of the day, don't overpress the details of the symbolism. As Leland Ryken reminds us:

The truth is that for the most part the images and symbols of Revelation are universal. . . .Its images are those of our waking and sleeping dreams—lamb, dragon, beast, water, sea, sun, war, harvest, bride, throne, jewels. Its color symbolism is equally universal—light for goodness, darkness for evil, red for bloodshed and perverse passion. Heaven is high, as we have always known it to be, and hell is low and bottomless. . . .The book of Revelation does not require a guidebook to esoteric symbols. It requires a keen eye for the obvious.[13]

Teaching the Church *Why* to Read Revelation

"I don't think I really *need* to read Revelation," said a woman in my church. "It doesn't make any sense, and the rest of the Bible already tells me what I need to know." In addition to giving the congregation hermeneutical help in reading Revelation, the preacher will want to give them devotional help by showing them *why* they need to read John's book. We know that God has promised a blessing to those who take hold of the words of Revelation (1:3). But what kind of blessings should our people expect? Here are seven ways I deepen my faith when I read Revelation:

I approach Jesus more humbly (ch. 1).

I was a BUICK—that stands for a Brought Up In Church Kid, and I saw the pictures of Jesus in flannelgraph with his white robe, blue sash, soft flowing brown hair, kind eyes, a lamb around his shoulders, and children on his lap. I saw a gentle Jesus, a nice Jesus, a Mr. Rogers Jesus. While Jesus is certainly meek and humble of heart, the danger for someone like me is that I can put Jesus in my theological dryer and shrink Him. He just becomes my XL Buddy. When you declaw the Lion of Judah, when He simply becomes a warm and fuzzy household pet, you can lose your reverence, fear, and awe.

But not if I read Revelation. In Revelation 1, I am overwhelmed by this glorious, dreadful vision of Christ. This is not the gentle Jesus with children on his lap. This Jesus speaks in Niagara thunder. He blazes with blinding supernova brilliance. This Jesus could play kickball with our planet. This Jesus could flick his finger and send our solar system spinning off into space. He is clothed in glory and majesty and splendor and power and authority, and this is not a Jesus in whose presence you can just casually stand around. This vision of Jesus washes over you, crushing you like a tidal wave and leaving you fighting for your life, your very breath. John fell at his feet as though dead (1:17).

So I am warned: Jesus is not a smiling buddy who winks at sin. He is not, as Tom Howard reminds us, "a pale Galilean, but a towering and furious figure who will not be managed."[14] When I read Revelation, I approach Jesus more humbly, more reverently, with awe.

I love the church more honestly (chs. 2–3).

I love God's idea called the church! When I read books like Ephesians and Acts, I catch God's vision for this vibrant, victorious community. I imagine a band of believers ablaze with love for Jesus, preaching the good news in the marketplace, embracing the sick and shameful with Christ's love, digging deeply into Scripture together. To be a part of a body like that — what a glorious joy! Sign me up!

But then I go to church and find people who sometimes care more about carpet color than compassion, who hold their money too tightly, who bicker and quarrel and know their TV Guide better than their Bible. I saw a book entitled *Church: Why Bother?* and when I see congregations shamed by immoral scandal or dulled by years of the same routine, I can get frustrated and feel like giving up on the church.

But not if I read Revelation. All churches have fallen short of the glory of God, and nowhere is that clearer than in Revelation 2–3. These churches are marked by immorality, sloppy teaching, apathy, and complacency. The churches are a mess — just like the ones I know. As my friend Mark Moore says, "We say we want to be the New Testament church. Congratulations, we made it!"

But the good news is: Jesus still loves these churches. It's tough love, to be sure. In these seven letters, Jesus challenges and corrects and confronts — moving them to maturity. But it's love nonetheless. "The Lord disciplines those He loves" (Heb 12:6). And with the confrontation is commendation. For each church except Laodicea, he affirms the good he sees mixed in with the bad. He loves these churches not because they're perfect, but because they're His. That's the essence of true love.

I heard about a girl breaking up with her boyfriend who said, "I will always cherish the initial misconception I had about you." Ouch! Real love doesn't happen in fantasy; it happens in reality. You can't love someone for who you wish they were; you must love them as they actually are—flaws and all. That's why Dietrich Bonhoeffer said that true Christian community begins with disillusionment. You aren't really loving your Christian brothers until they've disappointed you and you choose to stick by them anyway. That's what Jesus does for the churches in Revelation 2–3, and when I read these chapters, I too am inspired to love the church more honestly.

I enter worship more selflessly (chs. 4–5).

My wife and I have six kids. Can I tell you what a typical Sunday morning looks like at my house? I'd like to tell you that it's a focused time of joy and preparation, as my family smilingly helps each other get ready and then sings hymns in harmony on the van ride to church. But the reality is: Sunday mornings are crazy, it seems we're always running late, I can lose my cool with the kids, and too often I'm rushing into the sanctuary with a pounding heart and irritated soul. I'm not focused on God.

It's easy to focus on so many other things during worship—family issues or work or the ballgame or how someone's dressed or the music style or the misspelled PowerPoint slide. We can be thinking more about the excellence of the program than the excellence of God.

But not if I read Revelation. When you walk through the open door in Revelation four, you enter the throne room of heaven. You suck in your breath, shield your eyes from the dazzling light and drop to your knees in fear and wonder. Incense fills your nostrils. An angelic warhost so vast you have to count it by the ten thousands shakes the very foundations of the sky with their praise. The countless thundering voices rumble in your chest.

As you trace their attention, you find that every being is focused on the throne. At the center of that throne is a majestic God—so glorious the only way John can paint him is by dipping his brush in thunder, lightning, rainbows, and jewels. At the center of the throne is a merciful Christ—the lamb who gave His life as the ransom for men. And in the light of this sovereign God and this sacrificial Christ, we weep at our own pettiness. How can we have been thinking about anything else? All eyes are on the throne, and all anyone here is thinking about is the greatness of God and the goodness of Christ. When I catch a glimpse of God as I read Revelation, I enter worship more selflessly.

I endure suffering more confidently (chs. 6–9).

When the going gets tough, what do you do? Sometimes it gets tough because we live in a fallen world of tornadoes, cancer, car wrecks, and floods. The effects of sin affect us all. Sometimes the going gets tough because we're Christian. As Paul promised, "Everyone who wants to live a godly life in Christ Jesus will be persecuted" (2Tim 3:12). When the going gets tough, what do you do?

Revelation 6–9 teaches me to sing. The going gets tough in these chapters—war, famine, murder, earthquakes, stars falling to earth, warrior locusts. The slain believers in chapter 6 ask God, "How long will this suffering last?" In tough times, we wonder if God has forgotten us.

Phillip Yancey tells the story of some Americans in a World War II German prison camp who, unbeknownst to the guards, built a makeshift radio. One day news came over the radio that the German high command had surrendered, ending the war, but because of a communications breakdown, the German guards didn't yet know. It wasn't until four days later that the American woke to find the Germans had fled, leaving the gates unlocked. In the three interim days, those prisoners still suffered. They were still mocked, still abused, but they were changed. They waved to the guards, laughed at the German shepherd dogs, told jokes over meals, and in the midst of their captivity, they sang, because they knew their salvation was sure and soon.

In Revelation 7, the oppressed believers get a news bulletin about the near future. The time is coming when they will stand before the throne. The Lamb will be their shepherd and lead them to springs of living water, and God will wipe every tear from their eye. Because their salvation is soon and sure, they can sing the song in 7:10, "Salvation belongs to our God." So when my going gets tough, I too can sing. Heaven awaits and God has not forgotten me, so I can endure suffering more confidently.

I speak God truth more courageously (chs. 10–11).

These chapters can be hard to understand. How exactly can they help me in my Christian life? First, notice the main characters: John (chapter 10) and the two witnesses (chapter 11). Second, notice their activity. All three are commanded to speak the message of God. But all three discover that preaching is not all about congratulations and conversions. Notice the results: When John swallows God's message, it's bitter. When the witnesses finish speaking their testimony, they get killed. What does this teach me? Witnessing means telling God's truth, no matter the consequences. As one African-American preacher put it, "The church must be prophetic or it will be pathetic."

I don't know about you, but I need to be reminded of that. Our world does not like to hear God's truth and can get hostile. As Wayne Smith puts it, "If you carry the ball for Christ, you're going to get tackled." Sometimes, in the interest of keeping the peace, we can be tempted to keep silent. Nobody wants to be seen as intolerant or judgmental. It's easier to just be quiet.

Which is why we need these chapters. Notice: John doesn't write as much to instruct us *in* witnessing as much as to inspire us *to* witnessing. I don't need more explanation. I need examples. It's not information I lack. It's courage. Seeing these witnesses speak boldly for God shoots adrenaline through my soul. They paid the price for faithfulness. Surely I can speak up for Christ to my neighbor. Though the world may reject, God will reward (11:18). When I read Revelation, I say, "Make me like these guys. Make me a witness." I speak God's truth more courageously.

I see evil more clearly (chs. 12–18).

Looming over these chapters, John shows us evil personified as a violent dragon, two grotesque beasts, and a prostitute.

We need these shocking images because we don't always see evil as plainly as that. The world teaches us to call "un-nice" things by nicer names. Instead of cheating, it's creative accounting. Instead of lying, it's massaging the truth. Instead of profanity, it's freedom of expression. It's not gossip; it's concern. Satan is a deceiver, and his most effective strategy is dressing up ugly realities in beautiful words.

So in these chapters, John exposes the evil that seeks to deceive his readers. False religion and godless government are not simply well-meaning but misguided institutions. They are evil beasts who belong to the dragon. Follow the strings, and you will find they are marionettes of Satan, puppets of the prince of this world. The fallen culture around you may at first appear attractive, and it will seem that she is offering you the beginning of a beautiful friendship. But in Revelation 17, John unmasks her as a cheap, diseased streetwalker. She will be destroyed and all those with her, so don't be seduced.

This world is not a playground but a battleground, and the battle rages in the things I buy, movies I see, activities I pursue, conversations I have, priorities I set and beliefs I live by. In all of these, Satan will tempt me to make subtle compromises, and I must keep my eyes wide open. When I read Revelation, I see evil more clearly.

I will long for Christ's return more deeply (chs. 19–22).

John wants to teach us to pray, "Come, Lord Jesus." We are to have the attitude of Paul who said in 2 Timothy 4 that he longed for Christ's appearing. Mark Buchanan writes, "Our hearts are to have an inner tilt upward, the grain of our souls is to lean heavenward. We are to be heaven-bent. . . . Like the tug and heft of a huge unseen planet hovering near, the hope of heaven is meant to exert a gravitational pull on our lives that we cannot escape."[15]

But there was a time in my life when I prayed, "Come Lord Jesus . . . just not yet." I was young and had so much left I wanted to do—foods to taste, mountains to climb, books to read. I wanted to get married, have kids, enjoy life, and *then* see Jesus return. I was still attached to this world.

But I'm older now. I've seen the world for what it is really is—a place marred by sin. I'm tired of famine, abortion, murder, deceit, natural disaster, cancer, death, sin, and Satan running loose through this world. Jesus is tired of it too! The day is coming when He will come crashing through the clouds, the angelic warhost behind Him. Time will screech to a halt. In an *instant* (not some drawn-out Armageddon battle), Satan and sin and death will be defeated. They will be thrown into the lake of fire, and a new world will be ours!

When I read Revelation, my heart is captured by a new heaven and a new earth, a wedding banquet, a beautiful city, and a whole new kind of life. We will live in a city with no prisons, hospitals, cemeteries, or police stations. There will be no more sickness, no more death, no more pain, no more crying, no more night. We will live in a world with mountains and rivers and birds and trees so beautiful our souls will ache within us. We will see our loved ones who have died in Christ. We will work and play and laugh and dance. We will explore and learn and talk and worship together for eternity. And best of all, we'll see our Lord face to face. What a glorious day that will be! That's what our hearts long for. "Heaven is the ache in our bones. Heaven is the splinter in our heart. Heaven is our deepest instinct."[16] When I read Revelation, I pray, "Come, Lord Jesus. Come quickly."

Conclusion

O Preacher, your people need this book. On their darkest days, it is this vision that can keep them going. It is this vision that can strengthen their obedience, lengthen their endurance, and deepen their faith. It is no "haunted house," but a welcoming home to refresh and revive the weary of heart. So don't avoid it. Don't neglect it. Teach your congregation *how* to read Revelation. Teach them *why* they should read Revelation. Then let God's Word do the work that only it can do. Preach and teach the powerful truth of this book, and I promise you—no, God promises you—your church will be blessed!

PREACHING REVELATION IN THE TWENTY-FIRST CENTURY

J. K. Jones

Humility and Paradox: A Starting Point

Sometimes preachers forget. They can easily forget keys, cell phones, addresses, or names, but I am not talking about any of those things. I'm talking about something fundamentally essential to the meaning of proclamation. The preacher now and then forgets that preaching does not start with the crafting of a sermon. This is particularly true of preaching Revelation. Proclaiming the book of Revelation in the twenty-first century starts with a deep sense of humility.

Preachers need the kind of humility that does not push the text into saying something it does not say. They need the kind of humility that does not presume they understand everything about the "Revelation of Jesus Christ." They need the kind of humility that does not pretend to know something they do not know. Preachers need the kind of humility that approaches reading, praying, and contemplating the text in a deep spirit of yielding and trusting in the Holy Spirit, not with the "making" of sermons. The temptation toward hurrying the process is profound. After all, for those of us who preach regularly, it feels like Sunday comes every third day, but listening attentively to the biblical text and its historical context is essential and necessary to good preaching.

If there is the slightest bit of hesitation in you to tackle Revelation then you are probably a worthy candidate to preach it. On a very personal note, I found myself, even in the "making" of this chapter, nearly seduced into writing first and reading second. So, I went back and reread and reconsidered John's Revelation of Jesus Christ; it is appropriate that the teacher never stop being the student.

I observed that trait in Bob Lowery when I was a freshman Bible college student. In my early years of formative higher education Dr. Lowery modeled for me the kind of humility, love of Jesus, and biblical reverence I am attempting to describe. Almost thirty-five years have come and gone since I first encountered his passionate, supersonic, and sometimes confrontational teaching style. I saw in him the acute awareness that Scripture, by its very nature, is dangerous. We must, he often reminded us, approach it on its terms and not our own.

Many other good voices have taught us that the Bible should be marked with warning signs, such as: "Handle with Care," "Caution: Highly Combustible," and "Always Follow the Manufacturer's Recommendations!" Whatever the Holy Spirit, through John, is attempting to communicate: it is not boring! Challenging, demanding, even perplexing would be words that describe the preacher's adventure in attempting to proclaim this book in our time and place, but certainly not boring. When it comes to preaching Revelation, perhaps this is why, as far as I know, John Calvin never preached it and Martin Luther minimized its importance. I understand their reservation.

Preaching Revelation always makes me feel like I have been caught between two opposing views and two contrasting worlds. On one hand, I agree with Fee and Stuart in their classic assessment, "When turning to the book of Revelation from the rest of the New Testament, one feels as if he or she were entering a foreign country. Instead of narratives and letters containing plain statements of fact and imperatives, one comes to a book full of angels, trumpets, earthquakes, beasts, dragons, and bottomless pits."[1] There are moments in preaching when I wonder if I understand anything about the strange and mysterious apocalypse of Jesus Christ. On the other hand, I have some affinity toward C.S. Lewis' observation of Narnia and its resemblance for me to Revelation. "I have come home at last! This is the real country! I belong here. This is the land I have been looking for all my life, though I never knew it till now. The reason why we loved the Old Narnia is that it sometimes looked a little like this."[2] Now and then, when preaching Revelation, I have this surreal experience where I am completely at peace, entirely at home with John's wonderful portrait of the slain Lamb (13:8).

Even as I write I feel these conflicting perspectives looking and sounding like this: "I have no idea where I am and what this means," and "this is what I have been searching for my whole life." What a paradox! I assume you understand my struggle, as well as my excitement. Inherent to preaching this book is honestly facing this tug-of-war. If you have never felt this tension, there is probably no reason to read any further, though I hope and pray you will continue the journey. What I want to do in this chapter is not merely offer suggestions to preaching Revelation in our twenty-first-century context, but to actually walk into the text again and hear something of what John was attempting to describe about preaching in his first-century setting. We will get to the suggestions eventually, but let's start with the text first and especially with the preaching vocabulary of Revelation.

Proclamation in Revelation: Four Verbs

Some of you know that the NT writers used a variety of words to describe preaching. Since another chapter focuses on "teaching" (*didasko*) Revelation,[3] I will not include that word in this reflection. The preaching vocabulary of the NT includes such common and pedestrian words as "speak, talk, explain, discuss, admonish, persuade, reason, and refute" and such sizable and breathtaking words as "teach, evangelize, witness, and prophesy." By common and pedestrian I do not mean unimportant and by sizable and breathtaking I do not mean exclusive. I mean that the vocabulary of preaching in the NT is as varied as shoe sizes and snowflakes. What I am interested in talking with you about, though, are the words John uses for preaching in Revelation. To state it succinctly, John incorporates four primary verbs to proclaim the One at the center of the throne.

Martureo

The first preaching verb John draws upon is the word "*martureo*." In two distinct locations, once at the start of Revelation and once at the end of Revelation, the prisoner on Patmos uses the language of a preacher to describe the indescribable. Here is what he says. "He (God) made it known by sending his angel to his servant John, who *testifies* to everything he saw — that is, the word of God and the testimony of Jesus Christ" (1:1b-2). And later, "I, Jesus, have sent my angel *to give* you this testimony for the churches" (22:16). In this latter section John uses the verb two more times: "I *warn* everyone who hears the words of the prophecy of this book . . ." (22:18) and "He who *testifies* to these things says, 'Yes, I am coming soon" (22:20).

John's choice of preaching words here is intriguing in light of his arrest and imprisonment. Pagan political power and false worship produced a perfect storm that attempted to crush "Jesus-followers." Any person unwilling to confess "Caesar is Lord" was a target for persecution, imprisonment, and death. In this setting, John uses a word originating in the Greek courtroom. Classical Greek usage portrays a legal scene where "witnesses would appear in order to bear testimony or give evidence in a trial."[4]

John is the most prolific user of this verb in the NT. Of the seventy-six occurrences of "*martureo*," forty-three are located in John's writings.[5] I appreciate the succinct manner in which Craig Keener describes the importance of this word. He observes, "Roman Law always permitted the accused to speak in his defense, and Christians could use their hearings as an opportunity to proclaim Christ regardless of the consequences."[6] Preaching in John's context called for standing up and speaking up on behalf of Christ. That kind of hearty boldness might have a significant say in preaching Revelation in the twenty-first century.

Kerusso

The second preaching verb John uses is "*kerusso*." John writes in Rev 5:2, "And I saw a mighty angel *proclaiming* in a loud voice, 'Who is worthy to break the seals and open the scroll?'" John wants the reader to know that no one in all of heaven and earth is capable of opening what has been sealed. John, the pastor and preacher, weeps over this predicament. Only the victorious and paradoxical Lion/Lamb is able to open the seven seals. The lion is characterized by strength and power. The lamb is marked by traits of vulnerability and weakness. How strange that the Lion of Judah is also the Lamb of Passover. John pictures a strong angel with an equally strong voice bringing the news that a champion of champions is needed and Jesus alone answers the call.

This is the only place in Revelation where John uses the verb *"proclaiming."* Nonetheless, it is a significant usage! It sets the tone and mood for the rest of the book. Those of us who live in the world of preaching know that this particular verb gives us an ancient picture of a herald or spokesman who was entrusted to publicly announce what he had been told by a king, a military commander, or some other important official. In ancient Greek culture, the herald carried a scepter in hand to show the dignity and majesty of the task at hand. The status of the announcer was solely dependent upon the master he served. Other than a good voice, the chief requirement of this messenger was to deliver exactly what he had been told.

The sixty-one occurrences of the verb *"kerusso"* in the NT seem to put emphasis on the declaration of what God did for us in Christ. The event is what matters.[7] The implication for the preacher who desires to proclaim Revelation in the twenty-first century might be something as profoundly simple as telling the truth about Christ and not becoming preoccupied with speculation about chronology.

Euangelizo

The third word John uses in his preaching arsenal is *"euangelizo."* On two occasions he draws upon this verb. He writes, "But in the days when the seventh angel is about to sound his trumpet, the mystery of God will be accomplished, just as he *announced* to his servants the prophets" (10:7), and "Then I saw another angel flying in midair, and he had the eternal gospel to *proclaim* to those who live on the earth—to every nation, tribe, language and people" (14:6). In the fifty-four occurrences of this word in the NT, it is used to announce the Good News about the coming Kingdom of God, what God has done to save us, and what this salvation might look like. The emphasis is upon bringing a good report. The implication for preaching Revelation in our day might be to recall that in the most dire biblical texts and circumstances there is good news to be found. God is ultimately victorious! We will explore this a bit more when we look at some preaching possibilities.

Propheteuo

John's fourth and final preaching word in Revelation is *"propheteuo."* Once again, John records two occasions where he inserts this verb. First, "Then I was told, 'You must *prophesy* again about many peoples, nations, languages and kings'" (10:11), and second, "And I will give power to my two witness-es, and they will *prophesy* for 1,260 days, clothed in sackcloth'" (11:3). These two texts are located between the sixth and seventh trumpets of Rev 9:13 and 11:15. The imagery is powerful. John has just seen a mighty angel and heard loud and power-ful thunder. Then, John is instructed to eat the little scroll and told of the two witnesses who will prophesy.

Twenty-eight times in the NT, predominantly used in 1 Corinthians (11 times), we are told of Christians prophesying. It is true that the word used by John and other NT writers does have some sense of foretelling the future; however, the funda-mental notion behind this verb is the idea of declaring some-thing in the name of God.

> Primitive Christian prophecy is the inspired speech of charis-matic preachers through whom God's plan of salvation for the world and the community and His will for the life of individual Christians are made known. . . . He knows something of the divine mysteries . . . speaks out on contemporary issues . . . admonishes the indolent and weary . . . consoles and encourages those under assault.[8]

Revelation, with its references to itself as a book of prophe-cy (1:3; 22:7,10,18, and 19) has the feel and passion of forth-telling the message of Christ, in other words, of preaching about Jesus. The prophet has a message from the Lord in the here and now. Prophesying is not about a message from yesterday or even tomorrow. The preacher, then, has the opportunity to put the emphasis on Christ at this moment, rather than on the calendar of tomorrow.[9]

Preaching Revelation in the Twenty-First Century: Implications of the Four Verbs

Where, then, do these four preaching verbs lead us in proclaiming Revelation in the twenty-first century? Dr. Lowery underscored the need for preaching Revelation when he wrote:

I write as a preacher who wants to help people see the good news about Jesus (for those who embrace the gospel) and the bad news (for those who reject or abandon the good news) found in John's work. The message of the book needs to be heard in the twenty-first century just as much as it did in the first century, if not more.[10]

So, how do we accomplish that? Let's use the four verbs we've been talking about and allow them to give appropriate direction for our preaching.

Martureo *Preaching*

The book of Revelation encourages what I have called a "hearty boldness." As we preach, let's take up the courageous posture of standing up and speaking up. Call your listeners to a grace-filled and radical discipleship. Probe the obedience language of the Book. An important reminder to preachers is, "Revelation is filled with comfort for those who are being persecuted and with warning for those who are trying to avoid it."[11]

Revelation constantly reminds us of the danger of compromise, especially in chapters 2 and 3. Explore what is at stake when our love, commitment, words, purity, vitality, evangelism, and stewardship become compromised. A series of sermons from that particular section, shaped by the obedience talk of Rev 1:3 and 22:7 could usher in a new season of undivided loyalty to Jesus. Consider the seven churches of Asia Minor as examples of local congregations being "listening posts" for the articulate voice of God. Each church is challenged to act upon what it hears. The kind of "listening" that leads to "doing" starts with the preacher.

Kerusso *Preaching*

Whatever you decide to do in your preaching from Revelation, make up your mind right now to tell the truth about Jesus. Though it may sound trite and overused, remember to keep the "main thing" the "main thing." Don't forget that God wins in and through Jesus Christ. Let your preaching be Jesus-driven and Jesus-centered. Consider doing a book sermon that might look something like this: Jesus is on His throne in heaven (chapters 1–5), Jesus is on His throne on earth (chapters 6–19), and Jesus is on His throne in the new heaven and earth (chapters 21–22). Perhaps a preaching plan that announces the truth about Jesus' centrality in every reality of life would be appropriate in your place of influence. Here's a possible way of tackling that approach:

"Keep Jesus at the Center" – 1:1-20

"Keep Jesus at the Center of Our Listening" – 2:1-3:22

"Keep Jesus at the Center of Our Worship" – 4:1-5:14

"Keep Jesus at the Center of Our Battles" (Part 1) – 6:1-7:17

"Keep Jesus at the Center of Our Waiting" – 8:1-9:21

"Keep Jesus at the Center of Our Witnessing" – 10:1-11:19

"Keep Jesus at the Center of Our Battles" (Part 2) – 12:1-14:20

"Keep Jesus at the Center of Our Watching" – 15:1-18:24

"Keep Jesus at the Center of Our Celebrating" – 19:1-20:15

"Keep Jesus at the Center of Our Longing" – 21:1-22:21

In the shaping of your preaching plan don't forget that Revelation deals with three types of literature or genre: epistle, prophecy, and apocalyptic. The first two types typically do not give us difficulty, though sound hermeneutical principles are needed. However, apocalyptic material often challenges the best preachers among us. Remember this kind of material is grounded in ancient Judaism and was very popular from 200 BC to 100 AD, though first appearing in and around the fifth century BC.

The wise preacher should take the time to explore that period in order to gain some insight into why and how apocalyptic material was used. It is crisis literature that cannot always be taken literally and forces us to grapple with the symbols that are incorporated. It underscores the imminent arrival and reign of God that is cosmic in scope, set alongside an epic battle between good and evil. It is written to a minority group overwhelmed by opposition. It often rewrites past history into future events like in Revelation 12. The nature of apocalyptic material is that it invites and compels you to identify with someone in the drama. I remind you of this simple and powerful truth, "The central message of apocalyptic literature was the ultimate triumph of God's goodness over the evils of the present."[12]

Euangelizo *Preaching*

Put the emphasis on Good News as you prepare, ponder, pray, and ultimately preach through Revelation. I have been helped by the good counsel of Richard Melick at this point:

> Apocalyptic is doxological. The foundation and goal of all of the imagery and movements is the glory of God. . . . Although Satan and his envoys exercise intermediate control, even their actions result ultimately in God's glory. God overrules them. . . . (This) has several implications for preachers. First, God is the center of the drama. . . . Second, preachers cannot preach apocalyptic with a defeatist attitude. . . . Third, preachers cannot preach apocalyptic with a sense of triumphalism. Unbelievers will be punished and all who oppose God will receive their just rewards. . . . As always, preachers should preach these themes with compassion and heartfelt concern for those who reject God.[13]

I often remind myself that Good News is not Good News for everyone.

Nonetheless, a focus on the beatitudes in the book of Revelation might be a good way to get at *euangelizo* preaching. Consider these seven:

> "Blessed is the one who reads the words of this prophecy, and blessed are those who hear it and take to heart what is written in it, because the time is near" (1:3).

263

"Blessed are the dead who die in the Lord from now on" (14:13).

"Blessed is he who stays awake and keeps his clothes with him, so that he may not go naked and be shamefully exposed" (16:15).

"Blessed are those who are invited to the wedding supper of the Lamb" (19:9).

"Blessed and holy are those who have part in the first resurrection" (20:6).

"Blessed is he who keeps the words of the prophecy in this book" (22:7).

"Blessed are those who wash their robes, that they may have the right to the tree of life and may go through the gates into the city" (22:14).

Of course, a good word study on "blessed" and attention to the context where each beatitude is located is essential.

Propheteuo *Preaching*

My encouragement to you is to declare what God has already said, especially as it relates to the colossal themes of this book. Those gigantic subjects would include: the universal Lordship of Jesus Christ, redemption, hope, judgment, obedience, spiritual warfare, spiritual formation, worship, the church, the Trinity, etc. Jeffrey Arthurs is correct, "Apocalyptic preachers will preach on big themes with forms congruous to that scope. We present God as *pantocrator* ("ruler of all," see Rev 1:8 and eight other times in the book)."[14] This book, perhaps more than any other, can clear up misconceptions, especially those that surround God, Christ, the Holy Spirit, and the place of the church in a pluralistic and immoral society. Perhaps the twenty-first century is more like the first than any other previous century. A prophetic word is needed as never before.

Conclusion

Winston Churchill, just three days after Germany invaded Holland, addressed the British House of Commons, May 13, 1940. His words often remind me of the difficulty of being caught between our Lord's first coming and His ultimate and sure second coming.

> I have nothing to offer but blood, toil, tears, and sweat. . . . We have before us an ordeal of the most grievous kind. We have before us many, many long months of struggle and of suffering. . . . You ask, what is our policy? I can say: it is to wage war, by sea, land and air, with all our might and with all the strength that God can give us; to wage war against a monstrous tyranny, never surpassed in the dark, lamentable catalogue of human crime. . . . You ask, what is our aim? I can answer in one word: It is victory, victory at all costs, victory in spite of all terror, victory, however long and hard the road may be. . . .[15]

Whether the preacher, after much study and prayer, decides on an interpretive angle that is preterist, historicist, futurist, idealist, or some combination, Revelation shouts a victory cry as the faithful ones wait patiently for His glorious return! If that is not worth preaching, I don't know what is.

IN DEFENSE OF ESCHATOLOGY: DOES STUDYING REVELATION REALLY MATTER?

Shane J. Wood

Introduction

In teaching Revelation over the years, one particular question seems to surface with predictable frequency: "Does it really matter?" "Does the study of Revelation, the study of 'end times,' the study of 'eschatology'[1] really even matter?" This question is not limited to local church settings, college level classrooms, or even seminary hallways; instead, it is a question that can be found at all levels of study and inquiry— "Does it really matter?" To be honest, in my own study I have wrestled with this very question quite deeply. I do *not* want to waste my time pursuing arguments, reading thousands of pages, and lecturing across the world on a topic that has no significance for the Christian life. Therefore, I want to answer three questions in this chapter: (1) "What does 'eschatology' mean?" (2) "How does 'eschatology' function in the Bible?" and (3) "Does 'eschatology' really matter?"

Defining "Eschatology"

So what does "eschatology" mean? Eschatology is one of those $25 words that people often throw around but do not take time to define—both for other people and for themselves. This, however, does nothing but perpetuate confusion and a lack of clear communication, both of which lead to abuse and neglect of the study. As a result, three lines of inquiry will be used to elucidate the meaning of this enigmatic term.

First, the origin of a word can give clues to the general trajectory of its meaning. Used for the first time in the English language in 1844,[2] "eschatology" comes from two Greek words: *eskhatos* (ἔσχατος) and *logia* (λογία).[3] *Eskhatos* is translated "last" or "last things," while *logia* can be translated "the study of." Therefore, "eschatology," at the most basic level, means "the study of the last things."

While that ostensibly helps, the meaning of the word is still left somewhat nebulous—primarily because words are best defined in the context in which they are used. So, the second line of inquiry asks, "How is the word used today?" If you type "eschatology" into Google, the vast majority of the 945,000 websites that show up use other words besides just "eschatology" to describe their study, including: "end times," "last times," and more typically the "last days." Through the influence of the likes of Tim LaHaye[4] and Hal Lindsey,[5] many believe that the definition of "eschatology" is more accurately defined as "the study of the last days."

This definition, however, presents another problem: "How do we define 'last days'?" According to the aforementioned authors, the definition of the "last days" is: the time period leading up to and just before the final coming of Christ (i.e., the rapture, seven years of tribulation, 1,000 year reign, etc.).[6] Their supposed "eschatological" studies merely pursue timetables, antichrist identifications, and a constant focus on the activities of Israel—whom they incorrectly see as the key to eschatological events.[7] Nevertheless, in order to answer the question "How do we define 'last days'?" it is not necessary for us to ask the "prophecy experts;" instead, we need to ask in our third line of inquiry, "How does the *Bible* define 'last days'?"

The words "last days" or "last times" are used a total of seven times in the Bible,[8] and each time it is used with the same definition. The first usage, canonically speaking, is quite instructive for the meaning of the phrase throughout the Scriptures. In Acts 2:17, Peter, quoting Joel 2:28f., says, "In the *last days*, God says, 'I will pour out my Spirit on all people.'"[9] This quotation comes in the context where the Holy Spirit has just descended on the Apostles causing them to speak in "other tongues as the Spirit enabled them" (Acts 2:1-4). This event, as can be imagined, caused great bewilderment for the crowd hearing the Apostles speak in their "own tongues" (2:11). Finally, an explanation is offered: "They have had too much wine" (2:13).

In order to squelch this ridiculous assertion and deliver the true meaning of these events, Peter stands up and says, "Fellow Jews and all of you who live in Jerusalem, let me explain *this* to you; listen carefully to what I say" (Acts 2:14, *emphasis* added). Peter states that his intention is to explain "this" to the crowd — "this" referring to the outpouring of the Holy Spirit and phenomenon that has caused such disarray. He goes on to refute the accusation, "These men are not drunk, as you suppose. It's only nine in the morning! No, *this* is what was spoken by the prophet Joel. . . ." (Acts 2:15-16, *emphasis* added). Notice again, Peter is attempting to define "this." "This" being the moment they are experiencing; "this" being what the prophet Joel describes. The very next phrase that occurs in the text is: "In the last days. . ." (2:17a). Peter states in typical Jewish interpretation, "'*This*' is '*that*'" or "*This* outpouring of the Holy Spirit is *that* which Joel told us would happen in the *last days*." Consequently, Peter does not define "the last days" the same way that we do — the time period and events directly preceding the "end of all things." Instead, Peter says that "the last days" is the time period between the first and second coming of Christ, which began with his death, burial, and resurrection and will conclude with his second coming.

This definition, though, is not peculiar to Peter in Acts. Indeed, this definition of the "last days" is how all six of the other biblical references define the term (including "last times"). For example, in Heb 1:1-2, the writer states, "In the past God spoke to our forefathers through the prophets at many times and in various ways, but in *these last days* he has spoken to us by his Son. . . ." The author designates the "last days" as the time period in which he is writing (i.e., the first century C.E.) with the word "these," and he attaches the words and events of Jesus to the "last days." Or Jude 18, "But, dear friends, remember what the apostles of our Lord Jesus Christ foretold. They said to you 'In *the last times* there will be scoffers who will follow their own ungodly desires.' *These* are the men who divide you [now]. . . ."[10] Jude defines the scoffers who will appear in "the last times" as the men that are dividing the church to which he is writing in the first century C.E. Consistently throughout the NT, the words "last days" and "last times" are defined as: the time period between the first coming and second coming of Christ.[11]

According to this initial study, the definition of eschatology as "the study of the last days" seems to be much more involved than what we initially surmised. For we cannot simply define the "last days" as the events that lead up to the second coming of Jesus, but instead, we must adopt the biblical definition of the "last days" as the entire time period between the first coming of Christ and the second coming of Christ. What is at stake in common misunderstandings of the definition is not just incorrect information; rather, what is at stake is the function of eschatology itself. The implications of this are explored in the second question to be answered: "How does 'eschatology' function in the Bible?"

Prediction or Exhortation? — The Context of Major "Eschatological" Passages

Oftentimes eschatology is consigned to the realm of "who really cares?" because of the perception that the study is only concerned with awkward, enigmatic passages that only focus on the future with no concern for the present. But is this an accurate assessment of the "eschatological" passages of the Bible? Is this really how they function within the text and within the communities to which they were written? To answer the question "How does eschatology function in the Bible?" three key eschatological texts will be examined: the second coming of Jesus in Mt 24:36–25:46, the conflagration of the earth in 2Pet 3:1-14,17, and a brief overview of the book of Revelation — for some, the NT eschatological manifesto.

Matthew 24:36–25:46 — The Second Coming of Jesus
In Matthew 24:36, Jesus begins to answer the question regarding his second coming[12] — signaled by the emphatic "But

concerning . . ." to begin the text.[13] After describing the fact that the second coming will be completely without sign or warning—like "in the days of Noah" (24:36-41)—Jesus offers this caution in 24:42, "Therefore keep watch, because you do not know on what day your Lord will come." This warning is reiterated in 24:44, but this time "keep watch" is exchanged for the admonition to "be ready." These cautions are reiterated and explained in the text that follows.

The two warnings in 24:42-44 launch into four parables that stretch from 24:45-25:46—the parable of the faithful and wicked servants (24:45-51), the parable of the ten virgins (25:1-13), the parable of the talents (25:14-30), and the parable of the sheep and goats (25:31-46). Each of the four parables has the same two primary points: (1) Jesus' second coming is unexpected and unpredictable,[14] and (2) therefore we should always be doing what he asked us to do. Woven throughout the four parables are statements like: "It will be good for that servant whose master finds him doing [what he asked] when he returns" (24:46), "The master of that servant will come on a day when he does not expect him and at an hour he is not aware of" (24:50), and "Therefore keep watch, because you do not know the day or the hour" (25:13).

The final parable pictures a judgment scene that occurs "when the Son of Man comes in glory" (25:31). With "all the nations gathered before him" (25:32a), Jesus begins to separate the "sheep from the goats" (25:32b) or "the faithful from the unfaithful." In both the rewarding and condemning of these two groups, respectively, Jesus defines the exhortations to "keep watch" and "be ready" from the earlier passages: "I was hungry and you gave me something to eat, I was thirsty and you gave me something to drink, I was a stranger and you invited me in, I needed clothes and you clothed me, I was sick and you looked after me, I was in prison and you came to visit me" (25:35-36). The scene concludes with the faithful going to their place of reward, the unfaithful going to their place of judgment, and Jesus stating, "I tell you the truth, whatever you did not do for one of the least of these, you did not do for me" (25:45). So how does "eschatology" function in this text? The same as it functions in 2Pet 3:1-14.

2 Peter 3:1-14,17 — The Conflagration of the Earth

The Christians in the community to which 2 Peter was written had, apparently, been under attack by false teachers trying to deceive the faithful (2Pet 2:1-22). To bolster their faith, the author of 2 Peter reminds the first-century recipients that in "the last days"[15] people will scoff at their eschatological belief in a "coming savior." Second Peter 3:4 articulates the objection of the false teachers, "Where is this 'coming' he promised? Ever since our fathers died, everything goes on as it has since the beginning of creation." After pointing out the scoffers' oversight of the power and sovereignty of God (3:6-7), Peter assures them that God has not forgotten his promise or abandoned them; instead, he delays his coming because of his desire for "everyone to come to repentance" (3:8-9).

This discussion of the eschatological objection of the false teachers is followed in 3:10 with the description of the conflagration of the earth at the unexpected coming of Jesus, "But the day of the Lord will come like a thief. The heavens will disappear with a roar; the elements will be destroyed by fire, and the earth and everything in it will be laid bare." So what discussion does this description of the future, eschatological renovation of the entire cosmos at the second coming of Jesus prompt? An exhortation to be faithful servants:

> Since everything will be destroyed in this way, *what kind of people ought you to be*? You ought to live holy and godly lives as you look forward to the day of God and speed its coming. That day will bring about the destruction of the heavens by fire, and the elements will melt in the heat. But in keeping with his promise we are looking forward to a new heaven and a new earth, the home of righteousness. So then, dear friends, *since you are looking forward to this, make every effort to be found spotless, blameless and at peace with him.* (2Pet 3:11-14, *emphasis* added)

So how does "eschatology" function in this text? The same as it functions in the book of Revelation.

The Book of Revelation — The Eschatological Manifesto

Amidst all the ocean of images and visions in Revelation, a constant theme surfaces time and time again, like the waves on the shore, beating a single message home. While this book may seem confusing at first, the proclamation of the Apocalypse can hardly be missed—especially when three words are traced throughout the book: repent, deeds, and obey.[16]

The word for "repent" (*metanaeō*, μετανοέω) is used twelve times[17] and separates figures in the book into two distinct categories. First, the Christians in Asia Minor addressed in chapters two and three are repeatedly exhorted to "repent," often times in conjunction with a threat of judgment. The church in Ephesus is told, "**Repent** and do the things you did at first. If you do not repent, I will come to you and remove your lampstand from its place." Similarly, the church in Pergamum is advised, "**Repent** therefore! Otherwise, I will soon come to you and will fight against them with the sword of my mouth." This group of Christians whom Jesus rebukes with an exhortation to repent (3:19) is in direct contrast to rebellious humanity who refuses to repent. In Rev 16:9,11, this latter group is described as experiencing the plagues of God from the bowls of judgment, and even with this display of power, "they refused to **repent** and glorify him." This obstinacy from both the Christians and rebellious humanity is said to be met with punishment and ultimately judgment (2:22).

Colloquially, "repentance" is described as merely a cognitive shift in one's beliefs, but in Revelation, and the rest of the Bible for that matter, repentance is directly attached to the second word that litters the pages of Revelation—deeds. The word for "deeds" or "works" (*ergon*, ἔργον) is used twenty times,[18] and its usage intends to define what God demands in his proclamations of repentance. In five of the seven messages to the seven churches of Asia Minor in chapters two and three, Jesus states the same phrase: "I know your **deeds**."[19] In three of these passages the phrase is followed up by commendation;[20] the other two passages comment on the ostensible spiritual vitality (3:1-2) and the spiritual bankruptcy (3:15-18) of the respective churches. Sardis, for example, is told, "I know your deeds; you have a reputation of being alive, but you are dead. Wake up! Strengthen what remains and is about to die, for I have not found your **deeds** complete in the sight of my God" (3:1-3).

The intimacy with which Jesus knows the deeds of these churches is carried throughout the rest of the book. The agents of rebellion have their deeds keenly described throughout the text as well.[21] This relationship between Jesus and the deeds of others, though, is not merely cognitive (i.e., "I know . . ."), but rather, Revelation describes deeds as a tool of measurement for those who belong to Jesus at his final coming. Negatively, Jesus states in Rev 22:12, "Behold, I am coming soon! My reward is with me, and I will give to everyone according to what he has **done**!"[22] Positively, Rev 14:13 says, "Then I heard a voice from heaven say, 'Write: Blessed are the dead who die in the Lord from now on.' 'Yes,' says the Spirit, 'they will rest from their labor, for their **deeds** will follow them.'"[23] The evidence from the text, then, shows that the call for "repentance" in Revelation is inextricably linked to the "deeds" of the ones that choose to respond — both positively and negatively.

"Repentance" and "deeds" in Revelation are wed by the purpose of the Apocalypse, which surfaces in the study of the third word — obey (*tāreō*, τηρέω). Used eleven times in Revelation,[24] the exhortation to "obey" both bookends the text as well as fills the shelf in between. Within the first three verses of the Apocalypse, John states the desired reaction to the rest of the images that fill the book, "Blessed is the one who reads the words of this prophecy aloud, and blessed are those who hear and **obey** the things written in it, because the time is near!"[25] This same proclamation is made by Jesus to conclude the book in Revelation 22:7, "I am coming soon! Blessed is the one who **obeys** the words of prophecy in this book."[26] These promises of blessing, which bookend Revelation, keenly focus the audience on the book's purpose — a catalyst for obedience.

Revelation centers the conversation of obedience throughout its pages by linking it with the actual identity of those that follow Jesus. When the dragon failed to devour the male-child and his mother (Rev 12:1-6,13-16), the enraged creature turns its attention to the offspring or "those who **obey** God's commandments and hold to the testimony of Jesus" (Rev 12:17, **emphasis** added). Similarly, Rev 14:12 identifies the saints as "[those] who **obey** God's commandments and remain faithful

274

to Jesus."[27] Obedience, then, is not only a call to action, but in Revelation it is an invitation to an identity.

The "repentance" exhorted in Revelation that leads to the "deeds" of the faithful enacted through "obedience" to the call of their king becomes not just, then, a matter of personal piety but the means by which the individual and community claim their identity in Christ. Therefore, the eschatology (and by extension the imagery) that drives the book is merely a vehicle through which the Apocalypse challenges the Christian community to live life in the present faithful to the call of Jesus. So how does "eschatology" function in this text? The same way that it functions in Mt 24:36–25:46, 2Pet 3:1-14, and all of the other eschatological passages in the Bible. "Eschatology" functions to call Christians to live life in the present in light of the future and because of the past.

Living, Again, for the First Time: Becoming an Eschatological People

So now to ask the final question: "Does 'eschatology' really matter?" To answer this question, a more detailed definition of eschatology must be briefly stated in light of what we have examined thus far.

If "eschatology" is the study of the "last things" (e.g., the "last days") or the time period between Christ's first and second comings, then it focuses on three key aspects. First of all, "eschatology" focuses on what has shaped and formed the "last days." In other words, the study of "eschatology" must include a comprehensive understanding of the past history leading up to the "last days" to establish how we got to where we are. This would include examining the Creation and "Fall" of mankind, God's salvation history through the nation of Israel, and the effects of the incarnation of Christ on the curse of the "Fall" — i.e., the entire story of God written in the Old and New Testament. These are the formative events that shape who we are and what we experience here in the "last days" (i.e., the End, or Last Act, of the Story).

Second, "eschatology" looks forward to what the "last days" precede. Namely, this future aspect of the study of "eschatology" focuses on the ramifications of Christ's second coming, which includes: heaven, hell, the resurrection, judgment, salvation, etc. Jesus' parousia provides the consummation to events put into motion at the "Fall" and subjugated at the first coming of Christ. It is toward this climactic moment that we look forward to here in the "last days."

The third and final element is the key focus of the entire study of "eschatology." Namely, "eschatology" informs us how we are to live in the present (the "last days") based on what we know of our past and in light of what we know about the future. In other words, the goal of "eschatology" is not prediction but obedience. The goal of eschatology is not trying to crack the "prophetic timetable" with the newspaper in one hand and the Bible in the other—e.g., prognosticating the antichrist, the date of the rapture, or even the nations of "Gog and Magog." The goal of eschatology is the faithful witness in the *present* to the work of Christ in the *past* which secures our *future*. In other words, eschatology is about living life in the present in light of the future and because of the past. And, to me, that matters.

Dragons

Chapter One: Judaic Character (*Craig A. Evans*)

1. Grouping these writings together does not necessarily imply common authorship.

2. B.F. Westcott, *The Gospel according to St. John: The Greek Text with Introduction and Notes*, 2 vols. (London: John Murray, 1908) lxxiii-lxxxvii; idem, *The Epistles of St. John: The Greek Text, with Notes and Addenda*, 3rd ed. (London: Macmillan, 1892) xxxiii-xxxix. Westcott mostly speaks of Valentinian and Cerinthian docetism.

3. R. Bultmann, *The Gospel of John: A Commentary* (Philadelphia: Westminster, 1971) 7-12; idem, *The Johannine Epistles* (Philadelphia: Fortress, 1973) 28-29, 37-39. Even R.E. Brown, who rejects most of Bultmann's construct, sees elements of the Johannine Community swallowed by Gnosticism in the early second century. See R.E. Brown, *The Community of the Beloved: The Life, Loves, and Hates of an Individual Church in New Testament Times* (New York: Paulist, 1979). Bultmann's line of interpretation is followed by almost no one today.

4. The discovery and publication of the Dead Sea Scrolls gave major impetus to study of the Johannine writings, especially the Gospel of John, in the light of Jewish texts and not just the Scrolls. For studies that emphasize points of contact, see J.H. Charlesworth (ed.), *John and the Dead Sea Scrolls* (New York: Crossroad, 1990). For a more balanced assessment of the parallels between the Scrolls and the fourth Gospel, see R. Bauckham, "The Qumran Community and the Gospel of John," in L.H. Schiffman, E. Tov, and J.C. VanderKam (eds.), *The Dead Sea Scrolls: Fifty Years after Their Discovery — Proceedings of the Jerusalem Congress, July 20–25, 1997* (Jerusalem: Israel Exploration Society and the Israel Antiquities Authority, 2000) 105-115. Bauckham acknowledges the importance of the Scrolls, but rightly concludes that other Jewish sources offer better parallels for understanding the world of the fourth Gospel.

5. J.L. Martyn, *History and Theology in the Fourth Gospel*, 3rd ed. (Louisville, KY: Westminster John Knox Press, 2003 [orig., 1968]). In my *Word and Glory: On the Exegetical and Theological Background of John's Prologue* (JSNTSup 89; Sheffield: JSOT Press, 1993) I document the shift away from understanding the fourth Gospel against the background of Gnosticism to that of Jewish wisdom traditions and scriptural apologetics that reflect the Diaspora synagogue.

6. All scripture quotations are my own translation.

7. For further discussion of grammatical details and the practice of other Jewish writers in late antiquity, see F.J.A. Hort, *The Apocalypse of St. John I–III* (London: Macmillan, 1908) 11 ("taken simply as a name"); R.H. Charles, *A Critical and Exegetical Commentary on the Book of Revelation*

(Edinburgh: T & T Clark, 1920) 1:10; D.E. Aune, *Revelation 1–5* (Nashville: Nelson, 1997) 30-32.

8. See the discussion and the relevant primary literature (e.g., 1QM 12:8-9 "host of angels" = "host of spirits") cited in Aune, *Revelation 1–5*, 34-35.

9. The Hebrew of Exod 19:6 (מַמְלֶכֶת כֹּהֲנִים) is ambiguous and can mean either "kingdom of priests" or a "royalty of priests." See Aune, *Revelation 1–5*, 47.

10. See, for example, the artfully constructed menorah in the synagogue in Peki'in, Israel, from the Second Temple period. The menorah is featured on coins struck by Antigonus, c. 40 BC, the last of the Hasmonean rulers. And of course, the menorah is featured in the stone frieze inside the Arch of Titus, commemorating the triumph celebrated in Rome in AD 71, a triumph held in gratitude for the Roman victory over Judea (cf. Josephus, *J.W.* 7.148).

11. The Greek versions of both passages read somewhat differently (e.g., LXX, Isa 44:6 "I am first, and I am after these things").

12. For a survey of archaeological work undertaken at the seven cities of the seven letters, including the island of Patmos, see J. McRay, *Archaeology and the New Testament* (Grand Rapids: Baker, 1991) 243-275, 394-398. For assessment of ancient literary and inscriptional data, see C.J. Hemer, *The Letters to the Seven Churches of Asia in their Local Setting* (JSNTSup 11; Sheffield: JSOT Press, 1986).

13. For a survey of archaeological work done at Ephesus, see McRay, *Archaeology*, 250-261; A. Bammer, "Ephesus," in E.M. Meyers (ed.), *The Oxford Encyclopedia of Archaeology in the Near East*, 5 vols. (New York: Oxford University Press, 1997) 2:252-255.

14. The concept of "apostles," or "sent ones," is right at home in the Jewish world. The prophets are *sent* by God (e.g., Isa 6:8; 61:1). Moses is God's sent one (*shaliach*) in the rabbinic and Samaritan traditions (*Mek. Simeon ben Yohai* on Exod 3:10-11; *Exod. Rab.* 3.14 [on Exod 4:10]; *Memar Marqa* 5.3; 6.3). This is why those appointed by Jesus and sent to proclaim his message are called apostles. Jesus himself is sent by his heavenly Father (cf. John 20:21).

15. McRay, *Archaeology*, 272-274.

16. We have important coherence here with the opposition described in 1 John 2:22-23. It is the parallel with 1 John that clarifies the point of the blasphemy (or slander) emanating from the synagogue of Satan.

17. Remember that the meaning of *satan* is "opponent." Accordingly, the "synagogue of Satan" opposes those who confess Jesus. On synagogues in Asia Minor, see P. Trebilco, *Jewish Communities in Asia Minor* (SNTSMS 69; Cambridge: Cambridge University Press, 1991).

18. McRay, *Archaeology*, 266-272.

19. For a survey of possible references, see Aune, *Revelation 1–5*, 182-184.

20. See G. Vermes, "The Story of Balaam," in *Scripture and Tradition in Judaism: Haggadic Studies* (Leiden: Brill, 1973) 127-177.

21. The options are surveyed in Hemer, *Letters*, 96-104.

22. McRay, *Archaeology*, 244-247.

23. For a convenient summary of rabbinic legends about Jezebel, which for the most part accentuate her evil and idolatrous habits, see L. Ginzberg, *The Legends of the Jews*, 7 vols. (Philadelphia: The Jewish Publication Society of America, 1909–1938) 4:188-189.

24. See also *Joseph and Aseneth* 14:1: "So the Lord God listened to my prayer, because this star rose as a messenger and herald of the light of the great day."

25. C.H. Greenewalt, "Sardis," in Meyers, ed., *The Oxford Encyclopedia of Archaeology in the Near East*, 484-486; McRay, *Archaeology*, 261-265.

26. The Talmudic discussion of revising the Twelfth Benediction of the Amidah, in order to identify and remove heretics from the synagogue (*b. Berakot* 28b-29a) is seen in the early Medieval form of this benediction: "For apostates let there be no hope, and the dominion of arrogance do speedily root out. *Let the Nazarenes and Minim be destroyed in a moment, and let them be blotted out of the book of life and not be inscribed with the righteous.* Blessed are you, O Lord, who humble the arrogant!" The italicized portion is what is thought to be the later revision, perhaps dating to the end of the first century AD.

27. McRay, *Archaeology*, 246-247.

Chapter Two: Plagues of Exodus (*Gary Hall*)

1. *The Dictionary of Biblical Imagery*, s.v. "Exodus, Second Exodus," 253-255, provides a convenient list of 35 subplots or images.

2. R. Lowery, *Revelation's Rhapsody* (Joplin, MO: College Press, 2006) 93-94. An extensive study is J.S. Casey, *Exodus Typology in the Book of Revelation* (unpublished Ph. D. dissertation, The Southern Baptist Theological Seminary, 1982) which is summarized in F.D. Mazzaferri, *The Genre of the Book of Revelation* (Berlin/New York: De Gruyter, 1989) 367-373.

3. J. Hoffmeier, "Plagues of Egypt," *NIDOTTE*, 4:1058.

4. See D. Gowan, *Theology in Exodus* (Louisville, KY: Westminister John Knox, 1994) 134-137; J. Durham, *Exodus* (Waco: Word, 1987) 87 and passim (God's mighty acts are also a proof of his presence.); B. Waltke with C. Yu, *An Old Testament Theology* (Grand Rapids: Zondervan, 2007) 378.

5. J. Hoffmeier, "The Arm of God versus the Arm of Pharaoh in the Exodus Narrative," *Bib* 67 (1986) 378-387. He associates this concept with that of a cosmic struggle between Pharaoh and Yahweh, for in Egypt the Pharaoh had a major role in sustaining the cosmic order on earth. The nine plagues attacked his control.

6. Several scholars have advanced this idea including U. Cassuto, *A Commentary on The Book of Exodus* (trans. by Israel Abrahams; Jerusalem: Magness Press, 1967), and J.J. Davis, *Moses and the Gods of Egypt: Studies in Exodus* (Grand Rapids: Baker, 1986). N. Sarna asserts that the plagues are the first instance of the OT's war on polytheism (*Exploring Exodus: The Heritage of Biblical Israel* [New York: Schocken Books, 1986] 80).

7. T. Fretheim, *Exodus*, Interpretation (Louisville, KY: John Knox, 1991) 110.

8. P. Enns, *Exodus* (Grand Rapids: Zondervan, 2000) 230-231. Enns refers to several shared words between the plague accounts and Genesis 1. However, W. Propp is not convinced these connections are significant (*Exodus 1-18* [New York: Doubleday 1999] 345-346).

9. E. Peterson is adamant that the purpose of the ten plagues was a single theme: worship (*Reversed Thunder: The Revelation of John and the Praying Imagination* [San Francisco: Harper and Row, 1988] 143-144). The relevant texts are: Exod 4:31; 5:3; 7:16; 8:20; 9:1,13; 10:3 (see footnote 4 on chapter 10, p. 200; he also lists 8:11 which is probably a typo for 8:8). He further states that the judgment plagues are visited based on this issue and on this issue alone. Peterson comes to this conclusion from his interpretation of Revelation 15-18, and especially the hymnic portions. To say that worship is the single theme is an overstatement. I would suggest that the worship theme is subsidiary to that of knowing Yahweh. Who was Israel to worship? Israel as well as Egypt needed to discover that.

10. Enns, *Exodus*, 234; B. Childs, *The Book of Exodus* (Philadelphia: Westminster Press, 1974) 140.

11. Sarna, *Exodus*, 76; Enns, *Exodus*, 208, and others.

12. Sarna, *Exodus*, 77; Enns, *Exodus*, 208.

13. So G. Hort, "The Plagues of Egypt," *ZAW* 69 (1957) 84-103 and *ZAW* 70 (1958) 48-59.

14. See Hoffmeier, "Plagues of Egypt," 1056.

15. For signs see Exod 4:8,9,17,28,30; 7:3; 8:23(H-19); 10:1,2; for wonders see Exod 4:21; 7:9; 11:9,10. The purpose of the signs was to impart knowledge—7:5,17; 10:2. See P.A. Kruger, "אוֹת," *NIDOTTE* 1:331-333.

16. Gowan, *Exodus*, 132. See also the strong language in the Song of the Sea, Exod 15.

17. See G. Hall, *Deuteronomy* (Joplin, MO: College Press, 2000) for details. D. Stuart lists 27 categories of covenant curses culled mainly from Leviticus 26 and Deuteronomy 28 (*Hosea-Joel*, WBC 31 [Waco: Word, 1987], xxxiii-xl).

18. See J.A. Thompson/E.A. Martens, "שׁוּב," *NIDOTTE* 4:57, and W.L. Holladay, *The Root Subh in the Old Testament* (Leiden: Brill, 1958).

19. The triad also occurs often in Ezekiel. Some have suggested it was something of a "slogan" that may have arisen as a stereotypical phrase that originated in actual crisis. Perhaps Deut 32:23-25 is the foundation for the language.

20. G. Mayer, "דֶּבֶר," *TDOT* 3: 126-127.

21. J.A. Naude, "אֵשׁ," *NIDOTTE* 1:534-535; *DBI*, s.v., "Fire," 286-290.

22. Stuart, *Hosea-Jonah*, 241.

23. The other plagues, such as frogs, gnats/flies, and boils do not appear in judgment texts.

24. Ps 78 has the order of plagues 9, 1, 2, 4/5, 7, 8, and 10. Ps 105 has the order of plagues 1, 4, 2, 8, 7, 5, and 10.

25. J. Mays, *Psalms* (Louisville, KY: John Knox, 1994) 255-256.

26. Amos 4:6-11 lists seven covenant curses that God brought on Israel to induce them to repent, yet they did not. Two coincide with the plagues.

27. The seven bowls do not have an interlude.

28. The spheres of creation are: earth, sea, rivers, sun, realm of the wicked, the Euphrates, and the end. See G.K. Beale, *The Book of Revelation* (Grand Rapids: Eerdmans, 1999) 808.

29. Compare the seventh seal in 8:5.

30. If this is so, then all the plagues but the third and fourth (lice and flies) are alluded to in Revelation.

31. G.K. Beale and D.A. Carson, eds., *Commentary on the New Testament Use of the Old Testament* (Grand Rapids: Baker, 2007) 1120.

32. The phrase "signs and wonders" does not occur in Revelation. "Signs" (σημειον) occurs seven times. Positively, a woman clothed with the sun is a sign (12:1) and the seven angels are a sign (15:1). On the other hand the appearance of the red dragon is a sign (12:3). Furthermore, it is the beast (13:13-14) or the demonic spirits (16:14) or the false prophet (19:20) who perform signs, all designed to deceive people to follow the beast.

33. There is widespread agreement on this point. See the commentaries by Hendriksen, Ladd, Beasley-Murray, Osborne, Beale, etc.

34. R. Mounce, *The Book of Revelation*, rev. ed. (Grand Rapids: Eerdmans, 1998) 176-177, and G.R. Beasley-Murray, *Revelation* (Grand Rapids: Eerdmans, 1974) 156, see this as their main purpose.

35. Mounce, *Revelation*, 291.

36. Beasley-Murray, *Revelation*, 241.

37. Beale, *Revelation*, 465-467, and G.K. Beale, *John's Use of the Old Testament in Revelation* (Sheffield: Sheffield Academic, 1998) 205ff.

38. Beale, *Revelation*, 467, 471.

Chapter Three: "Witness" (Neal Windham)

1. *The New Testament Concept of Witness* (Cambridge: Cambridge University Press, 1977).

2. Ibid., 34-47.

3. Ibid., 45.

4. Ibid., 154.

5. Ibid., 171-172.

6. *The Mandate of the Church in the Apocalypse of John*, vol. 77 (New York: Peter Lang, 2005) 142-145.

7. Ibid., 144.

8. Themes like "encouragement, comfort, rebuke, warning, and promise," p. 138.

9. See B.K. Blount, *Can I Get a Witness? Reading Revelation through African American Culture* (Louisville, KY: John Knox, 2005) 38, and Blount, "Reading Revelation Today: Witness as Active Resistance" *Int* 54.4 (2000): 398-412, who argues that "witness" functions in acts of ecclesial resistance.

10. F. Mazzaferri, "*Martyria Iesou* Revisited," *BT* 39.1 (1988): 117, goes so far as to suggest that the cognate noun *martyrein* "equates with *propheteuein* in Revelation."

11. For more detailed analysis of the domain, see W. Bauer, F.W. Danker, W.F. Arndt, F.W. Gingrich (eds.), *A Greek-English Lexicon of the New Testament and Other Early Christian Literature*, 3rd ed. (Chicago: University of Chicago Press, 1999) 617-620.

12. Trites, *New Testament*, 156-158; and "*Martus* and Martyrdom in the Apocalypse: a Semantic Study" *NovT* 15.1 (1973) 75; J.P.M. Sweet, "Maintaining the Testimony of Jesus," in *Suffering and Martyrdom in the New Testament*, ed. by W. Horbury and B. McNeil (Cambridge: Cambridge University Press, 1981) 103-104; C.R. Koester, "The Church and Its Witness in the Apocalypse of John," *Tidsskrift for Teologi og Kirke* 78.3-4 (2007) 270.

13. G.W.H. Lampe, "The Testimony of Jesus Is the Spirit of Prophecy (Rev. 19:10)," in *The New Testament Age: Essays in Honor of Bo Reicke*, ed. by W.C. Weinrich, (Macon, GA: Mercer University Press, 1984) 1:253.

14. So G.K. Beale, *The Book of Revelation* (Grand Rapids: Eerdmans, 1999) 184. My colleague, Chris Keith, believes the genitive is appositional, a position which also makes good sense.

15. Especially in view of those texts which speak of witnesses who "have" the "testimony of Jesus" (Rev 12:17; 19:10).

16. See below.

17. Ibid. Yet another possibility comes from B. Dehandschutter, who argues that *marturia* may here mean "a good recommendation," as in 1 Tim 3:7. See his "Witness in the Apocalypse," in *L'Apocalypse johannique et l'Apocalyptique dans le Nouveau Testament*, ed. by J. Lambrecht (Leuven: Leuven University Press, 1980) 286.

18. Eus. *Eccl. Hist.*, 5.2.2-3.

19. Trites, "*Martus*," 73.

20. Ibid., 72-73.

21. Ibid., 73, 80.

22. M.G. Reddish, "Martyr Christology in the Apocalypse," *JSNT* 33 (June 1988) 86.

23. Ibid., 87.

24. Ibid., 89.

25. See, M.V. Lee, "A Call to Martyrdom: Function as Method and Message in Revelation" *NovT* 40.2 (April 1998) 174.

26. *Revelation* (Grand Rapids: Baker, 2002) 30-31.

27. The NIV is cited throughout this chapter.

28. P. Cotterell and M. Turner, *Linguistics & Biblical Interpretation* (Downers Grove, IL: InterVarsity, 1989) 244.

29. Ibid., 245.

30. K.A. Strand, "The Two Witnesses of Rev. 11:3-12" *AUSS* 19.2 (1981) 127-135.

31. See the helpful list of OT references in R.A. Lowery, *Revelation's Rhapsody: Listening to the Lyrics of the Lamb* (Joplin, MO: College Press, 2006) 175-197.

32. While Jesus at times refers to some part of the OT as the "Word of God" (Mt 15:6; Mk 7:13, etc.), Luke broadens the meaning of this phrase considerably (Acts 4:31; 6:2,7; 8:14, etc.).

33. G.R. Beasley-Murray, *The Book of Revelation* (Greenwood, SC: The Attic Press, 1974) 276, suggests that the commandment to worship God may carry "an indirect reference to the fact that the testimony of Jesus directs men to the Father . . . ," and that "Spirit-inspired prophets will do as [Jesus] did: point men to God."

34. Jesus did in fact call attention to the importance of worshiping God during his ministry (Mt 4:10; Lk 4:8; Jn 4:21-24).

35. As well as angel-worship (see Col 2:18).

36. The only text in Revelation which explicitly mentions worshiping God, but does not appear in the trajectory, is Rev 7:11.

37. Cf. 1:8 and 4:8,11 (where *kurios* refers to God) with 11:8 and 17:14 (where *kurios* refers to Jesus).

38. The chiasm works as follows:
    A. testimony
       B. Jesus
       B.' Spirit
    A.' prophecy

39. The verbs *ekousa* and *eblepsa*, "I heard and saw," introduced as they are by *hote* ("when"), recall John's attempt to worship the angel in Rev 19:10. John has trouble recovering from his costly mistake.

40. There is one key difference between 19:10 and 22:9. Where in 19:10 we have, "having the testimony of Jesus," in 22:9 the text reads, "keeping the words of *this book.*"

41. Lowery, *Rhapsody*, 54.

42. Ibid.

43. S.R.F. Price, *Rituals and Power: The Roman Imperial Cult in Asia Minor* (Cambridge: Cambridge University Press, 1984) 132, 233, 239-248.

44. E. Schüssler Fiorenza, *The Book of Revelation: Justice and Judgment* (Philadephia: Fortress, 1985) 192ff.

45. Ibid.,193.

46. A.Y. Collins, *Crisis & Catharsis: The Power of the Apocalypse* (Philadelphia: Westminster, 1984) 69-77. Collins sees the problems for John's churches more broadly (Christian problems with Jews and pagans, conflicts between rich and poor, Neronian persecution, which was not related to the imperial cult, etc.). See also L. Thompson, *The Book of Revelation: Apocalypse and Empire* (New York: Oxford University Press, 1990) 163-164. For a critical review of the positions of Schüssler Fiorenza, Yarbro Collins, and Thompson, see S.J. Friesen, "The Cult of the Roman Emperors in Ephesos: Temple Wardens, City Titles, and Interpretation of

the Revelation of John," in *Ephesos: Metropolis of Asia*, ed. by H. Koester (Valley Forge, PA: Trinity Press International, 1995) 245-250.

47. Thompson, *Revelation*, 164.

48. C.A.J. Coady, *Testimony: A Philosophical Study* (Oxford: Clarendon Press, 1992) 13.

49. Ibid., 248.

Chapter Four: Hymns (*Fred Hanson*)

1. R. A. Lowery, *Revelation's Rhapsody: Listening to the Lyrics of the Lamb* (Joplin, MO: College Press, 2006).

2. Commentators disagree as to the number of hymns in Revelation. However, potential hymns exist in 4:8; 4:11; 5:9-10; 5:11; 5:13; 7:9; 7:11; 7:15-17; 11:15; 11:16-18; 12:10-12; 14:3; 15:3-4; 19:1-3; 19:4-5; 19:6-8.

3. A seminal work for studying hymns is J. Sanders, *The New Testament Christological Hymns* (Cambridge: Cambridge University Press, 1971), but it, like many hymnic studies, fails to address Revelation. For articles addressing Revelation's hymns, see J.J. O'Rourke, "The Hymns of the Apocalypse," *CBQ* 30 (1968) 399-409; R. Smith, "'Worthy Is the Lamb' and Other Songs of Revelation," *CurTM* 25.6 (Dec 1998) 500-506; J.M. Ford, "The Christological Function of the Hymns in the Apocalypse of John," *AUSS* 36.2 (Aut 1998) 207-229; and W. Hulitt Gloer, "Worship God! Liturgical Elements in the Apocalypse," *RevExp* 98 (Wint 2001) 35-57.

4. For instance, see D.E. Aune, *Revelation 1-5* (Dallas: Word, 2002) 302, who, although surveying the probable liturgical background of the text, does not treat the grammatical influences. So too G.K. Beale, *The Book of Revelation* (Grand Rapids: Eerdmans, 1999) 331.

5. J.J. Collins, "Introduction: Toward the Morphology of a Genre," *Semeia* 14 (1979) 6, defines discourse in apocalypse as uninterrupted speech by the divine mediator of the apocalypse. In the case of many poems in Revelation, they are uninterrupted speeches by beings in the heavenly realm, but not necessarily the angelic mediator leading John through his heavenly journey.

6. M. Rutenfranz, "ὑμνος" *EDNT* (Grand Rapids: Eerdmans, 1993) 3:393.

7. "ΥΜΝΟΣ," H. Liddell, *A Lexicon : Abridged from Liddell and Scott's Greek-English Lexicon* (Oak Harbor, WA: Logos, 1996) 829. Philo's use of ὑμνος, in *Allegorical Interpretation II 82*, and *Agriculture 79*, among others, supports this gloss. See P. Borgen, K. Fuglseth, and R. Skarsten, *The Works of Philo: Greek Text with Morphology* (Bellingham, WA: Logos, 2005).

8. Forms of ὑμνος, hymns, or ὑμνεω, "I sing", appear in only six texts. The noun appears in Eph 5:19 and Col 3:16 and the verb in Mt 26:30, Mk 14:26, Acts 16:25, and Heb 2:12. In none of these instances is the content of the song included, rendering comparative grammatical analysis impossible.

9. ᾠδη, "song," appears only in Rev 5:9, 14:3, and 15:3. ψάλλω, "I sing," occurs in Rom 15:19, 1Cor 14:15, Eph 5:19, Jas 5:13. ψαλμος, "psalm," or "hymn," occurs only in 1Cor 14:26, when not referring to the canonical Psalms or coupled with ὑμνος in Eph 5:19 and Col 3:16.

10. This is not to say that all poems are hymns or homologies. Several of John's poetic arrangements follow similar patterns of other kinds of poetry, such as the Hebrew oracles of woe and judgment. For more on these genres, see D. Brent Sandy and R. Giese, *Cracking Old Testament Codes* (Nashville: Broadman & Holman, 1995).

11. Gloer, "Hymns," 116.

12. Regardless of hymn or homology, Revelation's poems are a part of what Collins terms, "auditory revelation [which] clarifies the visual." That is, the voices of the heavenly beings reinforce or interpret what John is seeing. See Collins, "Introduction," 6.

13. A similar list, though containing more categories and technicalities, exists in Gloer, "Hymns," 124-129. Gloer overstates his assertion concerning the use of rare language for an author as an indicator of hymnic presence. It is difficult to demonstrate, from such a small body of evidence, the extent of an ancient author's vocabulary. The most one can argue is that a word is rare in an extant corpus. To argue a rare word in Paul's written documents of the canon means the word is rare to Pauline vocabulary or did not originate with Paul goes beyond the bounds of sound logic. One cannot know the full extent of Paul's vocabulary. S. Horn, "The Author's Use of Hymns as Summaries of the Theology of the Book of Revelation" (PhD diss., New Orleans Baptist Theological Seminary, 1998) 27, correctly observes that "the list of characteristics of a hymn equals the number of those who write about the subject."

14. See Gloer, "Hymns," 124, for introductory formula regarding Pauline epistles.

15. Many of Paul's hymns appear, as without warning, in the midst of a text. That said, see note 13 above for Paul's use of the pronoun as a possible indicator rather than a verb signifying speech.

16. λέγοντες appears in most cases, though declinations such as λέγων and λέγοντας also appear. Observe 4:11; 5:9; 5:12; 5:13; 6:10; 7:10; 7:12; 11:15; 11:17-18; 12:10-12; 14:8; 14:13; 15:3-4; 16:5-6; 16:7; 18:2; 18:10; 18:16; 18:19-20; 18:21-24; 19:1-2; 19:4; 19:5; 19:6; 19:17-18; 21:3-4.

17. Those familiar with the Japanese Haiku will know that these poems divide by syllables: the first line possesses five syllables, the second seven, and the third five. Although biblical poetry does not possess any strict rules for syllabification, each individual poem may include its own rhythmic pattern of syllables.

18. E. Krentz, "Epideiktik and Hymnody: The New Testament and Its World," *BR* 40 (1995) 51-52, offers a brief discussion of dactyl in Greek hymns outside the NT.

19. M.S. DeMoss, "Isocolon," *Pocket Dictionary for the Study of New Testament Greek* (Downers Grove. IL: InterVarsity, 2001) 76.

20. A valuable analysis of John's poetry using homoioteleuta and paronomasia (repeated words or word stems), exists in H.O. Maier's, *Apocalypse Recalled* (Minneapolis: Fortress, 2002) 98ff. Although his excursus concerns the narrative prose of 7:4-8, it directly relates to hymnic poetry.

21. The "ou" sound from soup. A more formal rendering of these endings is, "to open the seals of it . . . you purchased for God with the blood of you . . . from every tribe and language and people and nation." The words "it, you, people, and nation," all rhyme in Greek.

22. These two words end with the pronunciation, "ace." The Greek lines end with priests, ἱερεῖς, and earth, γῆς.

23. Emphasis added.

24. Although the poetry of the Apocalypse is atypical in that John does not use a significant number of participles and infinitives in his stanzas, many NT hymns possess an abundance of them. For example, see Phil 2:6-11. The Greek student will note that Phil 2:6 and Col 1:15 begin with a pronoun, a common but not universal marker in hymns. Unfortunately, the more popular English versions, like the NIV and NASB, do not capture these pronouns.

25. Sadly, many poems, such as Col 1:15-20, lose their beauty via the English translator.

26. For many linguists, a text is a passage or verse under scrutiny. Its co-text is those words surrounding it within a literary environment. Its context refers only to the historical, social, and cultural background. Thus, a threefold use of text, co-text, and context, makes clearer one's analysis of a passage.

27. Collins, "Introduction," 9.

28. F. Hansen, "A Narrative and Exegetical Analysis of Joshua 2" (master's thesis, Lincoln Christian Seminary, 2002) 34.

29. R. Alter, *The Art of Biblical Narrative* (New York: Basic Books, 1981) 65.

30. For more on action sequences, see R. Culley, *Theme and Variation* (Atlanta: Scholars Press, 1992) 50.

31. R. Deichgraber, in J.L. Wu and S.C. Pearson, "Hymns, Songs: Revelation," *DLNTD* (Downers Grove, IL: InterVarsity, 1997) 524-525, rightly observes that Revelation's hymns are evenly dispersed throughout John's visions. The messages of these hymns serve as refrains and summaries for each vision.

32. Beale, *Revelation*, 784, asserts that 15:2-4 is the conclusion to the visions of 12:1–14:20, as well as an introduction to the related visions in the chapters to follow.

33. The NIV renders this, "King of the ages," based on two early manuscripts. However, "nations," as in the NASB, has tremendous manuscript support. The word "nations" also fits the co-text of verse 4 where all nations worship before God.

34. Rev 19:1-2 asserts that God's judgments are just. Therefore, between 15:3-4 and 19:1-2, God's people affirm in worship that God's works, God's ways, and God's judgments are true and righteous.

35. Students, preachers, and teachers should take care not to assert ideas based upon a single cultural or social identity. Each city addressed in John's apocalypse is multicultural and is quite diverse, similar to many cities today. At the very least, an overview of the Greco-Roman environment, as well as the Jewish environment, is necessary.

36. See this particular section of Pausanias's *Description of Greek* in its original Greek text at http://www.perseus.tufts.edu/hopper/text?doc=Perseus:abo: tlg,0525,001:10:12:10 (Accessed February 27, 2010). Pausanias's description is slightly different from John, though the sense is the same: Ζεὺς ἦν, Ζεὺς ἐστίν, Ζεὺς ἔσσεται.

37. R. Martin, "Approaches to New Testament Exegesis," in *New Testament Interpretation: Essays on Principles and Methods*, ed. by I. Howard Marshall (Milton Keynes, UK: Paternoster, 1973) 239.

38. As opposed to an archetypical model. Though the church would do well in proclaiming exactly John's hymns and homologies.

39. N.C. Habel and V. Balabanski, eds., *The Earth Story in the New Testament* (New York: Sheffield Academic Press, 2002) 13ff. It appears the Earth Bible Team suggests this reality in their ecojustice hermeneutics.

Chapter Five: Extrabiblical Literature *(Paul J. Kissling)*

1. D.A. deSilva, "Apocrypha and Pseudepigrapha," in *DNTB*, ed. by C.A. Evans and S.E. Porter (Downers Grove, IL: InterVarsity, 2000) 59, ". . . the line between Apocrypha and Pseudepigrapha is not clearly drawn and is blurred even further as one considers the relationship between Jude and 1 Enoch and Assumption of Moses."

2. For an accessible discussion of the contents and dates of 4 Ezra and 2 Baruch suggesting the priority of the former see G.W.E. Nickelsburg, *Jewish Literature between the Bible and the Mishnah*, 2nd ed. (Minneapolis: Augsburg Fortress, 2005) 270-285.

3. There is a consensus among experts that both 4 Ezra and 2 Baruch were originally written in Aramaic or Hebrew before being translated.

4. Fourth Ezra is found as chapters 3–14 of 2 Esdras in the Apocrypha in all traditions which accept the authority of the Apocrypha or "Deutero-canonical" books. Second Baruch was preserved by the Syriac speaking church.

5. R.A. Lowery, *Revelation's Rhapsody: Listening to the Lyrics of the Lamb* (Joplin, MO: College Press, 2006) 67-73.

6. In chs. 2, 7–12.

7. "The Jewish Apocalypses," in *Semeia 14: Apocalypse: The Morphology of a Genre*, ed. by J.J. Collins (Missoula, MT: Scholars, 1979) 9.

8. Unlike many apocalypses, the book of Revelation is not attributed to a heroic figure of the distant past in order to elevate its authority. Whether John is the apostle or another figure named John, he is a first-century contemporary of the original readers and not some distant-past hero like Enoch or Baruch or Ezra.

9. Second Baruch was written after the Roman destruction of Jerusalem in A.D. 70 and in light of that demoralizing set of events. Some think it may be dependent on 4 Ezra. A.J.F. Klijn notes, "Several passages determine the probable date of the Apocalypse of Baruch. 32:2-4 states that 'after a short time the building of Zion [i.e. the temple] will be shaken in order that it will be rebuilt. But that building [i.e. the rebuilt temple] will not

remain because it will again be uprooted'.'"(*OTP* 1, 616) While only this first example is completely convincing, Klijn has made his case. This seems to presuppose a second destruction of the temple, an event which occurred in A.D. 70. The quotation of 61:7 in *Barnabas* 11:9 makes the latest possible date sometime in the first third of the second century. Fourth Ezra is dated about 100 A.D. in part on the assumption that the 30th year referred to in the opening sentence (3:1) is counted from the destruction of the Jerusalem temple in 70 A.D.

10. Here I differ with Collins who anachronistically separates very Jewish but also Christian literature like the book of Revelation from other Jewish literature. He claims, "[I]n all the Jewish apocalypses . . . the situation of the historical author is concealed." (*Apocalyptic Imagination*, 51) This is not true of the book of Revelation which does not resort to pseudonymity but speaks openly of the author's own situation and the churches which are under pressure from the Roman government at the end of the first century A.D.

11. In 4 Ezra, this is the angel Uriel; in 2 Baruch it seems to be God himself.

12. So Nickelsburg, *Jewish Literature*, 283.

13. See M. Goodman, "Diaspora Reactions to the Destruction of the Temple," in *Jews and Christians: The Parting of the Ways A.D. 70 to 135*, ed. by J.D.G. Dunn (Grand Rapids: Eerdmans, 1992) 31-34.

14. For a careful discussion of the issue of the date of the book of Revelation see G.K. Beale, *The Book of Revelation* (Grand Rapids: Eerdmans, 1999) 4-27.

15. In the detailed indexes of Beale's rather comprehensive commentary on Revelation passages from the Apocrypha are cited on 475 pages (not counting pages with more than one citation of the same passage) and passages from the Pseudepigrapha are cited on 921 pages. These are not quotations but allusions and parallels. For comparative purposes the OT is cited about 4,000 times. Passages from 2 Baruch are cited on 85 pages and 4 Ezra on 128 pages of Beale's commentary.

16. Beale, *Revelation*, 125, n. 80.

17. Ibid., 446.

18. L.T. Stuckenbruck, "Messianic Ideas in the Apocalyptic and Related Literature of Early Judaism," in *The Messiah in the Old and New Testaments*, ed. by S.E. Porter (Grand Rapids: Eerdmans, 2007) 103.

19. Beale, *Revelation*, 874, helpfully charts the various theories identifying the seven and the eighth emperors.

20. Collins, *Apocalyptic Imagination*, 196.

21. G.R. Beasley-Murray, "Revelation, Book of," in *DLNTD*, ed. by R.P. Martin and P.H. Davids (Downers Grove, IL: InterVarsity, 1997) 1028.

22. Beale, *Revelation*, 18-19.

23. Nickelsburg, *Jewish Literature*, 271.

24. B.M. Metzger, "The Fourth Book of Ezra," *OTP* 1:517-518.

25. Nicklesburg, *Jewish Literature*, 277, 407.

26. Lowery, *Rhapsody*, 136-140.

27. Beale, *Revelation*, 770. He cites *PssSol* 9:6-9; 1Tim 5:24-25; *Barn* 4:12; *1En* 61:8; *2Bar* 14:12; 24:1; 4Ezra 7:35-36; 8:33 as parallels.

28. On the relationship between 4 Ezra and 2 Baruch, Nickelsburg, *Jewish Literature*, 285, comments, "In any case [no matter whether 4 Ezra is dependent on 2 Baruch or vice versa] we have two authors in the post-destruction period [Jerusalem in 70 A.D.] in dialogue with one another as they wrestle with the existential and theological questions that have arisen from the catastrophe of the year 70, and as they reshape tradition to fit what they perceive to be their situation and to fit the persona of the ancient figure with whom they identify their revelation."

29. See G.K. Beale, *The Temple and the Church's Mission: A Biblical Theology of the Dwelling Place of God* (Leicester: Apollos, 2004) 392-393.

30. deSilva, 62 [*emphasis* mine].

Chapter Six: Church Fathers (*Yulia Lubenets*)

1. I would like to offer this article to Dr. Lowery as a proof that I have completely forgiven him for playing a joke on me, his student, and surprising me with an *Old* Testament test after his *New* Testament class just to enjoy an expression of terror and bewilderment on my face. The valuable lessons I learned during his classes far outweigh a few moments of confusion and horror I experienced that day back in 1998. This work is a result of the profound desire inspired by Dr. Lowery to study various topics related to the New Testament and especially the book of Revelation.

2. H.B. Swete, *The Apocalypse of St. John*, 3rd ed. (London: Macmillan, 1909) ccvii.

3. R.H. Mounce, *The Book of Revelation* (Grand Rapids: Eerdmans, 1997) 21.

4. W.C. Weinrich, ed., *Ancient Christian Commentary on Scripture: Revelation* (Downers Grove, IL: InterVarsity, 2005) xix.

5. Ibid.

6. Mounce, *Revelation*, 22.

7. Ibid., 23.

8. I. Boxall, *Revelation: Vision and Insight* (London: SPCK, 2002) 149.

9. Mounce, *Revelation*, 23.

10. Ibid., 24.

11. Boxall, *Revelation*, 149.

12. Mounce, *Revelation*, 24.

13. Weinrich, *Ancient Christian Commentary*, xxi.

14. Jerome *The Lives of Illustrious Men* 24, *NPNF* 3:369.

15. Ibid. 61, *NPNF* 3:375.

16. Swete, *Apocalypse*, ccvii.

17. Mounce, *Revelation*, 24-25.

18. J.M. Court, *Myth and History in the Book of Revelation* (Atlanta: John Knox Press, 1979) 2.

19. Swete, *Apocalypse*, ccvii.

20. J.L. Gonzalez, *The Story of Christianity* (San Francisco: HarperSan-Francisco, 1984) 1:44, 46, 68, 84.

21. See Irenaeus *Against Heresies* 5.34, ANF 1:564-565.

22. A.W. Wainwright, *Mysterious Apocalypse* (Eugene, OR: Wipf and Stock, 2001) 22.

23. Ibid., 25.

24. Irenaeus *Against Heresies* 5. 35, ANF 1:559. Yet he adds, "we would not, however, incur the risk of pronouncing positively as to the name of Antichrist; for if it were necessary that his name should be distinctly revealed in this present time, it would have been announced by him who beheld the apocalyptic vision."

25. Tertullian *Against Marcion* 3.13, ANF 3:332.

26. Wainwright, *Mysterious*, 25.

27. Ibid., 30.

28. Clement *The Instructor* 2.8, ANF 2:268.

29. Weinrich, *Ancient Christian Commentary*, xxi.

30. Origen *Commentary on John* 5, ANF 10:348.

31. Origen *De Principiis* 2.11, ANF 4:297.

32. Methodius *The Banquet of the Ten Virgins* 7.5, ANF 6:336.

33. Ibid.

34. Jerome *Letter* 70.5, NPNF 6:151.

35. Ibid.

36. Jerome *Lives of Illustrious Men* 74, NPNF 3:377.

37. Weinrich, *Ancient Christian Commentary*, xxii.

38. Ibid., 334.

39. Ibid., 384-385.

40. B.E. Daley, *The Hope of the Early Church* (Peabody, MA: Hendrickson, 2003) 65.

41. Victorinus *Commentary on the Apocalypse of the Blessed John* 21.16, ANF 7:359.

42. Daley, *Hope*, 66.

43. Weinrich, *Ancient Christian Commentary*, xxii.

44. Wainwright, *Mysterious*, 29.

45. Victorinus *Commentary on the Apocalypse of the Blessed John* 7.2, ANF 7:352.

46. Wainwright, *Mysterious*, 29.

47. Gennadius *Lives of Illustrious Men* 18, NPNF 3:389.

48. Wainwright, *Mysterious*, 33.

49. Ibid.

50. Gennadius *Lives of Illustrious Men* 18.

51. As quoted in Weinrich, *Ancient Christian Commentary*, 120.

52. Wainwright, *Mysterious*, 35.

53. Gennadius *Lives of Illustrious Men* 18.

54. Ibid.

55. Swete, *Apocalypse*, ccx.

56. Ibid.

57. As quoted in Weinrich, *Ancient Christian Commentary*, 90.

58. R.H. Bainton, *Early and Medieval Christianity* (Boston: Beacon Press, 1962) 88.

59. Wainwright, *Mysterious*, 35.

60. Gennadius *Lives of Illustrious Men* 18.

61. W. Durant, *Caesar and Christ* (New York: Simon and Schuster, 1944) 657-658.

62. Wainwright, *Mysterious*, 36.

63. Bainton, *Early and Medieval Christianity*, 98.

64. C.R. Koester, *Revelation and the End of All Things* (Grand Rapids: Eerdmans, 2001) 7.

65. Weinrich, *Ancient Christian Commentary*, xxiv.

66. See Wainwright, *Mysterious*, 35, 37, or Durant, *Caesar*, 73.

67. Augustine *City of God* 15.1. NPNF 1-02.

68. Ibid. 20.7.

69. R.H. Charles, *Studies in the Apocalypse* (Edinburgh: T&T Clark, 1915), 13.

70. See Koester, Swete, Mounce.

71. Augustine *City of God*, 20.7, NPNF 1-02.

72. Ibid. 20.9.

73. Koester, *Revelation*, 8.

74. Wainwright, *Mysterious*, 38-39.

75. Ibid., 39.

76. Ibid.

77. Weinrich, *Ancient Christian Commentary*, xxiv-xxv.

78. As quoted in Weinrich, *Ancient Christian Commentary*, 12.

79. Wainwright, *Mysterious*, 39.

80. Charles, *Studies*, 13.

81. Jerome *Against Jovinian* 1:40, NPNF 2-06.

82. Weinrich, *Ancient Christian Commentary*, xxv-xxvii.

83. Swete, *Apocalypse*, ccx.

84. Daley, *Hope*, 178.

85. Weinrich, *Ancient Christian Commentary*, xxvii.

86. Ibid.

87. Daley, *Hope*, 180.

88. Wainwright, *Mysterious*, 44.

89. As quoted in Weinrich, *Ancient Christian Commentary*, 324.

90. Boxall, *Revelation*, 149.

91. Daley, *Hope*, 198.

92. Daley, *Hope*, 198; Weinrich, *Ancient Christian Commentary*, xxviii.

93. Weinrich, *Ancient Christian Commentary*, xxviii.

94. Charles, *Studies*, 12.

95. Swete, *Apocalypse*, ccxi.

96. Ibid.

97. R.A. Lowery, *Revelation's Rhapsody: Listening to the Lyrics of the Lamb* (Joplin, MO: College Press, 2006) 18.

Chapter Seven: Karl Barth's Understanding *(Otniel Ioan Bunaciu)*

1. Bob Dylan, "The Bible," *Theme Time Radio Hour*, Episode 19 (6 September 2006), quoted by Benjamin Myers, http://faith-theology.blogspot.com/2006/11/bob-dylan-on-bible.html (July 10, 2010).

2. N.T. Wright, "The Bible and Tomorrow's World," http://www.ntwrightpage.com/#lectures (July 10, 2010).

3. *CD* IV/2, 113.

4. The English translation is: *The Word of God and the Word of Man* (New York: Harper, 1957).

5. Probably Barth was influenced to make this change from his studies of Overbeck, Dostoyevski, and Kierkegaard.

6. W. Lindemann, *Karl Barth und die kritische Schriftauslegung* (Hamburg-Bergstedt: Herbert Reich-Evangelischer Verlag, 1973) 30.

7. K. Barth, *Prolegomena zur Christlichen Dogmatik* (Munich: Chr. Kaiser Verlag, 1927) 230.

8. Ibid., 344.

9. K. Barth, *Fides, Queaerens Intellectum, Anselms Beweis der Existenz Gottes* (Munich: Chr. Kaiser Verlag, 1931).

10. D.F. Ford, "Barth's Interpretation of the Bible," in *Karl Barth, Studies of His Theological Method*, ed. by S.W. Sykes (Oxford: Clarendon Press, 1979) 59.

11. Augustine, *Confessiones*, tr. Dr. Docent Nicolae Barbu (*Editura Institutului Biblic*: Bucureşti, 1994) X.38.

12. *CD* I/1, p. 104.

13. *CD* I/1, p. 118.

14. *CD* I/1, p.109.

15. *CD* I/1, p.124.

16. K. Barth, *The Word of God and the Word of Man* (Hodder & Stoughton, 1935) 62.

17. Ibid., 69.

18. Ibid., 73.

19. Ibid., 77.

20. The lectures were published under the title: *Biblical Faith and Natural Theology* (Oxford: Clarendon Press, 1993).

21. Barr, *Biblical Faith*, 123.

22. K. Barth, *The Epistle to the Romans* (London: Oxford Press, 1933).

23. *CD* IV/3, p. 44.

NOTES

John

Chapter Eight: The Witnessing Church (*Jeff Snell*)

1. All Scripture references are from the NIV, unless otherwise noted.

2. Neither "I heard" (ἀκούω) nor "I saw" (εἶδον) is found in Revelation 11, for John transitions from passive recipient to active participant. Of course, "told" (λέγων) in v. 1 implies that the command John received was delivered orally.

3. E.H. Peterson, "Apocalypse: The Medium Is the Message," *TToday* 26 (1969) 136.

4. S. Saunders, "Revelation and Resistance," in *Narrative Reading, Narrative Preaching: Reuniting New Testament Interpretation and Proclamation*, ed. by J.B. Green and M. Pasquarello III (Grand Rapids: Baker, 2003) 122.

5. Due to the parameters of and purpose for this essay, I will primarily write *from* an understanding of Rev 11 rather than arguing *for* one and will necessarily neglect a number of valuable and important issues.

6. W. Hendriksen, *More than Conquerors*, 2nd ed. (Grand Rapids: Baker, 1967) 23.

7. R.A. Lowery, *Revelation's Rhapsody: Listening to the Lyrics of the Lamb* (Joplin, MO: College Press, 2006) 137-140.

8. The witnessing church, clothed in sackcloth, forms a stark contrast (11:3). By adopting a common prophetic dress code, she both illustrates her message calling for repentance and models a posture of repentance.

9. As E. Peterson, *Reversed Thunder* (San Francisco: Harper, 1991) 115, notes, "The life of the two witnesses is reproduced in every act of witness."

10. The term μέτρησον (measure) applies to the worshipers as well as the temple/altar; this is blurred by the NIV's use of the term "count."

11. John's use of temple (ναός) elsewhere in Revelation is always with reference to the present or future heavenly temple (3:12; 7:15; 14:15-17; 15:5-8; 16:1; 21; 22).

12. I am grateful for a recent conversation with Robert Lowery in which he shared some yet unpublished insights that helped shape my perspective on this issue.

13. Some scholars deny any possibility the outer court could be a reference to God's people, based on the role of the outer court in Solomon's and Herod's temples. This difficulty is minimized by the recognition that Ezekiel's vision of the eschatological temple (Ezek 40–48) is the source of John's imagery. For further information, see G.K. Beale, *The Book of Revelation* (Grand Rapids: Eerdmans, 1998) 559-563.

14. ἐκβάλλω is used only in Rev 11:2; βάλλω is often used in judgment contexts whereby the recipient is "thrown" or "cast"; for further information, see O. Hofius, "βαλλω" in *EDNT*, ed. by H.R. Balz and G. Schneider (Grand Rapids: Eerdmans, 1990) 1:192. This usage is dominant in Revelation, especially after chapter 4 (28 occurrences: 2:10,14,22,24; 4:10; 6:13; 8:5,7,8; 12:4,9,10,13,15,16; 14:16,19; 18:19,21; 19:20; 20:3,10,14,15).

15. Forty-two months (11:2; 13:5) and 1260 days (11:3; 12:6) combine with "a time, times, and half a time" (Rev 12:14) to form a numeric pattern in Revelation whereby forms of the number 42 echo Daniel 7:25 and 9:27. These prophecies of persecution were initially fulfilled in Antiochus Epiphanes, a Syrian king, who ordered Jews to abandon their faith and who desecrated their temple in 168–165 B.C. This memorable period stood representative of other times when God's people suffered at the hands of godless and idolatrous political powers. Here, as in Daniel, the emphasis is on the severity of persecution rather than the duration of it (Beale, *Revelation*, 567).

16. The variation between the time designations in note 15 may underscore that the periods of the church's witness, God's protection, and ungodly antagonism occur simultaneously. R.H. Mounce, *The Book of Revelation*, 2nd ed. (Grand Rapids: Eerdmans, 1997) 221.

17. G.R. Beasley-Murray, *The Book of Revelation* (Grand Rapids: Eerdmans, 1978) 183.

18. Prophecy reflects its primary OT sense of "forthtelling" and only secondarily "foretelling." For further exploration of the reasons for and implications of this understanding, see Hill, "Prophecy and Prophets in the Revelation of St. John," *NTS* 18 (1971) 401.

19. L. Coenen, "Witness," in *NIDNTT*, ed. by Colin Brown (Grand Rapids: Zondervan, 1971) 3:1044-1046.

20. See A.A. Trites, *The New Testament Concept of Witness* (Cambridge: Cambridge University Press, 1977) 154. Also see his "*Martus* and Martyrdom in the Apocalypse," *NovT* 15 (1973) 72-80, for specific attention to Revelation 11. See also Neal Windham, "'Witness' in the Book of Revelation," in this volume.

21. Two witnesses were required for valid testimony according to Deut 19:15, but the idea of trustworthy testimony, while grounded in forensics, is relevant in other contexts as well (Lk 10:1). When John's readers pondered the allusions to Jesus and the OT prophets reflected in this passage and this vocabulary, they would probably have thought of those lives more holistically.

22. The reference to fire coming from the witnesses' mouths in v. 5 is also an allusion to Elijah, whose confrontation with the prophets of Baal (during the reign of Ahab) revolves around the literal and symbolic significance of fire.

23. See Beale, *Revelation*, 585ff., for detailed attention to these parallels and the significance of them.

24. For further development of the beast imagery, see Beale, *Revelation*, 588-589. The beast out of the sea represents the Roman government and the beast out of the earth signifies the imperial cult; the latter involved emperor worship as a means by which to unify the remarkably diverse Roman empire.

25. "Inhabitants of the earth" is John's most frequently used description for people who are opposed to God, His people, and His purposes (3:10; 6:10;

8:13; 11:10; 13:8,12,14; 17:2,8). The twofold use of the phrase in v. 10 is especially striking. Also notable is John's use of his universal formula, which he starts using negatively in Rev 10:11.

26. The term corpse (πτῶμα) occurs twice in v. 9 (though translated only once by the NIV), which further supports the interpretation that the witnesses are representative of the entire church, rather than two specific role categories within the church (such as missionaries and ministers, contra Hendricksen, *More*, 129) or two specific individuals. For a survey of alternatives proposed by those who think two specific witnesses are in view, see D.E. Aune, *Revelation 1–5* (Dallas: Word, 2002) 1:598-603.

27. Beale, *Revelation*, 598 wisely cautions against *assuming* literal resurrection is in view here. The strong linguistic parallels with Ezek 37–38 (where the restoration of Israel is not a literal resurrection, but rather restoration), and between 4:1-2 and 11:12 (indicating that the church's prophetic commission is being announced after the fact, like Elijah in 2Kgs 2:11, and yet in a way that parallels John's own commission) are striking. The relationship between John's commission in Rev 10 and the church's commission in Rev 11 is also noteworthy (the witnesses likely ascend to the same cloud from which the angel descends in 10:1, both John and the witnesses are called prophets in 10:11; 11:3,10,18, and it is implied that both announce judgment to every people, tribe, tongue, and nation (10:11; 11:9). By the same token, Beale is also aware that some Jewish scholars believed Ezek 37–38 would be fulfilled via literal resurrection, and it is hard to imagine that John's readers would have heard this section of *this* book without thinking at least secondarily of literal resurrection.

28. The other two uses of the noun φόβος (fear) are in Rev 18:10,15; this passage refers to God's judgment of Babylon (there symbolic of all idolatrous and persecuting power). There, as here, fear is the terror-filled response of those who realize the implications of God's vindication of the church. It also echoes the response of the Egyptians to the plagues and God's subsequent deliverance of Israel (Ps 104:38) as celebrated in the Song of Moses (Exod 15:16). This is especially striking since the plagues provide much of the conceptual framework for the trumpets in Rev 9–10.

29. Mounce, *Revelation*, 213.

Chapter Nine: Woman and Dragon (*Mark Scott*)

1. Mentioned in vv. 1,6,13,14,15,16,17.

2. Mentioned in vv. 3,4,7,9,13,16,17, and referred to as the accuser (10), the devil (12), and the serpent (15).

3. Major ones would include God (vv. 5,6,10,17), the Son/Christ or male child or lamb (vv. 4,5,10,11,13), and the rest of the woman's offspring (v. 17). Minor ones would include Michael (v. 7), the dragon's angels (vv. 7,9), the brothers (v. 10), those who dwell on the earth (v. 12), the great eagle (v. 14), and the nations (v. 5).

4. R.A. Lowery, *Revelation's Rhapsody: Listening to the Lyrics of the Lamb* (Joplin, MO.: College Press, 2006) 121-143.

5. This is the first reference to the noun, "sign," in Revelation (12:3; 13:13,14; 15:1; 16:14; 19:20). The verb first occurred in Rev 1:1. So John is clearly communicating in symbols. This woman is clothed in the sun and has the moon under her feet. Understood literally that would be the largest woman of all time.

6. Out of the 449 occurrences in the NT, the word "appear/see" occurs 103 times in Revelation. Revelation is a series of things John saw.

7. The other main characters in the chapter are more easily interpreted. The dragon is identified in 12:9 as the devil, and the male child that the dragon bears rules all the nations with an iron scepter (12:5) — a reference all too closely associated with Jesus (Gen 49:10; Ps 2:9; 110:2; Lk 1:32-33).

8. C.A. Davis, *Revelation* (Joplin, MO: College Press, 2000) 249-254.

9. Even today, high in the hills above Ephesus is the supposed house of Mary.

10. R.E. Murphy, "An Allusion to Mary in the Apocalypse," *TS* 10.4 (December 1949) 565-573. Murphy realizes that the image of the woman in John's vision is larger than Mary, but he still argues that John would not have used such an image had the significance of Mary not already been established. He concludes therefore that she is there by way of allusion (571). See also J.A. Schroeder, "Revelation 12: Female Figures and Figures of Evil," *WW* XV.2 (Spr 1995) 175-181. She cites R.E. Brown et. al. in *Mary in the New Testament* (Philadelphia: Fortress Press, 1978) 235, who suggests that early church writers didn't interpret Revelation 12 to refer to Mary until the fourth century.

11. It must be stated that apocalyptic symbols and literature do not have to follow any strict chronology. In fact, they often do not.

12. Dr. Davis may too quickly dismiss this third option. More will be said about it later, but if Eve is not only a real person but also representative of the holder of the promise of God to reverse the curse, then this might have much to commend itself.

13. Lowery, *Rhapsody*, 186-187. All the OT allusions from chapter 12 (and the other chapters of Revelation) are traced in this helpful appendix.

14. Also see 4Ezra 9:38–10:59.

15. The "bride" is identified as the new Jerusalem, she is faithful and loyal, she has wonderful names written on her, and she is transparent. The "harlot" is identified as Babylon, she is unfaithful, she has blasphemous names written on her, and she is full of abominations.

16. Davis, *Revelation*, 252. See also J.L. Sumney, "The Dragon Has Been Defeated — Revelation 12," *RevExp* 98 (Winter 2001) 103-115; A.Y. Collins, "The Combat Myth in the Book of Revelation," *Harvard Divinity Review* 9 (1976) 57-156; B. Witherington III, *Revelation* (Edinburgh: Cambridge University Press, 2003) 164-165.

17. While the most famous and most parallel would be the story about Zeus, Leto, Apollo, and Python, there were other myth stories as well (Babylonian, Egyptian, and Persian). G.R. Beasley-Murray, *The Book of Revelation* (Greenwood, SC: The Attic Press, 1974) 191, says, "It would

appear that in chapter 12 he has utilized traditions known all over the world of his day."

18. A statement attributed to Gardner C. Taylor.

19. Witherington, *Revelation*, 167.

20. Ibid., 166.

21. This is not to suggest that John saw Eve. But it is to admit that while Eve is real person (at least Paul thought so, 2 Corinthians 11:3; 2 Timothy 2:15), she also stands as the mother of the living. She contains inside of her the promise (Gen 3:15).

22. A legitimate argument against what is being espoused here is, "Is it hermeneutically justified to impose Pauline thinking to a Johannine text?"

23. This may not be a new option as much as a new way to state some of the options already given by Davis.

24. The word for "great" occurs 243 times in the NT and 127 times in Revelation.

25. The word for "red" only occurs in Revelation here and in 6:4 for the color of the second horse. Lowery, *Rhapsody*, 203, says it symbolizes violence, doom, and blood.

26. This word only occurs in Revelation. It occurs 13 times with 8 of those times being in chapter 12.

27. As is the beast out of the sea (13:1; 17:3,7,9).

28. The normal word for crown is not used here. The word διαδήματα occurs here, 13:1, and 19:12, where it is used of Jesus.

29. This is the only time in Revelation that this word occurs (ἡρπάσθη). It means to seize or take away. It occurs 14 times in the NT. Is it a reference to the event and the doctrine of the ascension? It is possible, but the events described here are larger than Acts 1:9-11. It is not a specific event as much as the enthronement of Christ above all powers (Eph 1:20-23).

30. Θρόνον (throne) occurs 62 times in the NT, but 45 of those times are in Revelation. Most of the occurrences are in chapters 4–5. They all refer to God's throne except in 2:13 (Satan's throne), 13:2, and 16:10 (the beast's throne), and in 20:4 (the Christian's or martyr's throne).

31. A period of suffering for God's people that goes back to Dan 7:25. See Lowery, *Rhapsody*, 201-202.

32. Often in Revelation when there is a "loud voice" what follows is song-like (5:12; 7:10; 11:15).

33. The Greek word πόλεμος occurs 18 times in the NT, but half of those references are in Revelation. The word means armed conflict, strife, and quarrel.

34. Sumney, "Dragon," 107.

35. Ibid.

36. Only mentioned here and in Jude 9 in the NT. The OT mentions him in Daniel 10:13,21; 12:1. In the Testament of Daniel (6:2) he is described as a mediator. But in the *TLevi* 5:7 he has a role similar to what he has in this vision—resisting the devil.

37. Rev 1:20; 17:7-14.

38. The other places it refers to a literal snake (Mt 7:10; Mk 16:18; Lk 11:11; Jn 3:14; 1Cor 10:9; Rev 9:19) or is used figuratively (Mt 10:16; 23:33; Lk 10:19).

39. Other than Rev 2:10, all the references to devil are in chapters 12 and 20. Some interpreters like to emphasize passages like Isa 27:1; Jer 51:34; Ezek 29:3-5; 32:2-8.

40. More significant than the etymology or the use of ἐβλήθη itself is the form and voice of the verb. This is an aorist passive indicative. The action is being done upon the dragon. The sovereignty of God is in the voice of the verb.

41. Other than an eagle, an angel, and the martyrs, the loud voice is usually God's in Revelation.

42. The word "authority" occurs 21 times in Revelation. Interestingly, God gives authority to lots of others in the book. Only here and in 16:9 is the authority solely his.

43. The term ἀδελφῶν only occurs five times in Revelation, but every time it refers to Christians.

44. The word ἐνίκησαν is a central theme in Revelation. While the white horse (6:2), and the beast (11:7; 13:7) are given ability to conquer, it is Christ and his followers who primarily conquer (chapters 2–3; 5:5; 17:14; 21:7).

45. "Woe" (οὐαὶ) occurs several times in just seven verses in Revelation. This "judgment in tears" onomatopoeia expression marks out the judgments of God or the pain that the ways of God will create. It is a word strongly associated with the prophets of the OT.

46. Earth and sea (Rev 13:1) is where the devil works and inspires his work.

47. The word ἐδίωξεν is a word that means to hunt down like an animal. It can mean to persecute.

48. This is a purpose clause in Greek meaning that the dragon went off with the specific purpose to make war against the offspring.

49. See especially Gary Hall's chapter on Revelation's use of Exodus in this volume.

50. Exod 19:4; Deut 32:11; Isa 40:31.

51. See 2Kgs 19:35-37.

52. Cf. Rev 12:14; 17:3. The image of desert (ἔρημον) multitasks in Scripture. It can be a place of punishment (Num 14), a place of testing (Deut 8:2), a place of revelation (Gal 1:17), a place of provision (Exod 16–17), a place of refreshment (1Sam 24:1), etc.

53. See Dan 7:25; 12:7.

54. The earth (ἡ γῆ) in Revelation often refers to that which stands opposed to God and opposite heaven (Rev 21:1).

Chapter Ten: Number of the Beast (Shane J. Wood)

1. All translations will be my own unless otherwise noted.

2. See "The Mark of the Beast (666)," *Evangelical Outreach*, 2 Feb. 2010 <http://www.evangelicaloutreach.org/markbeas.htm>, "The 'Mark' is Ready! Are You?" 2 Feb. 2010 <http://home.iae.nl/users/lightnet/world/mark.htm>.

3. Primasius (d. c. 560 C.E.) in his commentary on the book of Revelation suggested αρνουμε as the number 666 by taking the Greek letters and adding them together—i.e., α = 1; ρ = 100; ν = 50; ο = 70; υ = 400; μ = 40; ε = 5. The word αρνουμε, however, is not known to have any meaning as an actual word even though Primasius confidently translates the word as "I deny." Nevertheless, some have suggested that it could be related to αρνεισθαι—which means "to deny." See W. Barclay, "Great Themes of the New Testament: V. Revelation xiii (*continued*)," *ExpTim* 70.10 (July 1959): 296.

4. Arethas of Caesarea (c. 900 C.E.) suggested several options: (1) κακος οδηγος ("evil leader"): κ = 20; α = 1; κ = 20; ο = 70; ς = 200; ο = 70; δ = 4; η = 8; γ = 3; ο = 70; ς = 200; (2) αμνος αδικος ("evil lamb"): α = 1; μ = 40; ν = 50; ο = 70; ς = 200; α = 1; δ = 4; ι = 10; κ = 20; ο = 70; ς = 200.

5. Barclay, *continued*, 296 lists the following categories of slanderous options: (1) *Anti-Catholic Interpretations* - Ιταλικα εκκλησια ["Italian Church"]: I = 10; τ = 300; α = 1; λ = 30; ι = 10; κ = 20; α = 1; ε = 5; κ = 20; κ = 20; λ = 30; η = 8; σ = 200; ι = 10; α = 1; η Λατινη Βασιλεια ["The Latin Kingdom"]: η = 8; Λ = 30; α = 1; τ = 300; ι = 10; ν = 50; η = 8; Β = 2; α = 1; σ = 200; ι = 10; λ = 30; ε = 5; ι = 10; α = 1; Παπεισκος ["Pope"]: Π = 80; α = 1; π = 80; ε = 5; ι = 10; σ = 200; κ = 20; ο = 70; ς = 200; (2) *Anti-Protestant Interpretations* - Λουθερανα ["Luther"]: Λ = 30; ο = 70; υ = 400; θ = 9; ε = 5; ρ = 100; α = 1; ν = 50; α = 1; Σαξονειος ["Saxon" referring to Luther]: Σ = 200; α = 1; ξ = 60; ο = 70; ν = 50; ε = 5; ι = 10; ο = 70; ς = 200; (3) *Anti-Muslim Interpretation* - Μαομετις ["Muhammad"]: Μ = 40; α = 1; ο = 70; μ = 40; ε = 5; τ =300; ι = 10; ς = 200; (4) *Anti-Hitler Interpretation* - "If A = 100, B = 101, C = 102 and so on, the following result can be obtained: H = 107; I = 108; T = 119; L = 111; E = 104; R = 117; HITLER = 666!"

6. There are several different facets of the spiritual option, some of which include: [1] 666 as representative of man *falling short* of "perfection" (777)—G.E. Ladd, *A Commentary on the Revelation of John* (Grand Rapids: Eerdmans, 1972) 187; L. Morris, *The Book of Revelation*, Tyndale New Testament Commentaries (Grand Rapids: Eerdmans, 1988) 174; [2] 666 as self-worshiping idolatrous rebellion—A. MacPherson, "The Mark of the Beast as a 'Sign Commandment' and 'Anti- Sabbath' in the Worship Crisis of Revelation 12–14," *AUSS* 43.2 (2005) 282, n. 51; and [3] the symbol of sinful incompleteness—G.K. Beale, *The Book of Revelation* (Grand Rapids: Eerdmans, 1999) 722.

7. Barclay, *continued*, 295 writes, "[1] In A.D. 1213 Pope Innocent III called for a new crusade because he held that Muhammadan power was destined to last for six hundred and sixty-six years, and at that time that period was near to an end. [2] Certain others have taken it to refer to the six hundred and sixty-six years between Seleucus in 311 B.C. and the emergence of Julian the Apostate in A.D. 355."

8. W.G. Baines, "The Number of the Beast in Revelation 13:18," *HeyJ* 16 (1975) 195-196, suggests Vespasian (69–79 C.E.) due to the numerical value of 666 for the abbreviations on a coin that reads "Imp Caes Vesp Aug P M Cos IIII." E. Stauffer, "666," in *Coniectanea Neotestamentica* (Lund: CWK Gleerup, 1947) 237-241 suggests that the Greek uncial titles of Domitian (81–96 C.E.) (ΑΥΤΟΚΡΑΤΩΡΚΑΙΣΑΡ-ΔΟΜΕΤΙΑΝΟΣΣΕ-ΒΑΣΤΟΣΓΕΡΜΑΝΙΚΟΣ) that are abbreviated on some coins as Α ΚΑΙ ΔΟΜΕΤ ΣΕΒ ΓΕ add up to 666 and therefore point to the last emperor of the Flavian Dynasty. Further credence could be added to this last option in that the traditional date of the book of Revelation has been 95-96 C.E. — during the reign of Domitian.

9. So J.W. Roffey, "On Doing Reflection Theology: Poverty and Revelation 13:16-17," *Colloquium* 14.2 (May 1982) 54. G. Salmon, *Historical Introduction* (John Murray, 1886) 230-231, quips, "Any name, with sufficient ingenuity, can be made to yield the number 666. There are three rules by the help of which, I believe, an ingenious man could find the required sum in any given name. First, if the proper name by itself will not yield it, add a title; secondly, if the sum cannot be found in Greek, try Hebrew, or even Latin; thirdly, do not be too particular about the spelling. . . . We cannot infer much from the fact that a key fits the lock if it is a lock in which almost any key will turn."

10. So J.W. Marshall, "Parables of the War: Reading the Apocalypse within Judaism and during the Judaean War" (Ph.D. diss., Princeton University, 1997) 255; J. Christian Wilson, "The Problem of the Domitianic Date of Revelation," *NTS* 39 (1993) 587-605; K.L. Gentry, Jr., *Before Jerusalem Fell: Dating the Book of Revelation* (Victorious Hope Publishing, rpt. 2010) 193-219; L.J. Lietaert Peerbolte, *The Antecedents of Antichrist* (New York: Brill, 1996) 151; F. Sbaffoni, *Testi sull'Anticristo Secoli I-II* (Florence: Nardini, 1992) 358; P. Trudinger, "The 'Nero Redivivus' Rumour and the Date of the Apocalypse of John," *St. Mark's Review* 131 (September 1987) 43-44; D. Chilton, *The Days of Vengeance: An Exposition of the Book of Revelation* (Tyler, TX: Dominion Press, 1984) 350-351; C. Rowland, *The Open Heaven: A Study of Apocalyptic in Judaism and Early Christianity* (New York: Crossroad, 1982) 517 n. 87; A.A. Bell, Jr., "The Date of John's Apocalypse: The Evidence of Some Roman Historians Considered," *NTS* 25 (1978) 93-102; J.M. Lawrence, "Nero Redivivus," *Fides et Historia* 11 (1978) 54-66; A.Y. Collins, *The Combat Myth in the Book of Revelation* (Wipf and Stock, rpt. 2001) 174-175.

11. See below for the prominence of 616 as an alternative reading for the traditional 666.

12. For extensive evidence of the widespread use of gematria in the ancient world, see F. Bücheler, *Rheinisches Museum für Philologie*, New Series, 61 (1906) 307f.

13. A. Deissmann, *Light from the Ancient East* (New York: Harper & Brothers, 1927) 277. Also, Barclay, *continued*, 295, notes the religious connection of Jupiter with 717 — the numerical value of "the ruler" (ἡ ἀρχή).

14. *b. Nedarim* 32a as translated in Rabbi Dr. H. Freedman (trans.), *Hebrew-English Edition of the Babylonian Talmud: Nedarim* (London: The Soncino Press, 1985).

15. א = 1; ל = 30; י = 10; ע = 70; ז = 7; ר = 200.

16. See M.W. Holmes, *The Apostolic Fathers: Greek Texts and English Translations*, 3rd ed. (Grand Rapids: Baker, 2007) 372-373 for a discussion of the date.

17. While this interpretation may seem odd to some, it was not an isolated suggestion. In *Carm. Adv. Marc.*, iii. 4, Tertullian also sees the three hundred soldiers in Gideon's army as pointing to the cross due to the resemblance of the Greek letter τ to the shape of the cross.

18. So *SibOr* 1.324-9 — where "Jesus" is said to equal 888. For more examples, see Deissmann, *Light*, 275-277.

19. For arguments for the legitimacy of this transition from Greek to Hebrew to facilitate the gematria, see Barclay, continued, 296; F.X. Gumerlock, "Nero Antichrist: Patristic Evidence for the Use of Nero's Naming in Calculating the Number of the Beast (Rev 13:18)," WTJ 68 (2006) 359, n. 46; and F. Benary, "Interpretation of the Number 666 ($\chi\xi\varsigma$) in the Apocalypse (13:18) and the Various Reading 616 ($\chi\iota\varsigma$)," (Feb 1844) 85-86, trans. from "Zeitschrift für speculative Theologie," 1836, vol. I. part II. by Rev. Heny Boynton Smith.

20. The "n" added to the end of Nero is the necessary Greek grammatical form that is lost when translated into English. The numerical value of each letter is: נ = 50; ר = 200; ו = 6; ן = 50; ק = 100; ס = 60; ר = 200.

21. 666 is found in: א; A; $\mathfrak{P}^{47}$ 051 fam 1611[1611 2329] Andreas Byzantine; 025 fam 1611[1854], with only minor spelling differences occurring within these manuscripts that point to 666.

22. 665 is found in: fam 1611[2344].

23. 616 is found in: C arm[4] Tyc[2] p115 (P.Oxy 4499).

24. See Beale, *Revelation*, 719, n. 298.

25. For dating of this document, see J.N. Birdsall, "Irenaeus and the Number of the Beast: Revelation 13,18," in *New Testament Textual Criticism and Exegesis* (Leuven: Peeters, 2002) 349. To see the actual p115 fragment, go to: http://www.shanejwood.com/images/stories/p115.jpg. The 616 reference is in the fragment at the upper left hand corner. This document pushes the tradition within 200 years of the original composition of Revelation.

26. Against Heresies 5.30.1. Some of the suggested possibilities for 616 include: Caesar Romae (קיסר רום), Caesar God (Καισαρ Θεος), Caesar Gaius (Γαιος Καισαρ), and even Caesar Domitian (Kaiser Domitianus).

27. Birdsall, "Irenaeus," 352.

28. See Birdsall, "Irenaeus," 357.

29. See Irenaeus, *Against Heresies* 5.30.1.

30. Beale, *Revelation*, 719, n. 298.

31. נ = 50; ר = 200; ו = 6; ק = 100; ס = 60; ר = 200.

32. D. Brady, *The Contribution of British Writers between 1560 and 1830 to the Interpretation of Revelation 13.16-18* (Mohr, 1983) 292. The four German scholars are: Fritzsche, *Annalen der gesammten theologischen Literatur und der christlichen Kirche überhaupt*, Jahrg. I, Bd. 3, Heft 1 (Coburg and Leipzig, 1831) 42-64; Ferdinandus Benary, *zeitschrift für speculative Theologie*, Bd. 1, Heft 2 (Berlin, 1836) 205; Ferdinand Hitzig, *Ostern und Pfingsten: Zur Zeithestimmung im Alten und Neuen-Testament. Sendschreiben an Dr. L. Ideler* (Heidelberg, 1837) 3; and Eduard Reuss, *Hallische Allgem. K. Z.* (1837) Intell.-Bl., September.

33. This does not mean that Nero's name is not used in gematria at any point in early history (cf. Suetonius *Nero* 39), but rather, this is to point out that the modern option of Nero as the number of the beast advocated by the majority of scholars is a substantially late development with no early attestation.

34. Note: Nero does have four letters in his Latin and English names, but in his Greek name, as we have seen above, Nero is actually rendered "Neron."

35. This does not mean that the modern option is not right, but it is simply to suggest that the modern option is just that—modern.

36. Rev 1:8; 4:8,11; 5:9-10,13; etc.

37. Rev 6:1,3,5,7,10-11,15-17; 7:1-3; 8:2,5 (cf. the origin in Rev 4:5), 7,9,10,12; 9:1,4,5,13-14; etc.

38. Rev 1:4,8; 3:21; 4:2,3,4,5,6,8,9,10,11; 5:10; 11:15,17; 12:10; etc.

39. The application of this point is that the two beasts of the unholy Trinity have used many prostitutes to complete their tasks of persecuting Christians and deceiving the world to worship something other than the true God throughout the history of the world. This includes: Egypt in the time of Moses, Babylon in the time of Daniel, Greece in the time of Antiochus Epiphanes, Rome in the time of John, Nazi Germany in the time of Dietrich Bonhoeffer, and many others.

40. Although arrived independently, the following explanation can also be found in: M. Oberweis, "Die Bedeutung der neutestamentlichen 'Raetzelzahlen' 666 (Apk 13:18) und 153 (Joh 21:11)," *ZNW* 77 (1986) 226-241, and R. Bauckham, *The Climax of Prophecy* (London: T & T Clark, 1993) 384-452. This chapter differs significantly from Bauckham in that he affirms both the option that follows and the "Caesar Nero" option that was dismissed as "inadequate" above.

41. Contrasting my translation, you will notice that the NIV and others interpret this phrase in both places as: "the number of his name," but the Greek is as follows in 13:17: τὸν ἀριθμὸν τοῦ ὀνόματος αὐτοῦ and in 15:2: τοῦ ἀριθμοῦ τοῦ ὀνόματος αὐτου. The last three words, all in the Genitive form, are identical in the Greek. In the Genitive form, both the masculine and the neuter conjugations are identical; so, context needs to determine which interpretation you conclude for the noun. The NIV and others are assuming that the Genitive rendering is pointing to a male (hence, masculine), while I am assuming that the Genitive is not point-

ing to a male (hence, neuter). In fact, the closest referent in both passages is "beast," which is a neuter noun (cf. ESV).

42. Some may object by pointing to Rev 13:18b, which in the NRSV reads, "This calls for wisdom: let anyone with understanding calculate the **number of the beast, for it is the number of a person.**" On the surface this looks like the number is to be identified with an actual person, but two responses are in order. First, the Greek construction of this sentence actually points to a different interpretation. The Greek reads: ᾽Ὧδε ἡ σοφία ἐστίν; ὁ ἔχων νοῦν ψηφισάτω **τὸν ἀριθμὸν τοῦ θηρίου, ἀριθ-μὸς γὰρ ἀνθρώπου ἐστίν.** The section in bold begins with the phrase "the number of the beast," and it contains definite articles. The last phrase, however, is anarthrous—lacking definite articles. When a section is without definite articles, it can either be indefinite or qualitative. The NRSV takes the anarthrous phrase as indefinite: "it is the number of *a* person." The NIV, however, renders the phrase qualitatively: "If anyone has insight, let him calculate **the number of the beast, for it is man's number.**" Here the phrase in question is being used to qualify the information that precedes it (i.e., the number of the beast is man's number). The qualitative option of the NIV is to be preferred because in Greek if an anarthrous phrase follows a phrase in which definite articles are used, it is functioning qualitatively and not indefinitely. In other words, the definition is already given in the previous phrase. Second, in Rev 21:17 the exact same Greek construction is used, and it is translated unanimously as qualitative. "[The angel] measured its wall and it was 144 cubits thick, **by man's measurement**" (καὶ ἐμέτρησεν τὸ τεῖχος αὐτῆς ἑκατὸν τεσσεράκοντα τεσσάρων πηχῶν **μέτρον ἀνθρώπου**). The anarthrous phrase is used qualitatively here—in a similar situation found in Rev 13:18b. As a result, the qualitative option of the NIV is to be preferred, thereby explaining the phrase "the number of the beast" further by suggesting it is "humanity's number" or a number that belongs to the earth (i.e., Rev 21:17).

43. ת = 400, ר = 200, י = 10, ו = 6, ן = 50.

44. It is interesting to note that if the Greek word for "lamb" (ἀρνίον)—the name of Jesus in 14:1—and the nomina sacra for "God" (θΣ)—the name of Jesus' father in 14:1—are transliterated into Hebrew—"lamb" = ארניון and "God" = סח—and then added together, the total is 777 [(א = 1, נ = 50, י = 10, ו = 6, ן = 50), which equals 317 + (ת = 400, ס = 60), which equals 460]. This observation becomes even more intriguing when we take into account C.H. Roberts in *The London Times Literary Supplement* (10 Mar. 1961) p. 160, who concludes that the nomina sacra was a practice originating from the middle of the 1st c. C.E.

45. ת = 400, ר = 200, י = 10, ו = 6.

Chapter Eleven: Beast and Prostitute (*Brian Lowery*)

1. See O. Michel's article in *TDNT*, abgd. (Grand Rapids: Eerdmans, 1985) 451, and G.T.D. Angel's article in *NIDNTT* (Grand Rapids: Zondervan, 1986) 205.

2. The connection is solidified by more parallels between the beasts in Daniel's account and those in Revelation. While I'll leave it to the reader to do his or her own comparative analysis, I will point out the most fascinating — that the initial description of the beast in Revelation 13 blends imagery of a lion, bear, and leopard, which happen to be the three beasts that accompany the ghastly beast with ten horns in Daniel's account.

3. The horns will be covered in good time!

4. J. Ramsey-Michaels, *Revelation* (Downers Grove, IL: InterVarsity, 1997) 196, points out that sometimes John uses the same image to represent two distinct realities (seven heads=seven hills *and* seven rulers), just as he sometimes uses two images to represent one reality (seven lamps *and* seven eyes=seven spirits of God).

5. See L. Ryken, et al. *DBI* (Downers Grove, IL: InterVarsity, 1998) 367-368 ("Head").

6. See G.K. Beale, *The Book of Revelation* (Grand Rapids: Eerdmans, 1999) 869-875.

7. For an argument for and against this interpretation, see Beale, *Revelation*, 868-869.

8. See M. Eugene Boring, *Revelation* (Louisville: Knoxville Press, 1989), 11.

9. Again these are all symbolic numbers. In Jewish thought the number five often represents a small, but significant number within a mass. It is a "pointer" to abundance or totality. See Ryken, et al., "Five," 291. This means the sixth kind is probably not to be understood literally, but perhaps as a more general reference to the present-day leader/leaders.

10. Two notes of interest concerning the sixth and seventh rulers: First, John has chosen to pause at the sixth king. In a series of seven, John often pauses at six to "rally the troops" and prepare them for a final, climactic battle (see the seals, trumpets, and bowls). Perhaps the seventh and final king will be marked by greater evil. Also, the seventh king will "remain for a little while." In his commentary on Revelation, William Hendriksen, *More Than Conquerors* (Grand Rapids: Baker, 1983) 170-171, offers this intriguing thought: "In the language of the Apocalypse, this entire Gospel age is but for a little while (Rev 11:2, 3; 12:6, 14; 13:5)." Hendrickson makes a case that in the end, there is no use in trying to figure out who reigned the longest or shortest, lining up seven rulers that fit in some quaint timeline. The message that John is trying to get across is that there will be a complete time of suffering under an oppressive, antichristian empire with antichristian rulers.

11. The beast itself is actually listed as an eighth head (17:11), but this is just a symbolic way of saying the beast/kingdom and the heads/kings are so closely related — as the angel says, "[the beast] belongs to the seven" — that they create a circle of evil in which one cannot tell where or with whom the circle begins and ends.

12. Ryken, et. al., "Babylon," 68-69.

13. In some ways, typology is being employed in Revelation 17. Typology is "a method of interpretation that connects events, persons, or things in

one text (usually in the OT) to similar counterparts in a later text (usually in the New Testament) through strong parallelism, similar to foreshadowing and the culmination of foreshadowing." R.A. Lowery, *Revelation's Rhapsody: Listening to the Lyrics of the Lamb* (Joplin, MO: College Press, 2006) 216.

14. See H.G. Link and J. Schattenmann's article in *NIDNTT*, 714-716, and W. Foerster's article in *TDNT* (abgd), 428.

15. Still, some commentators speculate that the ten horns are in reference to ten Roman rulers of ten Roman provinces. See Beale, *Revelation*, 878, for a synopsis and rebuttal.

16. I.T. Beckwith, *The Apocalypse of John* (Grand Rapids: Baker, 1967) 317.

17. It's worth noting that the angel's reference to these ten horns/rulers playing a role in the final battle (17:13-14) does seem to set them up as eschatological figures that stretch out over time, including Rome and any other antichristian kingdom.

18. For thoughts on the meaning of "MYSTERY" in the prostitute's title — which, in the interest of space, I cannot cover, see Beale, *Revelation*, 858-859. Beale points out that "mystery" is used throughout Revelation to set apart stranger prophesies that will be fulfilled in the future (see 1:20 and 10:7). Beale also argues that the use of "mystery" creates a deeper connection with Daniel, who speaks of his own "mystery" in Dan 4:9.

19. See R.H. Mounce, *The Book of Revelation* (Grand Rapids: Eerdmans, 1977) 308. This is probably why the angel later interprets the "many waters" as "peoples, multitudes, nations, and languages."

20. See S.J. Kistemaker, *Revelation* (Grand Rapids: Baker, 2001) 464.

21. Wine is an image often associated with prostitutes in the ancient world. Many prostitutes would carry cups of wine to seduce the men into sleeping with them in their drunken stupor. See F. Hauck and S. Schulz's article on "wine" in *TDNT* (abgd.).

22. Mounce, *Revelation*, 84-87.

23. See Beale's chapter on Revelation 14 for an in-depth look at the trade guilds of ancient Rome.

24. Beale, *Revelation*, 859.

Chapter Twelve: Historic Premillennialism *(Craig L. Blomberg)*

1. R.A. Lowery, *Revelation's Rhapsody: Listening to the Lyrics of the Lamb* (Joplin, MO: College Press, 2006) 140.

2. Ibid., 135.

3. See esp. G.K. Beale, *The Book of Revelation* (Grand Rapids: Eerdmans, 1999) 972-991.

4. See esp. R.H. Mounce, *The Book of Revelation* (Grand Rapids: Eerdmans, rev. 1998) 229-262.

5. For these and related reasons for seeing Revelation 20 as occurring after the return of Christ, see C.S. Keener, *Revelation* (Grand Rapids: Zondervan, 2000). Cf. also B.S. Neall, "Amillennialism Reconsidered," *AUSS* 43 (2005) 185-210.

6. Lowery, *Rhapsody*, 42-48.
7. I. Boxall *The Revelation of Saint John* (New York: Continuum, 2006) 178-179, sees in the story of the woman beginning in this verse, "the sweep of salvation history from Eden to new Exodus in Christ."
8. G. R. Osborne, *Revelation* (Grand Rapids: Baker, 2002), 706.
9. Keener (*Revelation*, 467) explains that "because John envisions the whole church needing to resist the world system, he can portray the church as a martyr church, though his wording can allow for others who have withstood the beast but were not specifically martyred."
10. M.J. Erickson, *Christian Theology* (Grand Rapids: Baker, 1998) 1220-1221.
11. B. Witherington III, *Revelation* (Cambridge: Cambridge University Press, 2003) 249, notes that the most important parallel to this passage is Rev 2:8, in which Christ died and came to life through bodily resurrection.
12. The only possible exception is Lk 2:34, in which Simeon prophesies that the Christ-child will cause the falling and "rising" of many in Israel.
13. See D.E. Johnson, *Triumph of the Lamb: A Commentary on Revelation* (Phillipsburg, NJ: P & R, 2001) 294-299.
14. As in C.S. Lewis, *The Great Divorce* (New York: HarperCollins, 2001 [orig. 1946]).
15. Cf. S.S. Smalley, *The Revelation of John* (Downers Grove, IL: InterVarsity, 2005) 513.
16. See esp. throughout D. Brent Sandy, *Plowshares and Pruning Hooks: Rethinking the Language of Biblical Prophecy and Apocalyptic* (Downers Grove, IL: InterVarsity, 2002).
17. On the issue of two judgments, see G.E. Ladd, *A Commentary on the Revelation of John* (Grand Rapids: Eerdmans, 1972) 268.
18. On these verses, see esp. A.C. Thiselton, *The First Epistle to the Corinthians* (Grand Rapids: Eerdmans, 2000) 1257-1306.
19. D.E. Garland, *1 Corinthians* (Grand Rapids: Baker, 2003) 114-119
20. E.g., M.J. Harris, *The Second Epistle to the Corinthians* (Grand Rapids: Eerdmans, 2005) 408.
21. Cf. C.S. Keener, *The Gospel of John: A Commentary*, vol. 1 (Peabody, MA: Hendrickson, 2003) 653.
22. Cf. J.F. Walvoord, *The Revelation of Jesus Christ* (Chicago: Moody, 1966) 306-308.
23. Cf. Mounce, *Revelation*, 376.
24. On which, see the balanced perspective of D. Mathewson, "The Destiny of the Nations in Revelation 21:1–22:5: A Reconsideration," *TynBul* 53 (2002) 121-142.
25. See esp. *The Letters of 2 Peter and Jude* (Grand Rapids: Eerdmans, 2006) 282-287.
26. See esp. S.W. Chung, "Toward the Reformed and Covenantal Theology of Premillennialism: A Proposal," in *A Case for Historic Premillennialism*, ed. by C.L. Blomberg and S.W. Chung (Grand Rapids: Baker, 2009) 133-146.

27. Thus accomplishing the goals of B.R. Rossing, "For the Healing of the World: Reading *Revelation* Ecologically, in *From Every People and Nation: The Book of Revelation in* Intercultural *Perspective,* ed. by D. Rhoads (Minneapolis: Fortress, 2005) 165-182, but in a more exegetically defensible way.

Chapter Thirteen: Christian Millennium (*I. Howard Marshall*)

1. This is a revised version of a paper published in *EvQ* 72 (July 2000) 217-235. I am glad to give it a fresh airing both to honour Bob Lowery and to bring it to a wider public who are interested in solving the problems raised by Revelation 20. The constraints imposed by time and the need to shorten the original paper have prevented me from surveying and discussing recent literature to any great extent.

2. B.J. Dodd, "Millennium," in R.P. Martin and P.H. Davids (eds.), *Dictionary of the Later New Testament and Its Developments* (Downers Grove, IL: InterVarsity, 1997) 738-741.

3. M. Gilbertson, *The Meaning of the Millennium* (Cambridge: Grove Books, 1997) 14-15.

4. According to Irenaeus, *AH* 5.33.3-34; see M.W. Holmes, *The Apostolic Fathers,* 3rd ed. (Grand Rapids: Baker Academic, 2007) 750-753.

5. See Holmes, *Apostolic Fathers,* 738-739.

6. See *Barnabas* 15; Ascension of Isaiah 4:1-15.

7. J.M. Ford, in *ABD* IV, 834 (832-834). For a fuller survey, see R.J. McKelvey, *The Millennium and the Book of Revelation* (Cambridge: The Lutterworth Press, 1999) 13-41.

8. Cf. Dodd, "Millennium," 739.

9. F.F. Bruce, *1 and 2 Corinthians* (London: Oliphants, 1971) 147. See a more emphatic G.D. Fee, *The First Epistle to the Corinthians* (Grand Rapids: Eerdmans, 1987) 751-754.

10. E. Schnabel, *Der erste Brief des Paulus an die Korinther* (Wuppertal: Brockhaus /Giessen: Brunnen, 206) 927-929, holds that the question cannot be finally settled, but his presentation of the evidence tends, in my view, to favour a negative answer.

11. Among recent upholders of this view note G.R. Osborne, *Revelation* (Grand Rapids: Baker Academic, 2002) 697. See also, C.L. Blomberg, "Historic Premillennialism in the Book of Revelation," in this volume.

12. It was developed first by Joseph Mede (1586–1638). See R.J. Bauckham, "Millennium," in S.B. Ferguson, D.F. Wright and J.I. Packer, *New Dictionary of Theology* (Leicester: Inter-Varsity, 1988) 428-430.

13. D.E. Aune, *Revelation 17–22* (Waco: Word, 1998) 1104-1108, explains the passage in terms of the author thinking in this way; he notes the elements of duplication of the eschatological elements in 19:11–20:15 with the millennium inserted in the middle, and holds that John uses this awkward device to reconcile the two expectations of a future messianic reign and of a final realisation of God's eternal reign.

14. Bauckham mentions Thomas Brightman (1562–1607).

15. I. Murray, *The Puritan Hope* (London: Banner of Truth, 1971).

16. Dodd, "Millennium,: 741.

17. U. Schnelle, *Theology of the New Testament* (Grand Rapids: Baker Academic, 2009) 769.

18. *NDT*, 428-29; see further R.J. Bauckham, *The Theology of Revelation* (Cambridge: Cambridge University Press, 1993) 106-108; similarly, M. Gilbertson, *Meaning*, 13.

19. R.J. McKelvey, *Millennium*, 81-84, 92-94. It is essential to McKelvey's position that the "coming" in Rev 19:11-21 is not the parousia itself but a picture of the vindication of the martyrs.

20. G.K. Beale, *The Book of Revelation* (Grand Rapids: Eerdmans, 1999) 972-1038.

21. I.H. Marshall, "Martyrdom and the Parousia in the Revelation of John," in F.L. Cross (ed.), *Studia Evangelica IV* (Berlin: Akademie-Verlag, 1968) 333-339.

22. So earlier the amillennialist W. Hendriksen, *More than Conquerors* (London: Tyndale Press, 1962; rpt. 1940).

23. A point in favour of this interpretation is the parallel which Beale draws with 2Thes 2:6-12.

24. So M. Gilbertson, *Meaning*, 18 (following C. Rowland, *Revelation* [London: Epworth, 1993] 150).

25. This and other "insuperable difficulties" are listed briefly by G.R. Beasley-Murray, "Revelation," in D.A. Carson (et al.), *New Bible Commentary: 21st Century Edition* (Leicester: Inter-Varsity, 1994) 1452.

26. Some think that only the martyrs are included.

27. Cf. R.J. Bauckham, *Theology of Revelation*, 106-108.

28. G. Goldsworthy, *The Gospel in Revelation* (Carlisle: Paternoster, 1994) 127.

29. Yet Rev 20:3 seems otiose if there is nobody left for Satan to deceive!

30. This path is followed by J. Webb Mealy who has written a full-length reinterpretation of Rev 20, *After the Thousand Years* (Sheffield: Sheffield Academic Press, 1992); see G. Beale's summary and criticism of it, "Review Article: J.W. Mealy, *After the Thousand Years*," *EvQ* 66:3 (1994) 229-249.

31. See the discussion in G.R. Beasley-Murray, *The Book of Revelation* (London: Oliphants, 1974) 293-295; he thinks that 20:4a refers to the Church generally, but 20:4bc to the martyrs.

32. Something like this view was developed independently by E. Schüssler Fiorenza, *Priester für Gott. Studien zum Herrschafts- und Priestermotif in der Apokalypse* (Münster: Aschendorff, 1972) 291-332 (especially 323-325); cf. the summary and critique in J.W. Mealy, *Thousand*, 36-46. She rightly sees that the reign described as eternal in Rev 22:5 is apparently temporally limited in 20:4-6 if the thousand years is taken literally.

33. For example, as the text stands, Rev 20:4-6 seems to imply that the second death (which is surely the death that follows the final judgment) has no power over "them" but rather they will reign with Christ. The impli-

cation is that they then go on to reign rather than being caught up in the second death. If so, the picture here is of the final state. (There is also the problem that, as the text stands, it seems to exclude those who come to life after the thousand years [Rev 20:5] from exemption from the second death; this may, however, simply be a matter of loose expression.)

Chapter Fourteen: Release of Satan (*Shane J. Wood*)

1. All Scriptures will be cited from the NIV, unless otherwise noted.

2. The word "throne" (θρόνος) in Revelation is used 47 times (out of 62 in the NT). The word is connected with agents of God 44 times and applied to the agents of evil 3 times. Each time "throne" is connected to evil, it is on earth (2:13; 13:2; 16:10); conversely, each of the 43 times (excluding Rev 20:4-6) "throne" is connected to agents of God, it is in heaven. The only exception to this pattern in Revelation would be Rev 20:4-6. Moreover, the imagery of the "throne" comes from Dan 7:9-10,22 — located in heaven. Furthermore, "throne" is used 2 times in Rev 20:4's immediate context (20:11,12), both of which all millennial positions agree are in heaven. Since there are no clear indicators mandating that the reign of Christ and his saints occurs on earth in 20:4-6, it is logical to assume that the reign takes place in heaven — following the unanimous trajectory outlined in the rest of the book.

3. This is the fifth beatitude out of seven in Revelation (see 1:3; 14:3; 16:15; 19:9; 22:7; 22:14).

4. See the Appendix of OT allusions in R.A. Lowery, *Revelation's Rhapsody: Listening to the Lyrics of the Lamb* (Joplin, MO: College Press, 2006) 175-197.

5. Isa 11:12; Jer 49:36; Ezek 7:2. See also Mt 24:31; *1En* 18:2; 4Ezra 13:5.

6. Gen 22:17; 32:12; 41:49; Josh 11:4; Judg 7:12; 1Sam 13:5; Job 29:18; Ps 139:18; Jer 15:8; Hab 1:9. See also *Pr. Man.* 1:9; *Jos. As.* 1:2; *Gk. Apoc. Ezra* 2:32; 3:2; 1Mac 11:1.

7. 2Kgs 1:9-12; Ezek 38:22; 39:6; Ps 11:4-6. See also *PssSol* 17:24b; 4Ezra 13:9b-11; *1En* 48:8b-10a,10c.

8. "Gog" = 1Chr 5:4; Ezek 38–39; Amos 7:1 (LXX). "Magog" = Gen 10:2; 1Chr 1:5; Ezek 38–39. See also Jer. Targ. to Num. 11:27; *SibOr* 3.512; 3En 45:5.

9. The same lack of OT referent is also true of the "binding" and "imprisonment" of Satan. This imagery, however, is quite prominent in other Jewish and apocalyptic texts: 4Ezra 13:9b-11; *1En* 10:4-14; 14:4b-6; 48:8b-10a,10c; *Acts of Pilate* 22:2; *TLevi* 17. Cf. Mt 12:25-29; Mk 3:27; Lk 10:18; 11:17-22; Jn 12:31; 16:11; Eph 4:8-9; 1Jn 3:8b; Rev 12:11.

10. Postmillennial and Preterist perspectives are not included in the following analysis due to their general lack of attention paid to the release of Satan or their complete negligence of the topic.

11. This designation in this context refers to both Dispensational and Historic Premillennials. Although Historic Premillennials will take issue with this conflation, the descriptions and difficulties met by an earthly millennium kingdom are shared by both theological systems.

12. So T. LaHaye and J. Jenkins, *Kingdom Come: The Final Victory* (Carol Stream, IL: Tyndale, 2007) 31-32. N.B.: The OT referent for the millennial peace often imported into the premillennial perspective is Isa 11:6-9 and 65:17-25. These texts, however, do not share linguistic parallels to the events found in Rev 20:7-10 and the conceptual connections are tenuous at best; instead, the new heaven and the new earth described in Rev 21–22 consistently allude to these texts. This suggests that Revelation sees the new heaven and new earth as the fulfillment of Isaiah's vision and not the thousand years, *contra* premillennials.

13. LaHaye and Jenkins, *Kingdom*, 36, 53-54, 260, suggest that the "utopian millennium" will still have: brothels, drugs, alcohol, sexual sins, murder, robbery, and even pornography. This is peculiar in that premillennials reject amillennialism consistently on the grounds that "Satan could not be bound now with all of the evil in the world today." T. LaHaye, *Revelation Unveiled* (Grand Rapids: Zondervan, 1999) 323, even states, "History proves that the only means to secure a righteous era is for Satan to be bound; as long as he is loose, we will have trouble." So why is there still so much "trouble" when Satan is bound in LaHaye and Jenkins's *Left Behind* novels? Because they have to deal with the "release of Satan," which does not fit in their theological schema.

14. So Craig L. Blomberg, "Historic Premillennialism in the Book of Revelation," in this volume and T. LaHaye and J. Jenkins, *Glorious Appearing: The End of Days* (Wheaton, IL: Tyndale, 2004) 325; LaHaye and Jenkins, *Kingdom*, 25, 43-44, 61.

15. LaHaye and Jenkins, *Glorious*, 356.

16. LaHaye and Jenkins, *Glorious*, 356. For death in the millennium see: LaHaye and Jenkins, *Glorious*, 356; LaHaye and Jenkins, *Kingdom*, 32, 46-48.

17. G.K. Beale, *The Book of Revelation* (Grand Rapids: Eerdmans, 1999) 989, "But at the end of the age, directly preceding Christ's return, Satan will again be allowed, for 'a little time,' to stop the preaching of the gospel and to draw the curtain of delusion over the nations, especially with the goal of mounting a devastating attack against the people of God, as he did before in Eden, against Israel, and at the cross against Jesus, the true Israel."

18. There have been numerous attempts to answer this question. C.T. Chapman, *The Message of the Book of Revelation* (Collegeville, MN: Liturgical Press, 1995) 122, chooses to spiritualize the event to avoid the question, while V.A. Cruz, "Jesus Shall Reign: A Biblical Understanding of the Millennium," *Reformed Review* 52.2 (Winter 1998–1999) 89-90, suggests that God is simply setting up a divine mousetrap for evil humanity that has been dormant throughout the millennium. Others argue the event is God justifying his actions of judgment before man (see J.F. Walvoord, *The Revelation of Jesus Christ* [Chicago: Moody Press, 1966] 303), and still others suggest it is to reveal Satan's true nature for all to see (see J. MacKinney, *Revelation: Plain and Simple* [Longwood, FL: Xulon Press, 2006] 453).

NOTES

19. The term "key" (κλείς) is used four times in Revelation (1:18; 3:7; 9:1; 20:1). The initial usage in 1:18 should be used to govern the symbolic interpretation of the other three usages. In 1:18 the "keys" refer to Jesus' sovereignty over the agents of death and Hades, which was attained through his life, death, and resurrection. The "key" here in Rev 20:1 refers to the same sovereignty achieved through Christ's ministry and here used to exert authority over Satan in his binding and imprisonment.

20. Eleven times in the NT: Mk 5:3,4 [2x]; Lk 8:29; Acts 12:6,7; 21:33; 28:20; Eph 6:20; 2Tim 1:16; Rev 20:1. See also Wis 17:6.

21. R.H. Mounce, *The Book of Revelation* (Grand Rapids: Eerdmans, 1977) 361.

22. The prison in 20:7 is equivalent to the Abyss of 20:3, since that is the location into which he was thrown. See B. Witherington III, *Revelation* (Cambridge: Cambridge, 2003) 247; Beale, *Revelation*, 1021; and W.H. Shea, "The Parallel Literary Structure of Revelation 12 and 20," *AUSS* 23.1 (Spr 1985) 43.

23. E. Muller, "Microstructural Analysis of Revelation 20," *AUSS* 37.2 (Aut 1999) 232. The logic behind this conclusion is that the ways in which Satan was bound through Christ's life, death, and resurrection (i.e., cast out of heaven, conquered death, atonement for sins, grace for gentiles, outpouring of the Holy Spirit, etc.) have no possibility of reversal. See Mt 12:25-29; Mk 3:27; Lk 11:17-22; Eph 4:8-9; Col 2:15; 1Jn 3:8b; Rev 12:11.

24. W. Bauer, W. Arndt, and F. Gingrich, *A Greek-English Lexicon of the New Testament and Other Early Christian Literature*, 2nd ed. (Chicago: University of Chicago Press, 1979) 172.

25. See also Mt 26:54; Mk 8:31; 13:7; Lk 24:26,44; Rev 1:1; 4:1.

26. The Greek word for "released" is λυθήσεται—a third person, singular, future, passive, indicative verb.

27. For a thorough study of such imagery, see: P. Trebilco, *The Early Christians in Ephesus from Paul to Ignatius* (Grand Rapids: Eerdmans, 2004); L.J. Kreitzer, *Striking New Images: Roman Imperial Coinage and the New Testament World* (Sheffield: Sheffield Academic, 1996); C.J. Hemer, *The Letters to the Seven Churches of Asia in their Local Setting* (Grand Rapids: Eerdmans, 1986).

28. "Roman triumph" will be used throughout this chapter interchangeably with "triumphal procession" and should be seen as synonymous throughout.

29. S. Hafemann, "Roman Triumph," in *Dictionary of New Testament Background*, ed. by C. Evans and S. Porter (Downers Grove, IL: InterVarsity, 2000) 1004. Although some scholars argue for an Etruscan origin for the procession in the late sixth century B.C.E. (so D. Andrew Thomas, *Revelation 19 in Historical and Mythological Context* [New York: Peter Lang, 2008] 2, 21-24; H.S. Versnel, *Triumphus: An Inquiry into the Origin, Development and Meaning of the Roman Triumph* [Leiden: Brill, 1970] 55), M. Beard, *The Roman Triumph* (Cambridge: Harvard University Press, 2007) 305-318, suggests that there is no evidence for such a conclusion. For Roman triumphs mimicked in more contemporary events (i.e.,

Napoleon, celebration of the Spanish-American war, etc.), see: H. Kimpel and J. Werckmeister (eds.), *Triumphzüge: Paraden durch Raum und Zeit* (Marburg, 2001).

30. P. Marshall, "A Metaphor of Social Shame," *NovT* 25.4 (1983): 304. Triumphs in literature include: Plutarch, *Aemilius Paulus* 32-35; Polybius, *Histories* 30.25-26; Cicero, *Fam.* 7.1.2-3; Lucan 1.12; Silius Italicus 17.625-54; Ovid, *Ars Amortoria* 1.217-22; Varro, *RR* 3.2.15-16; Horace, *Carm.* 1.37, 29-32; Appian, *Punic Wars* 66; Dio Cassius 6.21;; 43.14-23; Suetonius, *Nero* 25; Josephus, *J. W.* 7.116-7.157. The *Fasti Capitolini* (also known as the *Fasti Triumphales*) has over two hundred triumphs inscribed on marble from the presumed first triumph of Romulus (735 B.C.E.) to Lucius Cornelius Balbus (19 B.C.E.). For more discussion, see Beard, *Roman Triumph*, 61-67.

31. Marshall, "Metaphor," 304. Some examples include: the arch of Titus (early 80s C.E.), the arches of Germanicus (19 C.E.), the Arch of Trajan (114 C.E.), the Forum of Augustus (Suetonius, *Aug.* 29.2; 31.5), and the temple of Pompey. For a description of Pompey's temple made out of the spoils of the triumph and dedicated to commemorate the event, see Beard, *Roman Triumph*, 21-29. For Roman triumphs in art, see: Pliny *Nat.* 35.27, 93-4; Servius (auct.), *Aen.* 1.294.

32. Kreitzer, *Striking*, 52-57, 126-144, 212-219. Concerning the function of the Roman triumph on coins, Beard, *Roman Triumph*, 20, writes, "Alongside their obvious economic functions, these coins would have been a prompt to reimagining the spectacle maybe years after, or miles distant from, its original performance."

33. Describing the pervasiveness of the Roman triumph in the aforementioned tools of propaganda, Beard, *Roman Triumph*, 18-19, writes, "Public spectacles are usually ephemeral events. . . . It is, of course, in the interests of the sponsors to ensure that the memory lasts, to give the fleeting spectacle a more permanent form, to spread the experience beyond the lucky few who were present on the day itself." (cf. Thomas, *Revelation 19*, 3, 27) The existence of triumphal procession imagery in Asia Minor will be discussed below.

34. So K. Hopkins, *Conquerors and Slaves* (Cambridge, 1978); E. Champlin, "Agamemnon at Rome: Roman Dynasts and Greek Heroes," in D. Braund and C. Gill (eds.), *Myth, History and Culture in Republican Rome* (Exeter, 2003): 295-319; Thomas, *Revelation 19*, 24-25. Beard, *Roman Triumph*, 80-106, however, challenges this view.

35. In the time of Augustus, the triumphal procession experienced a major shift in that the ritual was restricted only to members of the royal family — a political move to consolidate power and adulation to one man and one family (i.e., the emergence of the emperor Augustus *contra* the republic of Caesar). It was also at this time that the Roman triumphal imagery began to inundate the empire through coins, monuments, buildings, and other forms of propaganda. Beard, *Roman Triumph*, 296, sees this as the inauguration of "the age of the triumph." For a full discussion, see Beard, *Roman Triumph*, 294-305, and Thomas, *Revelation 19*, 29-30, 47-49.

36. This image was known as the *quadriga*. See Augustus, *RG* 35.1 and the monument of Marcus Aurelius' triumph (176–180 C.E.; Beard, *Roman Triumph*, 220, figure 31).

37. Suetonius, *Tib.* 6.4; Appian, *Punic Wars* 66; Dio Cassius 6.21. See also Beard, *Roman Triumph*, 19, figure 3, for numismatic evidence of Pompey's son riding on a horse next to the quadriga in one of his three triumphs in 80, 71, and 61 B.C.E.

38. P. Marshall, "Metaphor," 304; Hafemann, "Roman Triumph," 1005.

39. Hafemann, "Roman Triumph," 1005. More accurately, the crown usually was held above the head of the emperor by a slave that trailed behind him in the chariot. See Beard, *Roman Triumph*, 85-92, and Thomas, *Revelation 19*, 76-77.

40. D. E.Aune, *Revelation 17–22* (Nashville: Nelson, 1998) 1051. Livy, 10.7.10 says the emperor was "adorned in the clothes of Jupiter" and some scholars suggest that the face of the emperor was painted with red (to parallel Jupiter) based on Pliny, *Nat.* 33.1-2. These symbols (along with others) suggest that the emperor was intentionally portrayed as both god and king (so Versnel, *Triumphus*, 84-93; Thomas, *Revelation 19*, 42-58). For a complete discussion of the issues surrounding these descriptions, see: Beard, *Roman Triumph*, 219-256.

41. L. Ryken et al. (ed.), "Triumphal Procession," *DBI* (Downers Grove, IL: InterVarsity, 1998) 897. Tacitus, *Ann.* 2.41 states, "The procession displayed spoils and captives, replicas of mountains, of rivers and of battles." These depictions were displayed on placards carried in the parade. The placards contained the names of the conquered nations, number of captured cities and ships, amount of acquired money, and depictions of moments in the victorious battle (Plutarch, *Pomp.* 45.2; Appian, *Mith.* 117).

42. Hafemann, "Roman Triumph," 1005 states, "Most significantly, the victor led in his triumph representative samples of the vanquished foes and leaders, the former being paraded through the streets as slaves, the latter in mockery of their former royalty." Beard, *Roman Triumph*, 12 adds that sometimes enemies were forced to dress up in their "native costume" and forced to both march and enact moments of their defeat in the battle (cf. Josephus, *J.W.* 7.96, 147).

43. For a complete route of the triumphal procession, see: Beard, *Roman Triumph*, 335.

44. Josephus, *J.W.* 7.153.

45. Hafemann, "Roman Triumph," 1005. See Cicero, *Ver.* 2.5.77; Plutarch *Aem.* 33.3-34.2; 36.6; *Anton.* 84.2-4; Appian, *Mith.* 117; Livy, *Periochae* 67; Josephus, *J.W.* 6.433-434; 7.153. At some point in the procession, the enemies would be led away from the procession before reaching the final destination and a signal of their execution would ignite jubilation at the conclusion of the triumph. See Beard, *Roman Triumph, Roman Triumph*, 14, 128-132.

46. Ryken, "Triumphal Procession," 895-896; Hafemann, "Roman Triumph," 1005; Beard, *Roman Triumph*, 133-139, 214-218, 250-251.

47. Beard, *Roman Triumph*, 123, 181. See Josephus, *J.W.* 7.153-157; John Chrysostom, *In Praise of St. Paul* 2.3; Silius Italicus 17.629-30; Horace, *Ep.* 2.1.191.

48. Aune, *Revelation 17-22*, 1050-1052; Thomas, *Revelation 19*, 21-89. Thomas's conclusion, however, suggests that in addition to the Roman triumph, the Nero Myth plays an important role in influencing the images and language of Rev 19:11-21.

49. Furthering the Roman triumph connections here, Beard, *Roman Triumph*, 225, writes of the dress of Roman emperors in the triumph, "Though a military ceremony in many respects, there is no sign that the general ever appeared in military garbs. Quite the reverse: his war was over." So here with Christ – the cross and empty tomb were his battle and victory.

50. Hemer, *Letters*, 147, suggests, "Roman citizens wore a pure white toga at holidays and religious ceremonies, but especially at a triumph." (Plutarch, *Aemilius Paulus* 33) Cf. Thomas, *Revelation 19*, 79; Robert Payne, *The Roman Triumph* (London: Robert Hale, 1962) 148.

51. As acknowledged but dismissed by Aune, *Revelation 17-22*, 1052 and Thomas, *Revelation 19*, 4, 75-76.

52. A significant deviation from the four horse tradition is found in one of Pompey's triumphs in the first century B.C.E. In order to present himself like the god Bacchus, Pompey used elephants to pull his chariot— although his experiment was ultimately unsuccessful (see Granius Licinianus 36.3-4; Pliny, *Nat.* 8.4; Plutarch, *Pomp.* 14.4). The origin of the tradition of four white horses is traced back to the triumph of Caesar in 46 B.C.E. (Dio Cassius, 43.14.3), which was intentionally used to parallel Jupiter who was said to have his chariot drawn by white horses (Herodotus 7.40; Aeschylus, *Persians* 386-387). This, once again, empha-sized the triumphing general as more than a man – a victorious god. See Beard, *Roman Triumph*, 234-236 and Versnel, *Triumphus*, 67.

53. The date of Revelation is generally agreed upon by scholars as toward the end of the reign of Domitian (95-96 C.E.), although there are some dis-senters. For a detailed discussion, see Beale, *Revelation*, 4-27.

54. Josephus, *J.W.* 7.152; Suetonius, *Titus* 6; *Domitian* 2.1; Dio Cassius 65.15. See also Beard, *Roman Triumph*, 19, figure 3, for numismatic evidence of Pompey's son riding on a single horse.

55. Beard, *Roman Triumph*, 9 writes, "At Pompey's triumph in 61 [B.C.E.] the booty had flowed in so lavishly that two days, instead of the usual one, were assigned to the parade, and . . . still more was left over." So Plutarch, *Pomp.* 45.1.

56. N.B.: The first time the "one on the throne" is portrayed is in Revelation 4 – a scene that is heavily reliant on Ezek 1:1–3:13 in which God's throne and the events around it are portrayed in chariot-like depictions.

57. Dio Cassius 49.40.3-4; Plutarch, *Ant.* 50.4; Velleius Paterculus 2.82.3-4; Strabo 2.14.15.

58. Thomas, *Revelation 19*, 38.

59. The length of time between Satan's initial imprisonment and his "release" a thousand years later provides further connection to Roman triumphs. The triumph of the victor often times did not occur until several years after the war itself. This means that the prisoners would sometimes be kept in prison for years at a time until they were called upon to play their role in the imperial ideology by marching to their deaths in the triumphal procession (see Cicero, *Att.* 4.18.4; Dio Cassius 37.47-48; 39.65). For further discussion of this delay, see: Beard, *Roman Triumph*, 163-167, 202.

60. Single bound captive: Pliny, *Nat.* 35.27, 93-94 (the god "War"); Lactantius, *Divinae Institutiones* 1.11 (the god "Jupiter"). Bound captives: Ovid, *Ars Amor.* 1.2.19-52; frieze at the Temple of Apollo Sosianus in Rome (34-25 B.C.E.; Beard, *Roman Triumph*, 133, figure 23). In addition, the position of the chief leader bound in chains in front of the emperor's quadriga is a nonnegotiable element of the triumph. Beard, *Roman Triumph*, 124-125 writes, ". . . ancient writers are almost unanimous in identifying [the enemy's] place in the procession: *ante currum*, 'in front of the general's chariot.' . . . this phrase, in fact, is repeated so often that it seems almost the standard term in ancient triumphal jargon — both in literary texts and inscriptions — for leading a victim 'in a triumphal procession.'" See Cicero, *Pis.* 60; Livy 4.10.7; 6.4.2; Seneca, *Ep.* 71.22; Valerius Maximus 4.1.8.

61. Roman triumph imagery is found in various other Christian writings outside of Rev 19-21. Many authors agree that 2Cor 2:14 (see L. Williamson, "Led in Triumph: Paul's Use of Thriambeuo," *Int* 22 [1968] 317-322; Hemer, *Letters*, 147) and Col 2:15 (P. O'Brien, *Colossians, Philemon* [Waco: Word Books, 1982] 127) utilize the triumphal procession imagery — see also Thomas, *Revelation 19*, 63-66, for Eph 4:8 and T.E. Schmidt, "Mark 15.16-32: The Crucifixion Narrative and the Roman Triumphal Procession," *NTS* 41 (1995) 1-18. In addition, the third century Christian writer Lactantius, in *Divinae Institutiones* 1.11, pictures Jupiter (the chief Roman God) as being led in a triumph in chains in front of the triumphal chariot. See also John Chrysostom, *In Praise of St. Paul* 2.3.

62. Beard, *Roman Triumph*, 265.

63. Ibid., 333.

64. S.J. Friesen, *Twice Neokoros: Ephesus, Asia, and the Cult of the Flavian Imperial Family* (Leiden: Brill, 1993); idem., *Imperial Cults and the Apocalypse of John: Reading Revelation in the Ruins* (New York: Oxford University Press, 2001).

65. For the development of this phenomenon, see the seminal work: S.R.F. Price, *Rituals and Power: The Roman Imperial Cult in Asia Minor* (Cambridge: Cambridge University Press, 1984).

66. Friesen, *Neokoros*, 156. Suetonius, *Dom.* 13.

67. Today, this road leads to the impressive library of Celsus, which was not constructed until 135 C.E. For a diagram of ancient Ephesus and the location of the Temple of Domitian with this altar, see Price, *Rituals*, 139.

68. To view pictures of this altar taken by the author, go to: **www.shanejwood. com/images/stories/ephesusmuseumaltar.jpg**.

Every Grain of Sand

Chapter Fifteen: Images of Jesus (*Mark E. Moore*)

1. All scripture citations will be from the *NRSV* unless otherwise noted.

2. For a more standard Christology of Revelation, see: D. Guthrie, "The Christology of Revelation," in *Jesus of Nazareth: Lord and Christ*, ed. by J.B. Green and M. Turner (Grand Rapids: Eerdmans, 1994) 397-409; F. Matera, "Christ in the Theologies of Paul and John: A Study in the Diverse Unity of the New Testament Theology," *TS* 67 (2006) 237-256; S. Edwards, *Christological Perspectives* (New York: Pilgrim Press, 1982) 139-154; and J. Strauss, "Christology of the Apocalypse," in *Revelation* (Joplin, MO: College Press, 1972) 473-490.

3. The commonest approach to Christology in general and Revelation in particular is through the manifold titles applied to Jesus: Christ (1:1,2,5; 11:15; 12:10; 20:4,6); Faithful Witness (1:5; 3:14); Faithful and True (19:11); Firstborn of the Dead (1:5); Ruler of the Kings of the Earth (1:5); Son of Man (1:13; 14:14); First and Last (1:17; 22:13); Living One (1:18); Son of God (2:18); Amen (3:14); The Lion of the tribe of Judah (5:5); The Root of David (5:5; 22:16); Lamb (5:6,8,12,13; 6:1,16; 7:9,10,14,17; 12:11; 13:8; 14:1,4,10; 15:3; 17:14; 19:7,9; 21:9,14,22-23,27; 22:1,3); Lord (11:8; 22:20,21); King of Kings and Lord of Lords (17:14; 19:16); Word of God (19:13); Alpha and Omega, Beginning and End (21:6; 22:13); Bright Morning Star (22:16).

4. Cf. J. Christoffel De Smidt, "A Doxology to Christ (Rev. 1:5e-6)," *In die Skriflig* 40/2 (2006) 317-335.

5. A long robe and sash could be worn by persons other than priests. However, the following arguments point toward this being a priest. (1) The word for "robe" (ποδήρης) is used only here in the NT but twelve times in the LXX. Of those uses, eight designate the high priest or one of his associates; three are of an angelic harbinger (Ezek 9:1-11); only Sirach 27:8 uses the word as a poetic metaphor for a pure life (cf. Rev 19:8) without priestly implications. (2) Likewise, the sash (ζώνη) represents the priestly apparel in eight of its nineteen LXX uses and three more times it refers again to that same figure of Ezek 9:1-11. (3) The combination of images (sash, robe, and seven candlesticks) best describes a priest.

6. C. Rowland, "The Vision of the Risen Christ in Rev 1:13ff: The Debt of an Early Christology to an Aspect of Jewish Angelology," *JTS* 31 (1980) 1-11, offers an excellent survey of the developing angelology in 2nd temple Judaism. However O. Hoffius, "Das Zeugnis der Johannesoffenbarung von der gottheit Jesu Christi," in *Geschichte, Tradition, Reflexion: Festschrift für Martin Hengel zum 70 Geburstag*, ed. by Martin Hengel, et. al. (Tübingen:

NOTES

J.C.B. Mohr, 1996) 512-517, demonstrates that Revelation goes beyond any contemporary angelology in attributing divine characteristics to Jesus.

7. E. Boring, "The Voice of Jesus in the Apocalypse of John," *NovT* 34.4 (1992) 334-359, points out that the voice of Jesus and Yahweh are often indistinguishable in Revelation. "(a) Both God and Jesus speak in the Ἐγώ εἰμι form in the first person (21:6/2:23). (b) Both God and Jesus command the prophet γράψον (21:5/1:11; 2:1,8,12,18; 3:1,7,14). (c) Both God and Jesus claim to be τὸ ἄλφα καὶ τὸ ὦ (1:8; 21:6/22:13)" (340).

8. בֶּן־אָדָם is found in the OT a hundred and seven times, ninety-four of which are in Ezekiel (and the Aramaic בַּר אֱנָשׁ once, Dan 7:13). The remaining uses are Num 23:19; Job 25:6; 35:8; Ps 8:4; 80:17; 144:3; Isa 51:12; 56:2; Jer 49:18,33; 50:40; 51:43; Dan 8:17. Seven additional uses are found in the Apocrypha: Jdt 8:16; Wis 13:13; 14:15,20; 15:16; 2Esdr 8:6; 16:27.

9. "Son of Man" occurs 82× in the Gospels (Mt 30×, Mk 14×, Lk 25×; Jn 13×). Most surprising, perhaps, is the fact that it is almost exclusively a term used by Jesus for himself (excepting Lk 24:7 and Jn 12:34 where Jesus is quoted!). See also: *Barn* 12:10; Ignatius, *Eph.* 20:2.

10. M. Casey, *The Solution to the "Son of Man" Problem* (New York: T&T Clark, 2007) illustrates the use of this term for "generic humanity" with a number of texts: 1QapGen XXI.13; 11QtgJob IX.9 (Job 25.6); XXVI.3 (Job 35.8); cf. Dan 7:13; and in the plural Dan 2:38; 5:21; *1 En.* 7:3; 22:3; 77:3 (4Q Enastrᵇ 23); 1QapGen XIX.15; 4QGiants 426; 11QtgJob XXVIII.2 (Job 36:25). His assumption, however, that "Son of Man" is a generic term for humanity as opposed to a title for Jesus has rightly been challenged by B. Lindars, *Jesus, Son of Man: A Fresh Examination of the Son of Man Sayings in the Gospels* (Grand Rapids: Eerdmans, 1983); M. Müller, "Über den Ausdruck «Menschensohn» in den Evangelien," *ST* 31 (1977) 65-82; and M. Shepherd, "Daniel 7:13 and the New Testament Son of Man," *WTJ* 68 (2006) 99-111. Enoch, 4 Ezra, and Revelation all use the term as a title for an exalted figure.

11. E. Lohse, "Der Menschensohn in der Johannesapokalypse," in *Jesus und der Menschensohn*, ed. by Anton Vögle, et. al. (Freiburg: Herder, 1975) 415-420, and C.C. Caragounis, *The Son of Man: Vision and Interpretation* (Tübingen: Mohr, 1986). Cf. C.A. Evans, "Jesus' Self-Designation 'The Son of Man' and the Recognition of His Divinity," in *The Trinity*, ed. by S.T. Davis, D. Kendalls, and G. O'Collins (New York: Oxford, 1999) 29-47.

12. Cf. D. Charles, "An Apocalyptic Tribute to the Lamb (Rev 5:1-14)," *JETS* 34.4 (1991) 461-473.

13. It is not, however, altogether new. Philo ascribed to Moses divine honors (*Moses* 1.158), likely in contradistinction to Emperor Gaius (Caligula) [though still falling well short of what Jesus is offered here!]. It was political propaganda not unlike John's agenda with Revelation in the days of Domitian. Cf. P. Borgen, "Moses, Jesus, and the Roman Emperor: Observations in Philo's Writings and the Revelation of John," *NovT* 38.2 (1996) 145-159.

14. R. Morton, "Glory to God and to the Lamb: John's Use of Jewish and Hellenistic/Roman Themes in Formatting His Theology in Revelation 4–5," *JSNT* 83 (2001) 89-109.

15. D. Hannah is likely correct when he proposes that the throne of Yahweh is not merely surrounded by the living creatures but is composed of them. Literary and archaeological evidence depicts divine thrones as comprised of living creatures. Hence, Jesus, in the midst of these creatures, is, in fact, on the throne. Cf. "Of Cherubim and the Divine Throne: Rev 5.6 in Context," *NTS* 49 (2003) 528-542.

16. Cf. P. Munoa, "Jesus, the *Merkavah*, and Martyrdom in Early Christian Tradition," *JBL* 121.2 (2002) 303-325.

17. D. Charles, "Imperial Pretensions and the Throne-Vision of the Lamb: Observations on the Function of Revelation 5," *Criswell Theological Review* 7.1 (1993) 93.

18. W. Unnik, "'Worthy Is the Lamb': The Background of Apoc5," in *Mélanges bibliques en homage au R. P. Béda Rigaux* (Gembloux: Duculot, 1970) 445-461. See Wis 3:1-8.

19. A single pronoun refers to both God and the Lamb in 22:4, demonstrating that John views them not as two Gods but as one. He has not abandoned his radical monotheism in all the exaltation of Jesus to divine status (cf. Hoffius, "Das Zeugnis," 523).

20. Y. Khiok-Khng, "Christ the End of History and the Hope of the Suffering," *Asian Journal of Theology* 8.2 (1994) 318.

21. The only other conflation of Lion/Lamb appears to be in the *TJos* 19:8-9. There is, however, evidence of Christian interpolation in this passage.

22. The five LXX uses of this word have been used to suggest Jesus is actually a strong ram. However, each of them speaks to the lamb's weakness, not his strength. See Jer 11:19; 50:45 (LXX 27:45); Ps 113:4,6; Isa 40:11 (Aquila).

23. D. MacLeod, "The Lion Who Is a Lamb: An Exposition of Revelation 5:8-14," *BSac* 164 (2007) 336.

24. The theme of Jesus as the quintessential martyr is expanded by M. Reddish, "Marytr Christology in the Apocalypse," *JSNT* 33 (1988) 85-95.

25. B. Blount, "Wreaking Weakness: A Cultural Studies Reading of the Lamb in the Apocalypse," *Princeton Seminary Bulletin* 25.3 (2004) 289.

26. Cf. T. Longman, "The Divine Warrior: The New Testament Use of an Old Testament Motif," *WTJ* 44.2 (1982) 290-307, traces the Divine Warrior theme through the entire N.T., noting that Rev 19:11-16 is the most overt use of the imagery. He also notes that in the OT the enemies of Yahweh tended to be human forces while in the NT they are demonic or spiritual forces.

27. Cited in H.O. Maier, *Apocalypse Recalled* (Minneapolis: Fortress, 2002) 167.

28. This divine wedding motif is both ancient and Jewish (cf. Hos 1:2; Jer 2:2; 3:6-10; Ezek 16; Isa 54; 60:4; 5Q15). Cf. E. Cothenet, "L'église, épouse du

Christ (Eph 5; Apoc 19 et 21)" in *L'Eglise dans la liturgie*, ed. by A. M. Triacca and A. Pistoia (Roma: C.L.V. Edizioni liturgiche, 1980) 81-106.

29. The Targum of Isa. 63:5, the putative background of Rev 19:11-16, says this, "I saved them by my strong arm, and by the Memra [Aramaic for "word"] of my pleasure I helped them." Cf. J.R. Ronning, "The *Targum of Isaiah* and the Johannine Literature," *WTJ* 69 (2007) 263.

30. βάπτω ("dipped") is a cognate of βαπτίζω ("baptized") recalling Jesus' own description of his passion on the cross (Mk 10:38; Lk 12:50). This verbiage points more to Jesus' self-abnegation than his self-assertion and slaughter.

31. As M. Rissi suggests, "Und von einer Schlacht war noch gar nicht die Rede. Christus trägt sein blutiges Gewand vom Himmel her," "Die Erscheinung Christi nach Off 19:11-16," *TZ* 21.2 (1965) 89.

32. M. Bredin, *Jesus, Revolutionary of Peace: A Nonviolent Christology of the Book of Revelation* (Carlisle: Paternoser Press, 2003), offers an invaluable guide to the consistent nonviolent imagery of Jesus in Revelation.

33. "It has not often been noticed that Revelation rarely states unequivocally that it is God who acts when judgments occur. In fact, this occurs only in ascriptions of praise and thanksgiving to God for his acts of judgment (16:5-6; 18:8,20; 19:2; cf. also 14:7; 16:7)," R. Bauckham, "Judgement in the Book of Revelation," *Ex auditu* 20 (2004) 4.

Chapter Sixteen: Suffering and Hope *(Carmen Trenton)*

1. All scripture citations will be from the NIV, unless otherwise noted.

2. In this essay I will use *endurance* and *perseverance* interchangeably.

3. Anonymous. Several similar versions are ascribed to different authors.

4. *Merriam-Webster's Collegiate Dictionary*, 11th ed., s.v. "character."

5. NBC Evening News, March 10, 2010.

6. Dr. Lowery shows this in his forthcoming commentary on Revelation, his second book.

7. The Nicolaitans surface again at the Pergamum church (2:15), seemingly linked with idolatry and immorality. See D.E. Aune, *Revelation 1–5* (Dallas: Word, 2002) 148-149.

8. So the ESV and NRSV.

9. G.K. Beale, *The Book of Revelation* (Grand Rapids: Eerdmans, 1999) 230-232.

10. S.J. Kistemaker and W. Hendriksen, *Exposition of the Book of Revelation* (Grand Rapids: Baker, 1953–2001) 120-121.

11. Beale, *Revelation*, 240.

12. A. Roberts, J. Donaldson and A. Cleveland Coxe, *The Ante-Nicene Fathers* (Oak Harbor: Logos, 1997) 1:41.

13. The Asclepius snake image survives as a medical symbol today.

14. Kistemaker and Hendriksen, *Exposition*, 127.

15. Ibid., 136.

16. Beale, *Revelation*, 266, 269.

17. Kistemaker and Hendriksen, *Exposition*, 146-149.

18. R.H. Mounce, *The Book of Revelation* (Grand Rapids: Eerdmans, 1997) 92.

19. Mounce, *Revelation*, 98.

20. Kistemaker and Hendriksen, *Exposition*, 156.

21. L. Morris, *Revelation* (Downers Grove, IL: InterVarsity, 1987) 80.

22. C.S. Keener, *The IVP Bible Background Commentary: New Testament* (Downers Grove, IL: InterVarsity, 1993) 773.

23. Kistemaker and Hendriksen, *Exposition*, 156.

24. S. Gregg, *Revelation: Four Views – A Parallel Commentary* (Nashville: Nelson, 1997) 78-82.

25. Keener, *New Testament*, 774-775.

26. Ibid.

27. Beale, *Revelation*, 305.

28. D. Bonhoeffer, *The Cost of Discipleship*, trans. R.H. Fuller (New York: Macmillan, 1963) 99. Bonhoeffer was martyred by the Germans just before WWII ended.

Chapter Eighteen: Transformation *(Tony Twist)*

1. I still like R. Foster's statement in *Celebration of Discipline* (San Francisco: Harper & Row, 1978) about prayer and change. He points out that Prayer is "life creating" and "life changing," the "central avenue God uses to transform us." (p. 30). His later book, *Prayer: Finding the Heart's True Home*, (San Francisco: HarperCollins, 1992) is a good introduction to different expressions and forms of prayer that have been used throughout Judeo-Christian history.

2. P. Sheldrake, *A Brief History of Spirituality* (Malden, MA: Blackwell Publishing, 2007) 14-15, points out that a fundamental scriptural image for Christian spirituality is discipleship. A disciple responds to a call, receives an identity or status, breaks with the past (leaves everything) for the sake of the gospel and shares in the work of Jesus in bringing God's Kingdom into being.

3. If you would like a list of books and resources I have found helpful, please send me an e-mail requesting the list: **tony.twist@tcmi.edu.**

4. I would recommend C. Jones, G. Wainwright and E. Yarnold (eds.), *The Study of Spirituality* (Oxford: Oxford University Press, 1986), for a good survey of the History of Spirituality. Also, L. Bouyer, *A History of Christian Spirituality*, 3 vol. (New York: Seabury Press, 1963–1968).

5. D. Willard, *Renovation of the Heart: Putting on the Character of Christ* (Colorado Springs: Navpress, 2002), provides a good introduction to the process of inner transformation. I really love the image in Rev 7:9-12 of the great multitude from every nation, tribe, people and language in white robes finally transformed and home.

6. See M. Robert Mulholland, Jr., *Shaped by the Word: The Power of Scripture in Spiritual Formation* (Nashville: Upper Room, 1985), for a fuller treatment of spiritual reading. The classical progression of *lectio divina* is: silencio, lectio, meditatio, oratio, comtemplatio and incarnatio.

7. Rev 3:19-22 tells us that those He loves He rebukes and disciplines. He stands at the door knocking, waiting for us to open, to dine with Him, overcome and reign with Him and His Father.

8. I like this simple definition of spiritual formation given by Mulholland in his book *Invitation to a Journey* (Downers Grove, IL: InterVarsity, 1993) because it rightly points out that the purpose of spiritual maturity is service.

9. All scripture is from the NIV, unless otherwise noted.

10. R.A. Lowery, *Revelation's Rhapsody: Listening to the Lyrics of the Lamb* (Joplin, MO: College Press, 2006).

11. R. Guardini, *The Lord* (Washington, D.C.: Regnery, 1954) 591.

12. Ibid., 591.

13. Lowery, *Rhapsody*, 141-142.

14. At the last breakfast, Peter was asked to show his love by sharing this task nearest to God's heart. Nothing means more to a loving Father than protecting and providing for his children (Jn 21:15-25). Peter (like us) is reinstated after failure for the purpose of feeding and caring for His sheep by serving them completely like He modeled.

15. Willard, *Renovation*, 14-16.

16. The early church father, Irenaeus, used this wonderful illustration in his catechetical summary of Christian belief titled *Proof of the Apostolic Preaching*. See Jones et al., *The Study of Spirituality*, 107-109.

17. This image from William Blake is adapted for use by Thomas Merton in several of his works.

18. Willard, *Renovation of the Heart*, provides a helpful introduction to the process of inner transformation accessible to all Christians.

19. These thoughts on abiding are taken from my chapter on abiding prayer found in D.R. Crawford (ed.), *Giving Ourselves to Prayer* (Terre Haute, IN: PrayerShop Publishing, 2008) 269-270.

20. See Mulholland, *Shaped by the Word*, for a fuller treatment of spiritual reading (i.e., *lectio divina* above).

21. Mt 28:20: "I will be with you always, to the very end of the age."

22. John 21 gives us this abiding lesson. The last breakfast was more than a wonderful spiritual experience. Direction was given regarding what connecting (or reconnecting) with Jesus really means.

23. K. Leech makes the point that the God of the OT is the God of the wilderness, and it was in the process of wandering that Abraham and his children encountered the living God. See *Experiencing God: Theology as Spirituality* (Eugene, OR: Wipf and Stock, 2002).

24. In Jn 14:16-17, Jesus promised that the Holy Spirit would be with us "forever!"

Chapter Nineteen: Teaching Revelation in the Local Church
(Matt Proctor)

1. All Scripture quotations are from the NIV, unless otherwise noted.

2. F. Craddock, "Reflections on an Early Christian Sermon: Form," *Abilene Christian University Lectures on Preaching* (Abilene, TX: 1999).

3. J. Ortberg, *Experience God's Power* (Grand Rapids: Zondervan, 2002) 12.

4. T. Long, "The Preacher and the Beast: From Apocalyptic Text to Sermon," *Intersections*, ed. by Richard Eslinger (Grand Rapids: Eerdmans, 1994) 1.

5. E. Peterson, *The Contemplative Pastor* (Dallas: Word, 1989) 51.

6. Ibid., 47.

7. M. Graves, *The Sermon as Symphony* (Valley Forge, PA: Judson, 1997) 244-245.

8. T. Long, "Preaching Apocalyptic Literature," *RevExp* 90 (Summer 1993) 374.

9. R. Sider, *The Scandal of the Evangelical Conscience: Why Christians Are Living Just Like the Rest of the World* (Grand Rapids: Baker, 2005).

10. See R.A. Lowery, *Revelation's Rhapsody: Listening to the Lyrics of the Lamb* (Joplin, MO: College Press, 2006) ch. 7.

11. For those who don't follow sports, live in another country, or just slept through the '90s, go to: **http://en.wikipedia.org/wiki/Chicago_Bulls** for help in understanding the references.

12. See Lowery, *Rhapsody*, chs. 5-6.

13. L. Ryken and T. Longman (eds.), *A Complete Literary Guide to the Bible* (Grand Rapids: Zondervan, 1993) 460.

14. E. Peterson, *Reversed Thunder* (San Francisco: HarperCollins, 1988) 29.

15. M. Buchanan, *Things Unseen* (Multnomah, OR: Multnomah, 2002) 11, 24.

16. Ibid., 29

Chapter Twenty: Preaching Revelation in the Twenty-First Century *(J.K. Jones)*

1. G. Fee and D. Stuart, *How to Read the Bible for All Its Worth* (Grand Rapids: Zondervan, 1982) 205.

2. C.S. Lewis, *The Last Battle* (New York: Collier Books, 1978 rpt.) 171.

3. See in this volume, Matt Proctor, "From 'Haunted House' to Welcoming Home: Teaching Revelation in the Local Church."

4. A.A. Trites, "Witness," in *NIDNTT* (Grand Rapids: Zondervan, 1979) 3:1039.

5. While scholars are divided on whether or not the same John wrote the Gospel, the three epistles, and Revelation, the authorship issue does not lessen the importance of John's word selection.

6. C. Keener, *Revelation* (Grand Rapids: Zondervan, 2000) 56.

7. *TDNT*, 3:682-714.

8. *TDNT*, 6:848.

9. I have come to deeply appreciate the sound words of E. Peterson, *Reversed Thunder* (San Francisco: Harper and Row, 1988) xi, "Everything in the Revelation can be found in the previous sixty-five books of the Bible. The Revelation adds nothing of substance to what we already know. The truth of the gospel is already complete, revealed in Jesus

Christ. There is nothing new to say on the subject. But there is a new way to say it."

10. R. Lowery, *Revelation's Rhapsody: Listening to the Lyrics of the Lamb* (Joplin, MO: College Press, 2006) 15.

11. T.G. Carter, J.S. Duvall, and D.J. Hays, *Preaching God's Word* (Grand Rapids: Zondervan, 2005) 205.

12. M. Graves, *The Sermon as Symphony* (Valley Forge, PA: Judson Press, 1997) 250.

13. R. Melick, "Preaching and Apocalyptic Literature," in *Handbook of Contemporary Preaching*, ed. by M. Duduit (Nashville: Broadman Press, 1992) 386-387.

14. J. Arthurs, *Preaching with Variety* (Grand Rapids: Kregel, 2007) 193-194.

15. In R. Greene, *Words That Shook the World* (New York: Prentice Hall, 2002) 32-34.

Chapter Twenty-One: In Defense of Eschatology (Shane J. Wood)

1. This is pronounced "es-kuh-*tol*-uh-jee." What does it mean? Well, keep reading to find out.

2. G. Bush, *Anastasis* (1844).

3. *The Oxford English Dictionary*, vol. III, D-E (Oxford: Clarendon, 1933, rpt. 1969).

4. T. LaHaye, *Revelation Unveiled* (Grand Rapids: Zondervan, 1999).

5. H. Lindsey, *The Late Great Planet Earth* (Grand Rapids: Zondervan, 1970).

6. The subtitle of T. LaHaye and J. Jenkins's book, *Left Behind: A Novel of the Earth's Last Days* (Carol Stream, IL: Tyndale, 1995) betrays their "Last Days" definition. The books of the fictional series (of which this is the first) focus on the events of the rapture, the seven years of tribulation, and the inception of the millennial kingdom—i.e., the "Last Days," according to their view. For a critique of this perspective, listen and/or watch my lectures on these topics at: **www.shanejwood.com**.

7. For further discussion of this issue, watch my video lecture entitled, "Overview of the Gospel of Matthew" at **www.shanejwood.com**.

8. "Last days" = Acts 2:17; 2Tim 3:1; Jas 5:3; Heb 1:2; 2Pet 3:3 and "Last times" = 1Pet 1:20; Jude 18. Notice, I am distinguishing between the plural usage of these phrases and their singular counter parts: "Last day" (Jn 6:39,40,44,54; 11:24; 12:48) and "Last time" (1Pet 1:5; see also "Last trumpet" 1Cor 15:52).

9. *Emphasis* added. Unless otherwise noted, all scripture citations will be from the NIV.

10. *Emphasis* added. N.B.: 2Pet 3:3 has almost the same phrase used here but inserts "last days" for "last times."

11. For a thorough analysis of each of the passages, watch my lecture "Are We Living in the 'Last Days'? and What Is Prophecy?" at: **www.shanewood.com**.

12. Some interpreters will vehemently disagree with me about this section "beginning" the talk of the second coming of Jesus, in that: some will

suggest that the whole chapter has been talking about this topic and others will suggest that this passage never talks about his second coming. For a more thorough response to this issue, watch my lectures entitled, "Matthew 24:1-35 — The Destruction of the Temple," "The Rapture," and "Matthew 24:24:36–25:46" on my website: **www.shanejwood.com**.

13. The NIV inexplicably deletes this emphatic construction in the Greek: *Peri de* (Περὶ δὲ). The ESV, KJV, The NET Bible, and the NRSV, however, attempt to show a shift, with the ESV being the most accurate. See also Acts 21:25; 1Cor 7:1,25; 8:1; 12:1; 16:1,12; 1Thes 4:9; 5:1 for similar functions of the construction Peri de (Περὶ δὲ).

14. There is even evidence in these texts that a "long delay" for Jesus' second coming should be anticipated as well — so Mt 24:48; 25:5,9,19.

15. Cf. Jude 18. See discussion above for the biblical definition of the phrase "last days."

16. Together, these words are used forty-three times in only twenty-two chapters: 1:3; 2:2,5[3×],6,16,19,21[2×],22[2×],23,26[2×]; 3:1,2,3[2×],8,10[2×], 15,19; 9:20[2×],21; 12:17; 14:12,13; 15:3; 16:9,11[2×],15; 18:6; 20:12,13; 22:7,9,12.

17. Rev 2:5[2×],16,21[2×],22; 3:3,19; 9:20,21; 16:9,11.

18. Rev 2:2,5,6,19,22,23,26; 3:1,2,8,15; 9:20; 14:13; 15:3; 16:11; 18:6; 20:12,13; 22:12.

19. Ephesus (Rev 2:2); Thyatira (2:19); Sardis (3:1); Philadelphia (3:8); Laodicea (3:15).

20. Ephesus (2:2-3); Thyatira (2:19); Philadelphia (3:8). Ephesus and Thyatira, however, were not completely free from rebuke throughout their entire message (see 2:4-6,20-25), while Philadelphia (3:7-13) and Smyrna (2:8-11) are free from any rebuke.

21. Rev 2:6 [Nicolaitans]; 9:20 [rebellious humanity]; 16:11 [rebellious humanity]; 18:6 [Babylon].

22. *Emphasis* added. The word "done" is the same Greek word for "deeds" throughout the book of Revelation. See also Rev 20:12,13 where "the dead were judged according to what they had *done*. . . ."

23. *Emphasis* added. Some may suggest, at this point, that I am arguing for some form of "works righteousness," but that is simply misreading both the texts and my development thus far. Eph 2:8-9 ("For it is by grace you have been saved, through faith . . . not by works, so that no one can boast.") states that salvation is done through the work of Jesus, but Eph 2:10 instructs us of our appropriate response to this work: "For we are God's workmanship, created in Christ Jesus *to do good works*. . ." [*emphasis* added]. It is more theologically accurate, then, to say, "We have *not* been saved by our works, but we have been saved *for the purpose* of doing good works." Therefore, our works *do* in fact matter (see Jas 2:4).

24. Rev 1:3; 2:26; 3:3,8,10[2×]; 12:17; 14:12; 16:15; 22:7,9.

25. Rev 1:3, *The NET Bible* [*emphasis* added].

26. *New Century Version* [*emphasis* added].

27. *Emphasis* added. See also Rev 3:3,8,10; 16:15; 22:9.